EDUCATION
AND THE
PUBLIC TRUST

EDWIN J. DELATTRE is the Lynde and Harry Bradley Fellow in Applied Ethics at the Ethics and Public Policy Center. He was president of St. John's College, Annapolis, Maryland, and Santa Fe, New Mexico, from 1980 to 1986, and previously was director of the National Humanities Faculty and a professor of philosophy at the University of Toledo. He received a B.A. in philosophy from the University of Virginia and a Ph.D. in philosophy from the University of Texas. He is chairman of the advisory board of the Fund for the Improvement of Postsecondary Education, a lecturer at the FBI Academy in Quantico, Virginia, a member of the advisory board of the U.S. Naval Postgraduate School in Monterey, California, and chairman of the Southwestern Regional Panel of the President's Commission on White House Fellowships.

EDUCATION
AND THE
PUBLIC TRUST

The Imperative for Common Purposes

Edwin J. Delattre

Foreword by
William J. Bennett
Secretary of Education

ETHICS AND PUBLIC POLICY CENTER

Library of Congress Cataloging-in-Publication Data

Delattre, Edwin J.
Education and the public trust : the imperative for common
purposes / Edwin J. Delattre ; foreword by William J. Bennett.
p.   cm.
Bibliography: p.
1. Education—United States—Aims and objectives.
2. Education, Higher—United States—Aims and objectives.
3. Social ethics. 4. Values. I. Title.
LA217.D44 1987   370′.973—dc19   87–31170   CIP
ISBN 0–89633–114–8 (alk. paper)

Distributed by arrangement with:
National Book Network
4720 Boston Way
Lanham, MD 20706

3 Henrietta Street
London WC2E 8LU England

Ethics and Public Policy Center
1030 Fifteenth Street, N.W.
Washington, D.C. 20005
(202) 682-1200

To Winifred Lee Delattre

Acknowledgements

THIS BOOK HAS been written with generous support from the Lynde and Harry Bradley Foundation and the Ethics and Public Policy Center. I am indebted and grateful to Michael Joyce, Admiral Elmo Zumwalt, Donald Rumsfeld, Rabbi Joshua Haberman, and Ernest Lefever for the opportunities they have provided me.

Robert Royal, vice president for research of the Ethics and Public Policy Center, and Patricia Bozell substantially improved the manuscript. Other staff members of the Ethics and Public Policy Center have been most helpful, especially David A. Bovenizer, associate editor, and Cliff Frick.

Jude Dougherty, Austin Frum, Peter Greer, Arthur Kelly, and Kenneth Watson also provided valuable assistance.

Many friends and colleagues have read all or part of the text and given me the benefit of patient counsel: John Agresto, James Banner, William Bennett, John Burkett, A. Graham Down, Sydney Eisen, Charles Karelis, Leslie Lenkowsky, David Lynn, Jon Moline, Andrew Oldenquist, David Riesman, Michael Scully, John Silber, John Walters, and Peter Wehner.

Above all, I owe a profound debt of gratitude to Steven Tigner for repeated readings and many improvements. Ruth Pilsbury has worked tirelessly on the manuscript. My wife, Alice, has read text and given encouragement throughout.

To all of them, I am grateful. Naturally, I am responsible for any of the book's weaknesses.

Contents

Foreword

WHEN EDWIN J. DELATTRE decided to write this book, he committed himself to a formidable task: to argue in 1987 for a recovery of the intellectual and moral purpose in American education. He has met his task well.

Education and the Public Trust: The Imperative for Common Purposes is an intellectually and morally serious work. It calls on elementary and secondary schools, but particularly colleges and universities, to reflect on purpose and to commit to purpose. Above all, it challenges educators and educational institutions to take seriously, and guard jealously, the public trust that they have been given.

Since the release of the watershed 1983 report *A Nation At Risk,* we have seen an intense examination of the purpose and performance of American education. The scrutiny has now grown to include American colleges and universities as well as elementary and secondary schools. This is a welcome and, I believe, long overdue development.

At the heart of the debate lies the question of the expectations that we should rightfully place on our schools, colleges, and universities. As Dr. Delattre points out, we must "refuse to promise what education cannot deliver and insist on promising what it is obliged to deliver." What, then, is education obliged to deliver?

I have argued that we owe our students a good general education—indeed a far better general education in many instances than they now receive. At a minimum, we owe them a systematic familiarization with our own Western tradition of learning: with the classical and Jewish-Christian heritage, the facts of American and European history, the political organization of Western societies, the great works of Western art and literature, the major achievements of the scientific disciplines—

in short, the basic body of knowledge that schools, colleges, and universities once took upon themselves as their obligation to transmit, under the name of a liberal education, from ages past to ages present and future.

Indeed, the core of the American college curriculum—its heart and soul—should be the civilization of the West, source of the most powerful and pervasive influences on America and its people. It is simply not possible for students to understand their society without studying its intellectual legacy. If their past is hidden from them, they will become aliens in their own culture, strangers in their own land.

But our students deserve something more. They also deserve an educational institution's real and sustained attention to their moral well-being. To cultivate a student's intellect alone is not enough. As Harvard's Richard C. Cabot wrote more than six decades ago: "If there is not education of men's purpose, if there is no ethical basis at the foundation of education, then the more we know, the smarter villains and livelier crooks we may be. Knowledge is ethically neutral."

Education and the Public Trust: The Imperative for Common Purposes explores the relationship that exists between education's intellectual and moral responsibilities. It will encourage and inform the current examination of American higher education—its overarching duty to direct the minds and hearts of America's young.

Delattre cogently analyzes the need to identify specific educational ideals and purposes, recognizes the limits of formal education, and rejects what he calls "constituency mentality" in favor of a commitment to common purposes. He wisely rejects calling for new theories in education, focusing instead on the need to improve practice. And he asks, and expects, a great deal from those who would take it upon themselves to educate our young. This is as it should be.

But in the end, Dr. Delattre understands that no structure, no program, no technique—no government subvention even—can rescue the academy. He makes clear that real reform must come from inner vitalities of sensibility and intellect. Decay of all kinds—whether of an individual soul, a whole society, or of a school, college, or university—is removed by regeneration, and regeneration comes from within. What education requires above all else are men and women who, through their own vision, drive, and excellence, will protect and nurture the trust their students, their students' parents, and the citizens of the school community have placed in them. To breach that trust is to betray education's central mission.

Edwin Delattre has added his reflections and his rigorous, elegant voice to those who would insist that schools, colleges, and universities reclaim their high mission in American life. To read this book is to see afresh these responsibilities—and to feel a renewed sense of hope—as we look to the educational challenges that are before us.

William J. Bennett
Secretary of Education
May 21, 1987

Preface

THIS IS A BOOK about human institutions, especially schools, colleges, and universities. It is about human beings and the human condition, and the fabric of life into which formal education must be woven to do its best work. It offers considerations essential to educational reform. It argues that accredited educational institutions must, aside from a healthy diversity, have specific characteristics *in common* in order to fulfill the public trust to do all that they can to advance the well-being of students and the nation. It argues as well that we must try to become certain kinds of individuals if we are to build and sustain educational institutions worthy of us and our sons and daughters.

Much that is now written about formal education is a grim litany of disappointment and failure. We read of huge numbers of young people who are not learning to read or to think clearly, of teachers who are poorly trained or who "burn out" and lose all passion for teaching, of financial crises, of athletic scandals, of drugs, and suicide. Graduates of our finest institutions become cheaters and criminals.

Anyone who cares about the young and about the future must attend to this condition. We should also remember that helping the young to mature is one of life's greatest joys and most fulfilling occupations. Formal education—learning by study—is supposed to be rigorous and demanding, but not hateful or tedious.

In this book I argue that to bear the public trust, educational institutions must identify and declare those intellectual and moral purposes that they intend to strive conscientiously to fulfill. As the established accrediting agencies recognize, each individual school, college, and university must shoulder this responsibility. In the presence of fluctuating and diverse claims made upon it, each institution would be prudent to identify for itself specific ideals for which it stands—its particular mission and purposes—and establish its own best means to achieve them. It should make these ends and means clear to the public it serves and to the people within the institution. Each institution is obliged to gauge the coherence of its policies and practices with its stated ideals. This is not a job to be done once; rather, it should become an enduring part of the life of every institution.

This is not always easy. Human institutions are often enormously complex, and the sense of common purposes may be lost in disagreements over what should take priority, by failures of leadership, or by inadequate planning. But it is by conscientiously identifying their duties and undertaking them with a generous understanding of their colleagues and students that teachers, administrators, and trustees can make their institutions strong and trustworthy.

We sometimes think of bearing trust for the improvement of others as burdensome, wearying. But few things make life more fulfilling than important work. Young minds and hearts offer teachers and administrators the wonderful opportunity to invest the very best of themselves in splendid work. Yet we read little of such joy and fulfillment. Perhaps, like Flaubert's Emma Bovary, we destroy all chance of happiness by expecting too much. Rigorous and realistic expectations for ourselves and our students may allow us to find fulfillment in our opportunities.

In order to do this, we must keep in mind that the classroom is every bit as real as the rest of life. We must refute the false opposition between classrooms and the so-called real world. We must take seriously the ideals taught students and the quality of their instruction. Of course, as elsewhere in human life, some failures are inevitable even for the most conscientious adults. And, though all students have a natural desire to learn, to know, they may not always desire to learn what we want to teach them. We need the courage to give our best and to accept failure. The greatest teachers in history had their failures and yet persisted. So must we.

Educational institutions can do much to enable their personnel to live up to the trust they bear. By fostering intellectual community among faculty and administrators, they can make educational purposes more attainable and more understandable to students. Building institutions that respect intellectual discipline and personal and institutional decency is a far greater project than reforming a curriculum. It involves much broader domains of professional life and student environment. No educational institution rises above the quality of its own personnel, no matter what institutional forms, including curricular forms, it implements. This maxim has fundamental importance for financial, academic, and extracurricular planning and conduct in every school, college, and university.

Finally, we would do well to recognize the limits of what can be asked of formal education. Educational institutions may supplement the work of parents and help to advance the highest ideals of the nation, but if we expect them to replace parents or to stand alone in support of social goals, they can only disappoint us. If, as citizens and as parents, we expect formal education to help mold the young, we must bear some of this responsibility ourselves. We must encourage the ideals of education at home and in public. Specifically, we must help our children to learn their way, and we must take joy with them in their progress. Schooling cannot do this for us.

1

The Public Trust

Whatever one does, it is impossible to raise the standard of enlightenment above a certain level. Whatever facilities are made available for acquiring information and whatever improvements in teaching techniques make knowledge available cheaply, men will never educate and develop their intelligence without devoting time to the matter. . . . One of the characteristics of democratic times is that all men have a taste for easy successes and immediate pleasures. This is true of intellectual pursuits as well as of all others. Most men who live in times of equality are full of lively yet indolent ambition. They want great success at once, but they want to do without great efforts.[1]

—Alexis de Tocqueville

THROUGHOUT THE HISTORY of our country, many Americans have placed immense trust in the power of formal education to improve their own lot and that of their children. Sadly, many others have never had much faith in the worth of formal learning. Perhaps the great confidence many of us have in education tempts us to speak of "American education" as though it were something more than an abstraction.

"American education" is an abstraction, of course, but our people have placed their trust in something concrete—in individual schools, colleges, and universities. Each of these institutions bears an obligation grounded in that trust. The obligation is to identify and work conscientiously to fulfill intellectual and moral purposes.

Our confidence in the power of education itself is perhaps too great, and we frequently expect too much of schools, colleges, and universities. When they try to do everything asked of them,

1

they generally betray their legitimate purposes and their reasons for being.

Bearing the public trust does not mean indulging every public fancy or serving as an instrument of social reform at the expense of the arts of intelligence—the humanities, sciences, and fine arts. And it does not mean taking the place of family, church, and other social institutions. However inordinate our expectations, we have generously invested in education for centuries, so it is scarcely surprising that we should ask much in return.

In the American colonies, the authority of the Crown to charter educational institutions was well established. After independence, the Crown's authority did not pass to America's central government. Instead it passed to the respective states, first under the Articles of Confederation and later under the Constitution of 1787.

The states have exercised this authority broadly at all levels of education; they and their communities have chartered and established by legislation over 3,000 colleges and universities, 16,000 school systems, and 20,000 independent schools. The evolution of universal enfranchisement has been a central feature of America's experiment in ordered liberty,[2] and it has been attended by a similarly expansive experiment in marvelously diverse educational opportunity for an entire people.

These undertakings have been built on the growing conviction that educational opportunity—from compulsory, tuition-free precollege education to access to diverse forms of postsecondary and higher education—can improve individual lives, advance liberty and justice, and serve local and national political, social, and economic ends.

Americans have different ideas of how educational opportunity should improve both individual and national life. We have always held different and incompatible views about what should be taught. Early state constitutions, as in Massachusetts, as well as the Northwest Territories Act of 1787, assert that "schools and the means of education shall forever be encouraged" because the various means of education are to promote "religion, morality, and knowledge." These are "necessary to good government and the happiness of mankind."[3] Many of us now think it is not the business, at least of public education, to promote religion, and we wonder about the place of morals in education.

We ask, rather, what specific knowledge is necessary to good government and happiness.

Some of us think of education in terms of economic advantage and social mobility, while others talk of the development of fulfilling and useful talents. Some of us share Alfred North Whitehead's view that "the function of Reason is to advance the art of life"[4] and see formal education as a means of learning how to reason well and how to tell sense from nonsense.

Some think that citizenship requires the ability to make informed decisions, and that education must accordingly promote shared knowledge of our common heritage and nurture civic and personal virtue. For others, education can best improve life by redressing injustice and inhumanity we have, over time, deliberately or unwittingly visited on each other.

Our disagreements about what general education ought to cultivate, and how, are large. Sometimes our descriptions are vague. Yet, just as in a disagreement over the nature of the throaty beast growling in the darkness outside the tent, at least no one doubts that the matter is important.

The nation, the states, local communities, private and publicly held corporations, foundations, and individual benefactors have invested huge resources of time and wealth in educating the American people. A large part of the population invests much or all of its work and talents in teaching and educational administration.

Enormous federal, state, and local resources are spent on formal education to prepare people for citizenship and employment, to advance knowledge, realize personal potential, and perpetuate the institutions of civilization. Tax legislation encourages additional individual, corporate, and foundation donations. In 1986, U.S. expenditures for formal education from all sources totaled $260.2 billion; in 1987, the Department of Education estimates this figure will rise to $278 billion.[5]

Schooling is available tuition-free, and fees at most public and private colleges are considerably less than the costs. State appropriations, endowment income, and gifts make up the difference. Direct financial assistance to students is provided by federal, state, and local governments, by educational institutions themselves, and by corporate and union benefit programs. Any student with enough know-how and initiative can find educational opportunity. Sadly, many who are born with the potential to take advantage of the opportunity never do, often through no fault of their own. Others, with opportunity in their grasp, squander it.

Our large investment in education reflects our national purposes and hopes for our children. We see part, but not enough, of what Tocqueville saw so clearly—that men and women "will never educate and develop their intelligence without devoting time to the matter." But how is the time to be spent if raw intelligence is to mature into a well-disciplined and furnished mind and a worthy character?

LIBERTY AND TRUST

Our society allots years for learning. To that end, we maintain institutions with teachers, libraries, classrooms, laboratories, studios, playing fields, chapels, and theaters. And by law and practice we allow these institutions, particularly in postsecondary and higher education, freedom to choose their own purposes and the means to fulfill them. Within the limits of this freedom, educational institutions must meet standards of conduct and performance that justify the trust placed in them.

Educational freedom has been defended by the courts from the landmark case of *Dartmouth College* v. *Woodward* in 1819 to *Sweezy* v. *New Hampshire* in 1957. In the latter, Mr. Justice Frankfurter stressed "the dependence of a free society on free universities. . . . 'It is the business of a university to provide that atmosphere which is most conducive to speculation, experiment, and creation. It is an atmosphere in which there prevail "the four essential freedoms" of a university—to determine for itself on academic grounds who may teach, what may be taught, how it shall be taught, and who may be admitted to study.'"[6] Such liberty is not reserved exclusively to higher education. Precollege schools are normally subject to greater supervision and public influence, but the discretion exercised by schools and teachers is still considerable.

Such liberty entails the duty to identify educational purposes and to work responsibly toward their fulfillment. If liberty highlights the obligation to be conscientious, another fact drives the obligation home: we entrust the people we love most—our children—to schools and teachers we know little about, to educational influences and directions of which we are only vaguely aware. As laymen we tend to defer to education experts, and as citizens we frequently extend this trust virtually without qualification, especially after high school.

A school, college, or university is not a political institution, but each exists to serve the public. This suggests useful analogies.

For example, Francis Hutcheson's influential book, *A Short Introduction to Moral Philosophy,* was published in 1747. It was used widely in America's colonial colleges and concluded:

> Our children are dear to us, our wives are dear to us, so are our parents, our kinsmen, our friends and acquaintances. But our country contains within it all these objects of endearment, and preserves them to us.[7]

Hutcheson argued that constituted civil governments could treat our loved ones more securely, justly, and humanely than any others. He therefore argued that "the constituting of civil power is the most important transaction in human affairs."[8] Understandably, he insisted that civil authority requires the establishment of particular offices of government. People who serve in such positions are obligated to respect the law and to care for the public welfare.

Hutcheson concluded that these obligations are "very high and sacred." So profound is the duty to place nothing ahead of lawful and conscientious policy and practice in the public interest that it "shows rather more the high obligation on rulers to a faithful administration, than that on the subjects to obedience; and makes the rights of rulers rather less divine than those of the people, as the former are destined for the preservation of the latter."[9] Hutcheson took the sacredness of this duty to imply that "for crimes against the publik [sic] rights of a people, or for gross abuses of power, or attempts against the plan of polity to increase their own power or influence there should be no impunity."[10] To violate the trust of public office is an unpardonable crime.

Both the individual official and the constituted government have a limited liberty, a liberty secured for the sake of duty to the people. Lawbreaking is an obvious violation of duty. But so are ignorance, sloth, indifference, and cowardice.

Neither is the liberty of educational institutions unconditional. And in them, too, ignorance, incompetence, indirection, and failure of nerve betray the interests of the public they are obligated to serve.

The past three decades have brought new limits to the liberty of educational institutions. Federal and state programs include specific standards of institutional conduct, especially in personnel policies and practices. Columnist Smith Hempstone commented on recent reports about higher education: "Today colleges and universities are a heavily regulated industry, with the federal government determining who is admitted (by prohibiting discrimination), promoting affirmative action, ensuring accountability for research funds, guaranteeing suitable access for the handicapped, and controlling access to student records."[11]

In addition to federal regulations, all states have enacted legislation "espousing the principle that the business of public agencies should be conducted in public."[12] Judith Block McLaughlin and David Riesman argue that such Open Records and Open Meeting Laws, often called Sunshine Laws, have adverse effects on public educational institutions searching for top level administrative personnel: "Not only does public disclosure lose prospects, it also sacrifices candor."[13]

Lack of confidentiality in personnel searches is bound to have adverse effects because it deters some qualified people from applying. Many professionals cannot afford to be known as candidates for positions because their plan to depart can undermine their present work. Their devotion to the work in progress makes them unwilling to run this risk. Further, public disclosure constrains anyone from criticizing a possible future supervisor and therefore allows weaker candidates to escape warranted criticism.

There are certainly more regulations than there used to be, but higher education should not be described as "heavily" regulated. Many of the statutes prohibiting discrimination on the basis of sex, race, age, or handicap in admissions or employment do not generally *require* that applicants be admitted or hired. Many colleges and universities have criteria for selection that are entirely legal; they exercise the kind of authority and choice that Justice Frankfurter emphasized.

Precollege schools are more subject to outside influence and legislation. Since World War II, concern for the national defense has reduced local autonomy and even state authority by involving higher education and governmental agencies in the production of school textbooks and curricula, especially in physics and mathematics. Work in the 1950s at the University of Illinois, Harvard, and MIT was followed rapidly by efforts of the National Science Foundation to reform school curricula considered antiquated and deficient. At the time, as J. Myron Atkin, dean of the Stanford University School of Education, has observed, "No one seemed to doubt that the 'problems' were national in scope or that remedies required a national effort."[14]

The National Elementary and Secondary Education Act of 1965, including Title I, involved the federal govenment more extensively than before in school programs in urban poverty areas. Since that time, Atkin explains, schools have "become an arena for some of the country's major struggles for political power" with "special interest groups for the handicapped, for women, for minority ethnic groups, for homosexuals, and for the aged."[15]

But limits to educational liberty, including differences of opinion about the highest priorities, do not lessen the obligations of educational institutions. Indeed, the laws, both good and bad, presuppose that educational institutions as well as teachers, administrators, and trustees are obligated to identify and work faithfully to realize their educational purposes. To do so, educators must bring to their work the qualities of mind and character that make people fit to exercise liberty for the sake of others. It is not enough that educators respect the law: they must also be intellectually disciplined and morally honorable.

DUTY AND EDUCATIONAL MISSION

Those entrusted to administer and teach should be straightforward and lucid about the purposes they and their institutions are to serve. Unfortunately, conflicting pressures from various groups divert educational institutions from the task of identifying common purposes. If this task is assumed by others, such as public legislative bodies, the purposes identified may have little to do with education, and institutional liberty can be reduced or lost. As James B. Conant warned in a study of teacher education he undertook after his retirement as president of Harvard:

> *When disagreement concerning teacher education is forced into the legislature, unrelated conflicts may override the issue.* In state after state, legislators use arguments concerning academic or professional instruction to mask their concern with racial, economic, ideological, or partisan political factors . . . [and] professional and academic professors become pawns in disputes that in reality have little to do with the effective preparation of teachers. Moreover, by pressing for legislation to enforce their views, the academic professors restrict their freedom to control the curricula on their own campuses. [16]

The essential questions for each school, college, and university are: Where do *we* stand? What is the highest quality and range of benefits that *we* can legitimately offer to the segment of the public we are charged to serve or can responsibly aspire to serve? The greater the clarity of the answers to these questions, as expressed internally to staff and students and externally to the public, the greater the clarity shed on the appointed tasks and the more conscientious the performance. Those who are chosen to govern, administer, and teach must answer these questions that will illuminate their daily duties.

Educational institutions must take these duties seriously because public expectations of them have always been diverse. It is better, moreover, for each educational institution to clarify what may legitimately be expected of it than to disappoint unrealistic public expectations.

Public expectation has been great, and has led to abiding problems for educational institutions. In the 1930s, in the midst of economic depression and massive unemployment, every state made schooling mandatory. Whether this was done for educational reasons, to reduce unemployment, or to safeguard children from the sweat shops and mines, schools were expected to absorb a much larger portion of the population for a longer time than ever before.

In the 1940s, the GI Bill had a similar impact on higher education. "At the end of the 1939-40 academic year, U.S. colleges and universities conferred 216,521 degrees. By the end of the 1949–50 academic year, that number had more than doubled to 496,661."[17] The Carnegie Foundation and others assert that this rapid growth has "devalued" the college degree in America.[18]

If "devaluation" meant only that more people were earning college degrees, we would have no reason to worry. Actually, however, it means that college graduates are today less well educated than they used to be. But every graduate is a graduate of some *specific* college or university; the important questions are whether the graduate of any specific institution is less educated than used to be the case, whether this is an acceptable price to pay for having a larger portion of the American people today *better* educated than when fewer people went to college, and whether the standards of our institutions are high enough. The obligatory question is whether, *within each specific institution, it is possible to have it both ways.*

In 1954, *Brown* v. *Board of Education* rejected the 1896 *Plessy* v. *Ferguson* doctrine that equal education can be provided by racially segregated systems, and it led to greater integration of some schools. The principle and intention of the *Brown* decision were overdue in America's conception of justice. But the commitment of America to integration of neighborhoods, places of employment, and the social order itself has lagged. Schools were made the primary instruments of integration and thus presented with new and varied difficulties: busing, mutual racism and misconduct among students, differing standards of discipline, and parental concern that academic standards would not take into account diverse backgrounds.

In October 1957, the Soviet launch of Sputnik spurred increasing emphasis on mathematics and the natural sciences in American schools. Experts were pressed to accelerate development of curricula that would be "teacher-proof." Instead of emphasizing better education of schoolteachers in mathematics and science, textbooks were redesigned to compensate for the lack of teachers competent in those disciplines. When schools acquiesced in this compromise, they allowed teacher deficiencies and low professional standards to persist for years to come.

As recently as October 1986 Fred M. Hechinger observed in "Learning by Rote":

> Ultimately, teachers who do not need the crutch of educational packages must be freed from outside prescriptions of how to teach.

They must tell even the best intentioned reformers that it is insulting to give them "teacher-proof" programs.[19]

The remarkably low expectation for schoolteachers is demonstrated in the current Holt Basic Reading Series, a collection of readings and teachers' guides for grades K–12, typical of the "teacher-proof" approach to education. The guides promise that students will "acquire just the right combination of comprehension, vocabulary, phonics, and study skills."

This presumes that there is some such combination and that teachers know nothing of subject matter, students, or teaching. For example, the guides repeatedly urge teachers to ask about students' opinions and feelings: they then condescendingly explain that "answers vary." Definitions offered are false or misleading (nonfiction is defined as "narrative based on actual, real events"—at best a definition of historical fiction). And generalizations are often one-sided. For example, students are to be taught that "the more sophisticated communications technology becomes, the greater the opportunity for human growth."[20] This is at best ambiguously true. It recalls Lincoln's celebration of printing as the means by which people could learn that "their conditions [and] their minds were capable of improvement."[21] But, like other lessons in the teachers' guides, it does not allude at all to the magnificent achievements of individuals who lacked higher technology—such as Socrates, Epictetus, and Augustine—and it ignores the *negative* effects of communications technology.

By assuming that schools can be improved without qualified teachers, educational institutions have replaced substance with gimmick and have obscured fundamental purposes of education. This situation is primarily a product of political concerns during the Cold War, and forgets the overall well-being of schools as schools. International conflict is never to be taken lightly, of course; but the nation never becomes more secure by making schools weaker. Bruce De Silva asserts that today "many teachers demand books that are easy to use in the classroom" and that "many school superintendents want 'teacher-proof' books that will compensate for the varying talents of teachers."[22] In sum, many educational institutions and leaders have institutionalized what was at best an emergency measure and at worst a symptom of hysteria.

The 1960s and 1970s brought Vietnam and Watergate, and with them arose a renewed clamor for schools to teach values. The "values movement," however, has problems of its own because parents fear indoctrination in alien beliefs, as in the case of *Mozert* v. *Hawkins County Public Schools.*[23] But teachers, too, are hesitant to "impose" values, and many faculty and administrators have no particular competence in addressing moral questions. The problem of values in school is not new, of course; it was the principal object of Horace Mann's attention in his 1837 *Annual Report to the Massachusetts State Board of Education,* in which he insisted that "the fact that children have moral natures and social affections, then in the most rapid state of development, is scarcely recognized."[24]

The 1980s have given rise to widespread belief that education should expand students' job opportunities and enable them to perform at least in entry-level jobs. Students are routinely taught, to their disadvantage, that a career is no more than a succession of jobs, rather than a life of work worth doing. But pressure for immediate job placement tends to ignore questions about how students will spend their working lives. Disastrous public phenomena—alcoholism, drug addiction, teenage pregnancy, and epidemic diseases such as AIDS—have taken their toll as well. Many educational institutions devote time and resources to trying to help students with such problems.

As public or media attention changes, expectations of educational institutions tend to change accordingly. As recently as 1986, for example, in response to an alleged increase in youth suicide in America, the House of Representatives considered a Youth Suicide Prevention Act. The bill, H.R. 4650, proposed a discretionary grant program "in the U.S. Deparment of Education to assist local educational agencies and private nonprofit organizations in establishing and operating youth suicide prevention programs." The bill would have spent $1 million to "establish model programs that increase the awareness of the problem among families, school personnel, and community leaders" and to "train school personnel and community leaders in schoolwide suicide prevention strategies."[25] The future of this legislation was unclear when the 100th Congress convened.

As social problems are identified in America, educational institutions are often asked to address them—whether or not they are equipped to do so. The people and the government rarely understand the limits of time, professional experience, and money that prevent schools and colleges from being everything to everybody. It is up to the educational institutions themselves to explain what they can and cannot do, because, so long as there is confusion about such issues, the question of fidelity to the public trust cannot be clearly answered.

LIMITS OF EDUCATIONAL PURPOSE

To what extent, then, can schools, colleges, and universities serve as instruments of social reform to combat social injustice and social, civic, economic, and military weaknesses?

Few deny that the country is confronted by severe problems, even crises, both domestically and internationally. The gravity of these problems persists even though the media and others often leap from one concern to another. If educational institutions try to keep up with whatever happens to occupy center stage, their responses are bound to be hasty, episodic, and short-lived. Yet the learning of students is supposed to stand the test of time and serve them as a foundation; if it is to be durable learning, it cannot consist of superficial responses to the fashions of the moment.

Superficial teaching and learning are dispiriting to teachers and often recognized as such by students. Students therefore have reason to be indifferent to or even contemptuous of their studies. Further, if their studies jump from one topic to another without some distinction between the fundamental and the trivial, the result is likely to be intellectual shallowness, even promiscuity. Consequently, it is not surprising to hear people say they would rather read *TV Guide* than Shakespeare: superficial learning does not prepare students to read Shakespeare with pleasure or insight.

Surely students should learn by study enduring lessons in the human condition—that individuals and institutions are everywhere fallible; that justice is hard to achieve and equally hard to maintain; that temptations to intemperance are not of recent invention; that ignorance and cowardice militate against civility; that love is more demanding and can lead to greater heartache and greater fulfillment than selfishness and indifference; that the price of freedom is eternal vigilance; that evil sometimes prevails over good; and that disappointment can sometimes be tempered with humor. All of these are reasons for making ourselves and our institutions as reliable, effective, and honorable as possible. They are reasons for the hard work needed to develop our talents and to apply them to our circumstances. When these lessons are being learned, attention to current events has a point, and there is reason to hope that over time general public awareness will be raised.

Our problems, however, do not generally admit of quick-fix remedies outside education or within it. Schools, colleges, and universities are obliged to appoint and retain personnel who can help students to *think* better and to *act* as mature, responsible adults. To address our problems as a nation, large numbers of us must become responsible adults. If, for example, we want the widespread use of drugs to stop, then as adults we should not use drugs. By our own habits we can teach our children what we take seriously and thereby support the efforts of formal education. If we do less in questions of justice, patriotism, financial restraint, sexual promiscuity, and the like, we do our children a disservice that their formal education is not likely to redeem.

But educational institutions must expect to be asked to do many things by many groups, more than they can find the time, resources, or personnel to satisfy. How, then, are they to identify and explain their fundamental purposes?

First, administrators in each school and college can describe their institution's distinctive mission, the means to its fulfillment, and the problems and solutions in progress.

Second, an institution has to do more than repeat platitudes and make vague recommendations. The institution should declare what it stands for so that it can ask its members for serious attention to its goals. Only then it can reasonably expect board, administration, faculty, staff, and students to devote themselves to those purposes and to try always to insure that their particular work is consistent with and supportive of these ends.

Third, insofar as the institution is designed for teaching students—as distinct from scholarly and scientific research—it must be explicit about what it intends the students to learn. Are literature, history, languages, philosophy, sciences, mathematics, and the fine arts central? Or are they on a par with other kinds of learning through athletics, social organizations, and the like? Or is the institution principally interested in inculcating entry-level job skills, the promotion of a specific religious faith, and so on?

In what follows, our concern is with schools, colleges, and universities that are obligated by charter and legislation, and by their own account, to put the academic disciplines above everything else. Such an obligation applies to all institutions of higher education, though not to all postsecondary institutions, to all public schools, and to all private schools that are offered as an alternative to public schooling. We will not discuss vocational schools or those community colleges that design their programs to fit local public interest. Although these have value, this study concentrates on the kinds of institutions that are most frequently pressed to do things separate from, and often detrimental to, their central mission.

When the scholarly and scientific disciplines are intended to be central to teaching and learning, it is essential before all else to say so. This enables straightforward deliberation about the coherence of various policies and practices with educational purposes. Sometimes this coherence is neglected, and sometimes it is hard to achieve even with considerable effort. But this coherence—this wholeness or integrity—matters most of all.

INSTITUTIONAL INTEGRITY AND PERSONAL AND INSTITUTIONAL DISCIPLINE

Devotion to common purposes, like any real devotion, requires the members of an institution to place certain ideals above narrow personal interests or desires, and above and beyond the special interest of any group. Some of the ways we talk and think obscure how vital these common purposes are to institutional integrity.

In recent years, for example, educational agency officials, foundation personnel, administrators, faculty, and writers have tended to refer to a school's "constituencies." This suggests that we are primarily concerned about entitlements or rights and only secondarily about duties. In a typical passage in *Faculty Participation in Decision Making,* Carol E. Floyd uses such language: "Faculty are less comfortable . . . with the involvement of nonfaculty constituencies in the revised senate structures established in the late 1960s and early 1970s and continue to seek means to minimize the influence of those constituencies."[26]

Such language suggests that each group is divided from and has interests that are distinct from, and perhaps at cross purposes with, other groups. This leads us to think of schools as collections of factions. Unless we learn that every group in the institution has its reason for being in shared purposes, our institutions will not be coherent. The public trust demands that we—and our students—achieve and show a more generous and expansive understanding of ourselves and our work together.

Governance, administration, and maintenance—from investment management and fund-raising to cleaning the cafeteria—are supposed to contribute to institutional purposes. Since these purposes are most directly pursued in the daily work of faculty and students, every other group—counselors, coaches, board members, dormitory advisors—exists to support *academic* work. The constituency mentality thwarts commitment to common purposes. Insofar as it becomes dominant, it leads to fragmentation rather than to integrity.

Some institutions have lost sight of common purposes, Edward Shils of the University of Chicago contends, by institutional reforms that have "democratised" universities: "The reforms . . . have denied that there can be consensus and solidarity about common aims in the university and that the university can be a community devoted to intellectual things, despite the divisions of age, function, status, and specialization."[27]

No educational institution can afford to allow a so-called pluralism to dictate that everything whatsoever has a rightful place in education. Because institutions must respect reason, they must hold that pluralism is limited in its embrace to differences that can be and are represented by reasonable people of good will. This is the difference and disagreement cherished in academic liberty, and its limits prevent institutional chaos. Pluralism has no further claim on education; if it did, it would destroy the very possibility of systematic teaching and learning.

As sociologist Gerald Grant observes in "Education, Character, and American Schools," our institutions can be pluralistic only on the premise of the *common* beliefs of a free country:

[A]lthough we respect differences of opinion on many issues, there are some salient or core beliefs to which all subscribe. Pluralism is in fact not possible without agreement on some kinds of values: the minimal order required for dialogue, the willingness to listen to one another, respect for truth, the rejection of racism (or openness to participation in the dialogue), as well as those transcendent values that shore up the whole society—a sense of altruism and service to others and respect for personal effort and hard work. Without such agreement one does not have a public, but a kind of radical relativism; not pluralism but mere coexistence.[28]

The constituency mentality and confusion about pluralism are not the only obstacles to institutional integrity and shared purposes. If, as Tocqueville argues, all men in democratic times "have a taste for easy successes and immediate pleasures," the same is true for children and for adults who grow older without growing up. No school can afford to indulge this human tendency because aversion to work obstructs systematic teaching and learning.

Though standards of discipline must be established for all, they are most pressing with regard to students. Gilbert Highet claims in *The Art of Teaching* that "The young do not like work. . . . Nor do the young like authority. . . . Also, the young hate concentration. It is an effort, an unfamiliar and painful effort."[29] This description is not universally true, but it applies to many students. We must beware of this tendency at all levels of education.

Obviously, not all significant learning by either children or adults is a matter of careful planning, intense concentration, deliberate work, or authoritative standards. Small children normally have quite a remarkable grasp of language by the time they are four years old, without any program of study or extended concentration. In my own experiences as a father, none is more unforgettable than a moment with our three-year-old daughter Donna. On a fall day, as the wind blew leaves into little rising spirals of color, Donna hopped up and down in sympathy with the leaves and said, "Look, Daddy, the leaves are dancing." Her description was startling and strikingly apt. How she learned to see what she saw I do not know, but it was certainly not by any concentrated form of study.

Experiences of this sort may incline us toward the idea that the ends of education can easily be achieved. Certainly, we will want educational enviroments to allow room for the free play of intelligence and imagination. But systematic, rigorous, informed intelligence, ordered and coherent grasp of subject matter, and deliberate application of thought to specific issues depend heavily on planned study.

Discipline and self-discipline do not diminish in importance even if few institutions operate any longer *in loco parentis*. As Highet insists, "It is useless to attempt to teach tough youngsters as long as they are allowed to run free in bad surroundings."[30] It may be even *more* important for formal education to emphasize self-discipline for students whose parents devote little time to the behavior and habits of their children. Furthermore, as Immanuel Kant explained two centuries ago, the success *of any kind of instruction* depends on the establishment of discipline:

> It is discipline which prevents man from being turned aside by his animal impulses from humanity, his appointed end. Discipline, for instance, must restrain him from venturing wildly and rashly into danger. Discipline, thus, is merely negative, its action being to counter man's natural unruliness. The positive part of education is instruction.
>
> Unruliness consists in independence of law. By discipline men are placed in subjection to the laws of mankind, and brought to feel their constraint. This, however, must be accomplished early . . . for when this has not been done, it is difficult to alter character later in life. Undisciplined men are apt to follow every caprice. . . . [I]f a man be allowed to follow his own will in his youth, without opposition, a certain lawlessness will cling to him throughout his life.[31]

What is an institution to do with students who are undisciplined? It must be explicit about standards of behavior and performance; it must be resolutely intolerant of conduct that does not satisfy these standards; it must encourage and celebrate success; and it must insist that failure has consequences. To achieve integrity, an institution must live up to coherent standards of its own; it cannot merely try to please everyone.

The cumulative effect of discipline problems can scarcely be overestimated. In "Patterns of Black Excellence," Thomas Sowell explains:

> The destruction of high-quality black schools has been associated with a breakdown in the basic framework of law and order. Nor did it require mass violence to destroy these or other black schools.

Again and again those interviewed who were working in the field of education pointed out that only a fraction—perhaps no more than one tenth of the students—need to be hard-core troublemakers in order for good education to become impossible.[32]

The vital question, as Sowell adds, is "whether there is, in fact, a solution—whether we have it in our grasp today, and whether we shall allow the 'problem' to take its fullest destructive toll before such indefinite time as we have it 'solved.'"[33]

Facing such problems is unpopular because there is virtually no remedy that does not include the suspension or expulsion of students. Strong measures run the risk of appearing to be discriminatory. Furthermore, if troublemakers are out of school, they will cause trouble elsewhere; traditionally, truancy statistics match neighborhood crime statistics. But if the misconduct of others is not to deprive students of educational opportunity, administrators and teachers will have to accept criticism and defend fair and responsible standards of conduct. It is not the job of schools to prevent crime by keeping troublemakers off the streets, nor can they leave students mercilessly exposed to the wantonness of others. Their job is to teach those who are willing to learn and to attempt to cultivate the will to learn in those whose behavior permits.

The worst troublemakers usually opt out of formal education before reaching college, or fail to gain admission. Yet even in college the problem of discipline is serious, sufficiently so that Georgetown University President Reverend Timothy Healy, S.J., insists that since the concept *in loco parentis* has disappeared, "what we really need is a new theory."[34]

Actually, educational institutions do *not* need a new theory. They need *standards* and the courage to enforce them. If college students act like children, they do not belong in college, and should be treated accordingly. Students cannot be granted adult prerogatives without undertaking adult responsibilities.

In practice, the issue is more complicated, since the stages of human maturation span both childhood and adulthood. Many students in schools, colleges, and universities are adolescents or youths who can be quite mature at one moment and remarkably childish in the next. It is worth remembering that, in many cases, such patterns of behavior occur only because the students are young and not because they are somehow off the track of healthy development. Accordingly, disciplinary measures that have no sympathy for the sheer exuberance of youth can be self-defeating, particularly if they seem to treat having fun as a bad thing. But educational institutions have to rely on standards of conduct consistent with their educational expectations and with intellectual progress.

Just as there must be standards for the individuals in an institution, there must be standards that the institution applies to itself. Every institution conducts or permits a variety of nonacademic activities, potentially instructive and therefore valuable. Most of them are susceptible to excesses that make a mockery of teaching and learning and traduce personal decency and institutional character. Foremost among these are conditions of student life, athletic programs, and political activity.

Student social life, for example, is crucial. Learning to play constructively and to enjoy leisure with companions is among the most fulfilling of joys. Making friends and meeting people with different backgrounds is broadening and enlightening. But when social life runs amok, and involves drugs, abuse of alcohol, or other destructive behavior, it flies squarely in the face of educational purposes.

What can institutions no longer acting *in loco parentis* do about misconduct and failure to satisfy institutional expectations? They can grade according to merit and penalize absenteeism. They can instruct security forces and administrators to enforce the laws against violence, drug abuse, and underage drinking; discipline promptly; and impose sanctions on the social organizations involved. They can work with local police to patrol the areas surrounding the institutions—areas where drug dealers do their selling—and implement student orientation programs designed to prevent self-destructive behavior and uphold institutional standards. They can refuse to tolerate comparable misconduct by their own faculty and staff.

None of these steps depends on *in loco parentis* authority. Institutions that will not use the authority they already have can scarcely hope to have a campus life conducive to educational purposes. As Ernest Boyer of the Carnegie Foundation asserts, "Every study of the impact of college education makes it very clear that what happens outside the classroom is absolutely crucial."[35]

The same general points can be made about athletics. Athletics belong in education; they are the source of much that is magnificent and joyful. But overemphasis on intercollegiate athletics for the sake of publicity and financial support generates more embarassment than glory. Overemphasis consists in placing athletics outside, above, or exempt from the academic mission. It attracts the gamblers involved in point-shaving scandals, or drug dealers, and, with them, corruption in every form; it thereby leads students, especially athletes, into temptations they are ill-prepared to handle. The scale of our national shame in such matters is a blight on education everywhere.

The national scandals in higher education since 1984—recruiting violations at Clemson University, star athletes convicted of drug dealing at the University of Virginia, the drug death of Len Bias at the University of Maryland, repeated scandals at Southern Methodist University—tend to divert our attention from community or junior colleges and pre-college schools. Yet there, too, problems in athletics surface, and they are problems of alarming proportion.

For example, on October 23, 1986, the basketball coach of Erie Community College said that he had changed the grades of fifteen players in order to help them get scholarships to Division I four-year schools. The coach said he was "frustrated by the lack of tutoring received by his players" and criticized "the system" for not caring about minority student-athletes. The coach has since resigned.[36] On October 8, 1986, Langley High School in McLean, Virginia, dismissed its varsity football coach for eavesdropping on wireless radio conversations of opposing coaches during a game.[37] The seriousness of this occurrence is compounded by the fact that Langley is one of the finest high schools in America. Though both of these schools quickly dismissed the offenders, an overemphasis on athletics is tempting and calls for special care.

Some institutions allow student and faculty involvement in social and political causes to excuse them from their educational responsibilities. Certainly students should become interested in the political questions facing a free people and should shed their best moral lights on America's future. But they deserve to learn from their teachers that moral fervor is no substitute for diligent and systematic learning. There is little indication that student demonstrations since the 1960s have reflected conscientious study of the relevant issues—whether in history, philosophy, government, economics, or the sciences.

This criticism should not be confused with an attack on moral conviction or freedom of speech; rather, it describes the institutional failure of allowing students to set aside—and even to obstruct—the educational purposes for which the school, college, or university has been founded. In practice, such failure gives the impression that, in matters of moral import, passion and action are substitutes for knowledge and deliberation. The rational pursuit of truth central to teaching, scholarship, and research is thereby dimmed, and educational purposes are slighted or even dismissed.

This absence of study was apparent in the fervor of protests against the war in Vietnam, and it is equally apparent concerning South Africa today. In each instance, the moral principle to which protesters have appealed is above reproach: in the first, that America should avoid unjust wars; in the second, that apartheid is wrong.

No serious person questions these principles. But there is no responsible way to judge how they should be applied without study of each specific case. Educational institutions have an obligation to promote responsible judgment and the informed application of principles. Those who forsake this duty by acquiescing in student demands teach the lesson that moral virtue can be separated from intellectual conscientiousness, that noise and pressure are acceptable substitutes for reasoned discourse, and, finally, that the end justifies the means. Students deserve institutions that stand on higher intellectual and moral ground— in classrooms and outside them.

Some institutions, following the path of least resistance, have allowed classroom and administration buildings to be shut down by student and faculty demonstrators. Such closings replace moral discourse with exhibitions of power. They fly in the face of intellectual inquiry and obstruct institutional duties.

The decisions of Yale and Johns Hopkins to treat shanties as an acceptable expression of opposition to apartheid in South Africa are a dramatic example of following the path of least resistance at the expense of educational purposes. Building shanties may attract attention, but it does not apply intelligence to important moral and political issues, and it is no substitute for study. As John Silber, president of Boston University, argues, to treat students "who are perfectly capable of harnessing their mouths to their minds as if they are incapable of articulate speech is a confession of bankruptcy."[38]

It is dangerous and self-defeating to believe that every injustice is intolerable and must be immediately remedied, no matter the method. Yet many demonstrations are based on this misconception. A person who can tolerate no injustice cannot live in the world, because the world always includes conditions of injustice; but such a person cannot consistently opt for social change either, because all substantial change is attended by injustice as well. The pressing questions are how to reduce particular injustices without causing others, and how to reduce injustice without betraying other ideals such as liberty, privacy, and civility. These are often hard questions.

Surely education ought not indulge "symbolic expression" when to do so encourages students to suppose that they have done what morality requires *without making* the effort to answer the hard questions. To teach such bad lessons is to forego respect for the civilized intelligence that education both presupposes and hopes to nurture. Indulging members of an educational institution in such political activities poses a greater threat to institutional integrity and the public trust than any external pressure.

By contrast, when I was president of St. John's College and concerns about South Africa began to spread across America, the college administration and the Finance Committee of the Board of Visitors and Governors took the initiative. Rather than base their obligations on the merely topical, they undertook an inquiry in the tradition of the comprehensiveness of the liberal arts. That is, they did not ask, "Should St. John's, as a protest against apartheid, divest itself of all holdings in companies that do business in South Africa?" Instead, they posed the question, "What should be the relation between social, political, and moral concerns and the investment policies of a college devoted to the liberal arts?" The committee invited students, faculty, alumni, staff, and board members to submit the best essays, editorials, and papers they could find on the question and collected them into a book for the use of the college community. It then arranged seminars at the college and with alumni groups throughout the country. Asking that no one attend the seminars before reading the book, which contained diverse points of view, the committee deliberated for eighteen months through these public forums.

By engaging the community in a dialogue among reasonable people of good will, the committee gave opportunity for fruitful disagreement. It sustained civility, limited adversarial tension, and revealed the folly of supposing that when two people disagree one of them is invariably bad or morally insensitive. All this was possible because the board and administrators were clear about the college's educational purposes and were resolved to act in fidelity to them. It was also possible because the board clearly recognized—and taught—that it had both the authority and the duty to govern.

Integrity and fidelity to the public trust require not only clarity of purposes and expectations, but individual teachers and administrators with the courage, judgment, patience, and willingness to act decisively and to accept responsibility for their decisions. That many problems are hard to address helps explain why some institutions shy away from them and conceal rather than face them. It may also explain why so much putative reform is no more than inconsequential curricular change or administrative tinkering that does nothing to clarify institutional purposes or expectations. To tinker is simply easier than to articulate institutional purposes and bring them to life in the academic and nonacademic areas of a school.

Many schools seem to fear the consequences of clear thinking on this subject. For example, if a college determines that it has a drug problem and sets out to overcome it, the existence of the problem will very likely be reported by the media and possibly by standard guides to colleges. This may hurt short-term enrollment, and therein lies the temptation to concealment.

Specifically, it is easier to play with curriculum or governance structures and to pander to transient and narrow interests of various groups than to refuse to promise what education cannot deliver and to insist on promising what it is obligated to deliver.

FAITHFUL PROMISES

Our fondest hopes for our children are that they will flourish and leave the world a better place. Education cannot promise either. Not everyone with a good education will have a happy and fulfilling life. Not everyone with sound educational opportunities will live a decent, honorable, or noble life. The best educated among us are not always the best.

But there are promises that are owed every student and parent, every taxpayer and benefactor: Classroom performance, study, and homework will come ahead of everything else. Standards of work and subjects studied will not permit indifference or merely casual attention to learning. In every respect, the conduct of the institution will serve formal study, and neither institutional nor personal behavior will be allowed to undermine learning in solitude or in the company of other students and teachers.

These are promises every school, college, and university can keep if it wants to—if its personnel are up to the challenge. They are straightforward promises. They are promises that students will be treated, above all, as students.

They do not mean that school is all work and no play. They do not threaten lively activities of student life or fruitful interscholastic, intercollegiate, and intramural sports. They mean that the nature of student life, including political activity, social conduct, and athletic programs, will neither conflict with nor make a mockery of educational purposes. They mean that student work comes first because student work *is* learning by study.

Yet the obstacles are great. The most difficult problems are not easily solved. The reasons it is difficult for institutions to identify and achieve common purposes run deep in the human condition and in our nature as human beings.

It is most difficult for any group of people in any setting, including an educational one, to achieve by deliberation a sense of common purposes. We are divided by samenesses, as well as by differences, and it may be more difficult for highly educated, or at least scholarly, people to achieve common purposes than for any others.

Advanced education, we all hope, increases critical capacity, abundance of imagination, refinement and subtlety of thought. These expand the domain of possible disagreement and dissent, and they tend to increase respect for intellectual liberty and expression in disagreement.

George Will may be right to insist, in the spirit of George Orwell, that "It is axiomatic that there are some ideas so grotesquely false and morally frivolous that only intellectuals will believe them."[39] What is certainly true is that in any educational institution there is a great likelihood of disagreement on any question of substance or procedure, and that in any argument there will be not one side or two but many sides. This is one of the reasons that an educational institution can be intellectually fertile and advance knowledge while cultivating critical intelligence in students. It is part of the genuine power of formal education, because, at its best, such critical intelligence keeps inquiry open and vital, while disagreement spurs diligent work.

At the same time, advanced critical intelligence and respect for freedom have no direct connection to humility, civility, moral sensibility, kindness, patience, temperance, courage, and justice, or loyalty to institutional purposes. Without these, disagreement can be divisive, and educational institutions, as much as any others, can and sometimes do lose all sense of purpose because of their absence. There is no relief in any measure that tries to prevent reasonable disagreement: no ideal of education can be sustained by forced conformity.

Many of the problems in education can be faced only by successfully negotiating the path between abdication of authority on one hand and authoritarianism on the other. The challenge of fidelity to the public trust is for each institution to serve common educational purposes without becoming slavishly ideological. To meet this challenge, institutions must be able to rely on the intellectual and moral powers of their personnel. We turn next, then, to the problems of identifying and achieving common purposes in human institutions without destroying the liberty, and the independence of mind and action, of the individuals who live and work in them.

2

Common Purposes

Have we not already seen enough of the fallacy and extrava-
gance of those ideal theories which have amused us with
promises of an exemption from the imperfections, the weaknesses, and the evils incident to society in every shape? Is it
not time to awake from the deceitful dreams of a golden age
and to adopt as a practical maxim for the direction of our
political conduct that we, as well as the other inhabitants of the
globe, are yet remote from the happy empire of perfect
wisdom and perfect virtue?[1]

—*Alexander Hamilton*

A MONG THE EVILS incident to society and to education are
fragmentation of purposes and lack of purposes. These sap
both institutions and individuals. Nations, and institutions
within them, tend to flourish when their members are devoted to
common purposes that transcend the gratification of narrowly
personal interests and desires.

Where there is fragmentation, there is often adversarial tension and, attendant upon it, corruption and betrayal of institutional purposes. If a country or an institution is without common
purposes and therefore without direction, it can be manipulated
by special interests. This is one reason that it is crucial for
institutions to identify their own individual purposes if they are
to fulfill their daily obligations.

But the achievement of common purposes is a difficult thing
and sometimes the means exact a price that overrides the
benefits. For example, by American ideas of liberty, justice, and
opportunity, citizens should learn to read. Universal literacy
should be a common purpose of the nation. But while this is a

national issue, it does not follow that it admits of a national remedy.

Instruction in reading is the work of individual schools, colleges, and universities—each with its own students—and it is the duty of each of them to build faculty, academic programs, and conditions of institutional life to achieve this end. When we suppose that all national goals can be achieved by steps taken at the national level, we undermine the responsibility of individual educational institutions by making them redundant. This is an unacceptable price, because it keeps the schools from identifying the specific problems that, finally, no one else has the ability to solve. As Alfred North Whitehead insisted, "The first requisite for educational reform is the school as a unit, with its approved curriculum based on its own needs, and evolved by its own staff."[2]

This point has been made repeatedly in the history of American education. As the Commission on Financing Higher Education put it in 1952:

> What most protects freedom of choice in America is the great diversity of its institutions. . . . The structure of American higher education exemplifies this. Its liberty is buttressed by the variety of its institutions. Our colleges and universities engage in healthy competition within the broad outlines of a common purpose. They grew up to meet the needs of the country. They reflect the particular interests of different communities. . . . [They] differ because of their location . . . and also with sponsorships. No arbitrary pattern, no central plan, has ever been imposed.[3]

Our concern, then, is with the achievement of common purposes within individual educational institutions. This, too, is difficult, because we are all very much alike in some ways and very different in others. Oddly, our similarities often have as much power to divide or isolate us as our differences.

SAMENESSES THAT DIVIDE

There are some striking samenesses in all of us: We are all born in spectacular ignorance, and we all die with much of it intact. We have a natural tendency to love ourselves, and to give inordinate weight to our individual desires and perceptions of things and to our own worthiness to be loved by others. We tend toward self-preoccupation, and we often act selfishly. These characteristics obviously tend to divide us.

Our self-indulgence tends to make us satisfied with our own opinions rather than judicious and thoughtful. Descartes captured this in a penetrating insight in 1637—striking evidence of how little we change over the centuries:

> Good sense is of all the things in the world the most equally distributed, for everybody thinks himself so abundantly provided with it that even those most difficult to please in all matters do not commonly desire more of it than they already possess.[4]

We seldom suppose that we need any more good sense than we have. Instead, all of us tend to question the good sense of those who disagree with us. It is another likeness that divides.

Augustine identified an even more dangerous human element twelve centuries earlier. He argued that in the City of Man (temporal existence on earth), unlike the City of God (Heaven), there will always be war because everyone is alike in desiring peace. The catch is that everyone desires peace in accordance with his or her own vision of what forms of peace, what conditions of coexistence, are acceptable. We fight for a peace that is never acceptable to all the combatants, and so there is no war to end all wars.[5]

This has been recognized in our century, too. In 1940, Antoine de Saint Exupéry wrote, "War must be waged . . . but, as the fundmental problem is never tackled, this war will only end with the momentary exhaustion of one of the adversaries."[6] Subsequent events have proved how right he was.

These facts about us—that we can be set apart from each other by both sameness and difference—can make the human condition rough-edged, stressful, and sometimes violent. Not much can be accomplished unless we can live and work together, unless we can share common purposes. But our samenesses, let alone our differences, are so divisive that the fundamental question of political philosophy is, and always has been: How are we to enjoy some peace and security together—to say nothing of opportunity for meaningful work—without subjection to a tyrant sufficiently powerful to keep us from each other's throats?

CYNICISM

Cynics have two answers to this question. One is that without tyranny we will tear each other to pieces. This version of cynicism generally holds, with Thomas Hobbes, that the only durable and reliable bond among human beings is fear: people can always be motivated to act in a particular way through fear. Thus, we must repose power in a tyrant. The power must be sufficient to generate whatever measure of terror is necessary for the tyrant to force people to act in behalf of common purposes.

Hobbes articulates both the theory and the practice of this position. The theory is that the dark side of human nature—our natural passions—is utterly dominant and subject to restraint only by external force. In a natural condition without a tyrant to subdue us, our lives are "solitary, poore, nasty, brutish, and short."[7] Only tyranny can save us from ourselves:

> "For the Lawes of Nature, (as *Justice, Equity, Modesty, Mercy,* and (in summe) *doing to others as wee would be done to,)* of themselves, with out the terrour of some Power to cause them to be observed, are contrary to our naturall Passions, that carry us to Partiality, Pride, Revenge, and the like. And Covenants, without the Sword, are but Words, and of no strength to Secure a man at all."[8]

Thus, the practice of achieving common purposes consists in the forfeiture of each individual will to a single sufficiently powerful will:

> He who submits his will to the will of another conveys to that other the right of his strength and faculties. Insomuch as when the rest have done the same, he to whom they have submitted hath so much power, as by the term of it, he can conform the wills of particular men into unity and accord.[9]

Even though, in Hobbes's view, some people are less selfish than others, all will do what they can to serve their own ends, even if their excesses are only for the sake of their own safety and security. The worst among us, the most ruthless, will destroy the rest whenever it is to their advantage.

This is the cynical warrant, the only warrant, for tyranny: Take the most demeaning view possible of humanity—that no one can *ever* be trusted—and then control disparate human wills by institutionalized terror. The natural immoderation of men can be constrained, and common purposes preserved, only by building institutions that have the capacity to visit totally immoderate power on everyone.

The twentieth century is replete with tyrants, from Stalin and Hitler to Idi Amin and the Ayatollah. And most of these tyrants invoke pure hatred against all who are not their subjects: dissidents, members of other religions, other nations, other economic systems, other races, and so on. Tyrannies best sustain common purposes by hatred and destruction. Hatred of others effectively diverts attention from the humiliation of personal subjection and thus serves the tyrant well.[10]

The encouragement of hatred and even lust for blood by the tyrant comes easily, of course, because the sole justification for his power is that we are all irrevocably contemptible. Individuals and individual lives cannot matter, humanity must be faceless, because we are all alike in our inordinate self-interestedness.

Nothing which has a price can be priceless, and the idea of dignity cannot apply to anyone who would stop at nothing to get ahead. If the tyrant is even crudely logical, he must see all of humanity, including himself, as unworthy of respect; thus, there is no reason, aside from personal survival or perpetuation of power, for the tyrant ever to exercise restraint. Many tyrants strive with great passion to avoid this conclusion, to believe instead that they are superior to others. Thus Philo could report Caligula's conviction that either kings are gods or men other than kings are beasts. In either case, the tyrant is exempt from every moral restraint.

Something deep inside us responds to the comforts of subjection, and allows the would-be tyrant to invite us to sacrifice liberty and its allowance of individual differences. Perhaps the fact that not all tyrants behave equally badly appeals to us. Or, more probably, that many of us seem to be addled even by the tension generated when reasonable people of good will disagree, at least up to a point, on matters of the greatest importance. Many of us find comfort and security only in homogeneity, whether of sex, race, ethnic background, language, opinion, or judgment. Even though we may actually achieve security from ruthless men by banding together, our tendency to avoid tension can make us easy prey for the tyrant.

It is this human tendency that leads Isaiah Berlin to say:

One belief, more than any other, is responsible for the slaughter of individuals on the altars of the great historical ideals—justice or progress or the happiness of future generations, or the sacred mission or emancipation of a nation or race or class, or even liberty itself, which demands the sacrifice of individuals for the freedom of society. This is the belief that somewhere, in the past or in the future, in divine revelation or in the mind of an individual thinker, in the pronouncements of history or science, or in the simple heart of an uncorrupted good man, there is a final solution.[11]

Tyranny is the way of life that declares itself the final solution.

The appeal of this solution must not be underestimated. Many human institutions achieve common purposes by a dominant power. Not only countries, but sometimes corporations, schools, churches, families, armies, street gangs, social organizations, and athletic teams work, consciously or unconsciously, on a tyrannical model.

The price of achieving purpose by this first method of the cynic is steep, whether we visit it on ourselves or it is visited on us. Liberty falls. Justice falls. Courage falls. Self-respect is replaced by arrogant self-righteousness and fanaticism. Since all limits to power fall, the tyrant's excesses and errors in politics, economics, and war cannot be checked. These effects are normally measured in thousands or millions of dead, slaughtered on the altar of the tyrant's ambition or even of the tyrant's sincere belief that his answer is final.

The cynic cannot escape Lord Acton's truism that absolute power does destroy whoever possesses it—does corrupt absolutely. The corruption consists partly in the very sincerity with which the tyrant says that his ends justify his means. He believes this. And, in his self-satisfaction, he lives beyond all limits. This is not unhuman; it is rather what Descartes saw as our inordinate confidence in our own good sense carried to its final excess. It is all too human.

For this reason, many cynics pose an alternative solution to enable us to live together, but this second solution forfeits any aspiration to common purposes. This second position holds that because of the dark side of human nature, no one can be trusted with *any* power, so that all questions must be settled by unanimous consent.

The difficulty with this view—aside from a deep contempt that denies the possibility of human achievement even before life begins—is that it cannot sustain both durable equality and common purposes. Even if it protects us from the tyrant, it cannot protect us from the tyranny of individuals or the tyranny of the minority. It saves us from the tyrant by destroying legitimate authority and responsibility. Thus, it gives us over to the worst in everyone.

In practice, this egalitarian ethos based on universal impotence leads to the resolution of disagreements by the passion of the people involved: the most insistent prevail or else there is no resolution and no hope of shared purposes. Perhaps worse, all questions of substance become secondary to questions of procedure; the issue is always whether everyone consents, never whether what they are consenting to is true or right, just or reasonable. Consent itself becomes a procedural tyranny, suppressing concern for substance. At worst, shared, slavish devotion to procedure amounts to nothing more than pure litigiousness.

When such a spirit of distrust pervades all, the group has no chance to be a community and to be joined in common purposes. Concern for the common good, and civic and moral authority sufficient to advance it, become impossible.

Ironically, the model of universal consent even defeats the likelihood of compromise. As Michael Crozier explains in *The Trouble With America:*

> When social barriers collapse, broken down by ease of access to decision making and the freedom of all concerned to follow their own paths to the bitter end, the rule of law becomes harder and harder to impose. Adjustments continue to be made of course, but their pace keeps slackening, as the system closes in on itself. The short-term gradually absorbs the long-term, there is no longer the time or the freedom needed to reflect and invest for the future.
>
> And once the long-term ceases to be adequately represented, it pays for each player in the political game to press his short-term demands to the limit. With much more latitude than he ever enjoyed before, the individual (or group) now has the luxury of displaying a fine intransigence. Thus, adjustments become more difficult, and they no longer contain the elements of flexibility and risk taking that once provided a way out of the zero-sum game dilemma (where it makes no sense for anyone to take the chance of collaborating with another person, since A's gain is B's loss).[12]

In effect, this putative solution to the problem of common purposes offers to settle for mere coexistence. And it cannot promote even that.

How different this is, for example, from the explicit position of Abraham Lincoln: "no man is good enough to govern another man without that other's consent. I say this is the leading principle—the sheet anchor of American republicanism."[13] Lincoln insisted on the principle of consent in the establishment of specific governments, but he did not deny that there should be government or that men and women should be entrusted with the authority and powers of office.

It is scarcely surprising that the two forms of human coexistence envisioned by the cynic should lead to such unsatisfactory conclusions. We *do* have the weaknesses the cynic attributes to us: self-indulgence, excess, vanity, abuse of power, envy, and folly. But this is not the whole truth about us. If all of us are by nature capable of the seven deadly sins—gluttony, lust, sloth, pride, greed, anger, and envy—then we must be in some measure capable of their corresponding virtues, or else they would not be sins. A being constitutionally incapable of anything but gluttonous behavior could not be a sinner, any more than a machine could be.

To this, it may be replied that we are in error to think of any human conduct as sinful, wrong, blameworthy, or reprehensible. The cynic may insist that we are constitutionally incapable of acting on principle under pressure; he may, without contradiction, hold that every person can be bought, and deny that there is anything evil, weak, or lamentable in humanity. The cynic may treat this only as a fact about us to be taken into consideration depending on what we want. If we want common purposes, safety, and homogeneity, then we should establish tyrannies; and, if we fear the excesses of tyrants, then we should establish universal impotence. On this view, all normative questions are simply questions about the effectiveness of our means; nothing human is good or evil except insofar as it promotes or fails to promote our ends, which are not in themselves good or evil, but whatever we happen to want.

In support of this position, the cynic might insist that studies of criminals and their behavior provide the model for all of

humanity. Such studies, as James Q. Wilson and Richard Herrenstein explain in *Crime and Human Nature,* provide "mount-
ing evidence that, on the average, offenders differ from non-
offenders in physique, intelligence, and personality."[14]
"Criminals are more likely to have mesomorphic body types, to
have fathers who were criminals, even in the case of adopted
sons who could not have known their fathers, to be of somewhat
lower intelligence, to be impulsive or extroverted, and to have
autonomous nervous systems that respond more slowly and less
vigorously to stimuli."[15] The future may show that there are
genetic factors relevant to criminal behavior or disposition to
criminality; it may someday confirm that some human beings are
not malleable in the sense that neither education nor normal
socialization can prevent them from being criminals. The cynic
may then argue that we are all like criminals—that the relevant
differences among us are mere matters of degree.

This conclusion does not follow, of course. The genetic make-
up of some criminals may spare them from responsibility, i.e.,
from normal human obligations of self-control and restraint.
They are not sinners but victims of a genetic flaw.

But because this flaw is identifiable as such only by contrast to
the make-up of human beings who are not victims of it, it cannot
be used as the basis of an account of human beings in general.
Instead, if the research proves out, we may develop a more
considered idea of our obligations to people with the flaw. We
can, for example, seek medical means of improving the responsiveness of their nervous systems so that they can derive satisfaction from human relations without the spur of violence,
danger, or drugs.

If the cynical argument should prevail, several consequences
will follow. If nothing human is good or evil, then it will not
matter to us whether we have common purposes. If we do have
common purposes, it will not matter what they are. And if
nothing is genuinely right or wrong, then we will find nothing
wrong in betraying the public trust. Should these ideas become
humanity's supposed "final answer," the point of civilization
and education will be destroyed. Should future generations of
human beings ever try to recover from this nihilism, they will
have to rebuild the humanly possible from ashes far more deadly

than any created by nuclear weapons. For nuclear weapons have the power only to destroy life. Cynicism destroys the very reasons for life.

Because the cynic holds that the dark side is the whole truth about us, he or she cannot appeal to anything *but* institutional forms to resolve the problems of coexistence and common purposes; the cynic has eliminated the possibility of appeal to anything *better* in us that might give vitality to the human enterprise. But the forms of institutions of themselves cannot solve the problems of living, breathing beings; forms have no more vitality than the faith and conviction and drive those beings pour into them. For the cynic, because we are empty vessels, we have nothing to pour in, and the forms must sustain themselves.

Forms, without the investment of human vitality and aspiration, are lifeless, not self-sustaining. The limitation on mere forms was clearly recognized by James Madison and other Federalists, and was essential to the formation of the United States. The Federalists were not naive about the importance of formal structure in governance as a constraint to abuse of power and to our capacity for factional violence. In fact, Madison insisted that "the latent causes of faction are . . . sown in the nature of man,"[16] and he therefore argued:

> If men were angels, no government would be necessary. If angels were to govern men, neither external nor internal controls on government would be necessary. In framing a government which is to be administered by men over men, the great difficulty lies in this: you must first enable the government to control the governed; and in the next place oblige it to control itself.[17]

But as alert as Madison was to the samenesses and differences that divide us, he knew that the cynical solution to the problem of common purposes is no solution at all, and that its premise is incomplete:

> As there is a degree of depravity in mankind which requires a certain degree of circumspection and distrust, so there are other qualities in human nature which justify a certain portion of esteem and confidence. Republican government presupposes the existence of these qualities in a higher degree than any other form. Were the pictures which have been drawn by the political jealousy of some among us faithful likenesses of the human character, the inference would be

that there is not sufficient virtue among men for self-government; and that nothing less than the chains of despotism can restrain them from destroying and devouring one another.[18]

Such a vision was essential to the establishment of the United States; its reliability is confirmed by the fact that our experiment in ordered liberty is still underway, two centuries later.

The dynamism of the experiment is due not merely to the genius of our system of checks and balances—our forms. It arises as well from the humanly possible—the potential in human beings to be and to do what deserves "a certain portion of esteem and confidence."

The American Union could never have been sustained by mere forms; it could not have survived in 1861 without the desire of men and women committed to its preservation *or* without the civility, constraint, and decency of those who fought to secede from it. Thus we can admire both Abraham Lincoln and Robert E. Lee, despite the fact that from 1861 until 1865 they were adversaries in war.

Nor are our problems today solvable by mere forms any more than we could resolve racial discrimination by having everyone learn the forms by reading the Constitution. It is not that the cynic needs greater imagination in the construction of forms; it is, rather, that the merely formal solutions to which the cynic is limited cannot answer the question of common purposes.

INNOCENCE

If cynicism will not do, neither will innocence or naïveté. If innocence of the human capacity for excess, even for depravity, were enough, we would not need to teach our children to refuse candy from strangers. That this lesson is so imperative, that it must be taught so firmly and so early in the life of any child, is ample evidence that we can find no hope of achieving common purposes by appealing to the notion that men and women are by nature decent, restrained, cooperative, and tolerant. To believe this is to invite disappointment, and to teach this to a child is to instill a notion that later experience will transform into full-grown cynicism. For cynicism is nothing more than innocence disappointed and lost, rather than innocence overcome by generous instruction in the facts of life.

Naïveté, because it denies evil, grants evil a license to flourish. Alexander Solzhenitsyn cautioned against naivete and its consequences in his now famous Commencement Address at Harvard University in 1978. Commenting on Western society's "scarce defense against the abyss of human decadence,"[19] Solzhenitsyn observed that "this tilt of freedom toward evil has come about gradually, but it evidently stems from a humanistic and benevolent concept according to which man—the master of this world—does not bear any evil within himself, and all the defects of life are caused by misguided social systems, which must therefore be corrected."[20]

It is for this reason that Reinhold Niebuhr insists in *The Children of Light and the Children of Darkness* that "a free society prospers best in a cultural, religious, and moral atmosphere which encourages neither a too pessimistic nor too optimistic view of human nature."[21] Both excesses tend toward totalitarianism precisely because they ignore the facts of our nature taken so carefully into account in the formation of the United States. Neither cynicism nor innocence can serve the cause of common purposes in a condition of liberty.

Where, then, are we to look?

BEYOND CYNICISM AND INNOCENCE

We must look to institutional forms, at least in part. Madison reminds that we are neither angels nor beasts. So we must look to ourselves, because we *are* human. We must see what we have in us, and what we may come to rely on in ourselves that can enable us to work together without becoming mindless drones. How can we be faithful to anything other and greater than the satisfaction of our own private desires, whims, and tastes?; better, how can we live and work together with a mutual desire for common purposes and individual liberty? How can we achieve loyalty to specific institutions without becoming servile to them?

Educational institutions have usually answered these questions with a respect for the methods of rational inquiry and deliberation; they have sought, or at least claimed, to be institutions where cooperative deliberation on relevant evidence leads to decision making without tyranny or caprice.

This ideal is no more potent in practice, however, than the spirit of the individuals who aspire to it. In education that spirit has often been weak because for many faculty and administrators educational institutions are instruments of personal ambition rather than vehicles for service to students. J. Myron Atkin argues that what is generally true of human institutions is especially true within education:

> We are ambivalent about our government. These days each presidential candidate seems to run against Washington and thereby strikes a deep, responsive chord in the body politic. At the same time, government is used as a blunt instrument to advance one's own favorite cause. It is difficult to know what any one person can do, particularly in the United States where there is not a group of well-regarded individuals speaking out on education issues. Education administrators these days do not represent the profession in the United States. Indeed, their major preoccupation is survival, and they are usually in an adversarial relationship with the teachers. Leaders of teachers unions are seen as self-serving. . . . Teachers themselves, of course, have become a powerful special interest group, though it is not clear that their power is being used with special skill or wisdom.[22]

At the same time, the many pressures within and outside academic institutions have pulled teachers and administrators in many directions away from any sense of common purposes. Edward Shils observes:

> The disorders both in the student body and in the teaching corps have all left marked traces in the diversion of attention from some of the central tasks of academic life. Many teachers have continued to do their duty, and, of course, great numbers of teachers have applied themselves unreservedly to research. Nevertheless, in recent decades, the sure moral touch has weakened and the self-confidence of the academic profession in its devotion to calling has faltered. There is need for the profession to clarify in its own mind and to reaffirm the fundamental obligations inherent in its undertaking.[23]

Because of these conditions, exacerbated by the constituency mentality, the governance of educational institutions frequently does not embrace reason to identify and to serve common purposes. At worst, it is reduced to efforts to accommodate the supposed "rights" of various groups that are identified as "constituencies."

A preoccupation with so-called rights is a grim sign in any institution. When we think of our relations to each other exclusively in terms of rights, we implicitly acknowledge that we have no hope of common purposes and shared effort through the more intimate bonds of affection, mutual respect, kinship, personal virtue, and decency. This bodes ill for students because it focuses administrative leadership on satisfying the putative rights of other groups, deflecting attention from the absolute priority of educational mission.

Of course respect for individual human rights and representation of individual interests is essential to civilized life. But when we emphasize our rights to the exclusion of all else, the destruction is enormous: What would we make of a marriage in which spouses are faithful to one another only because each acknowledges that the other has a right to fidelity? What would we say of friends who were truthful only because of their respective rights? Of parents who do not beat children only because of their children's rights? Of people generally whose only regard for others is based upon rights? We would say that such relations were far superior to the barbaric conditions under which no rights are acknowledged, but *inferior*—far inferior—to human relations in which some sense of mutuality, of shared interest and concern, is abidingly present. Only then is it possible to speak of marriage, friendship, parenthood, or collegiality.

And yet, perhaps unavoidably, the structure of educational institutions sometimes tends to create interest groups. Schools, colleges, and universities, whether public or independent, are normally divided into relatively isolated departments. Good reasons for departmental structures include the achievement of depth in scholarly and scientific disciplines, organization of undergraduate and graduate courses, supervision and assessment of the work of junior colleagues in a field, and localized budgetary authority and responsibility. Without departments, no college or university could ever hope to achieve the same breadth of expertise and educational opportunity for students. But there is a negative side to this division: departments commonly share little in the way of mutual purpose, and temptations of academic prestige, institutional power, and allotments of money can lead to ruthless competition.

Faculty members are frequently isolated as well, often by their own choice. Many faculty view research, scholarship, and publication—not teaching or participation in the life of an educational institution—as the priorities of their profession.

This view is often reinforced by the practices and rewards of their schools. In some institutions, books, articles, and grants for research may figure more in determination of rank, tenure, and salary than effective and conscientious teaching.

Furthermore, universities consist of numerous faculties and colleges, undergraduate, graduate, and professional. Communication among them may be limited, interest in each other relatively low, purposes quite distinct. Only sound leadership can create the needed unity within diversity.

Yet many of the people entrusted to administer or teach are so busy trying to get through each day's immediate tasks that they have little time to devote to institutional planning, let alone planning for common purposes and liberty. The lives of many administrators are more akin to the lives of firemen waiting for the next alarm than to institutional planners. They have much to learn from such leaders as Marcus Aurelius, who cautioned that people whose days are busy whirls of reaction to events never manage to focus all their effort and thought on fundamental goals. They become "triflers"; being without focus, they cannot lead.[24]

With such leaders, motivation to identify and achieve common purposes is low, and many institutions would have scant idea where to begin even if they wanted to. They accommodate interest groups rather than lead different groups in the mutual task of educating students.

Problems of structure cannot be remedied by administrative tyranny. If educational institutions are run by tyrants, they cannot respect intellectual liberty, and so they can neither advance knowledge nor help students toward mature freedom. Universal impotence fares no better. If institutions have no considered places for the authority of trustees to govern, of administrators to administer, and of faculty to teach and conduct research, no one will be responsible for the institution's work. In either case, there is no way to bear faithfully the public trust. Authority and accountability must be based on an institutional structure that serves the establishment of common purposes *and* the protection of liberty. But unless structure is designed for the sake of the institution's work, and unless that work is clearly articulated and understood throughout the institution, structural change is mere tinkering.

There are many ways to organize the structure of an institution so that it can fulfill its educational mission. But structure alone does not provide such a mission and it is never a substitute for the personal attitudes and virtues that make sound teaching and learning possible.

John A. Beach, who has served as president of the National Association of College and University Attorneys, addressed this point in a telling way in "The Management and Governance of Academic Institutions":

> The attitudes of individuals involved in university governance and management are more telling than general analysis of governance or organizational management.
>
> There is quite a lot of literature on academic governance. I do not think it is really possible to gather enough data, let alone assign them all their proper weights, to satisfy the formulae often urged upon us as essential to decision making. Moreover, I do not think tinkering with governance or organizational structures will help very much. For better or worse, it is the attitude of human beings that will control the university management and governance structures and not vice versa.[25]

The spirit of service that administrators and teachers bring to their institutions cannot be overestimated. Where groups are more divided by concern for their own rights than they are joined by their devotion to students, the consequences are dire. At worst, as Beach explains, institutions can become preoccupied with procedures for deliberation among "constituent" groups to the extent that they are unable to resolve any question; such institutions become victims of academic gridlock.

My own experience as a college president confirms this. In one instance, for example, a coed was confronted in her dormitory by an intruder. Fortunately, she was not done serious injury, but the institution was faced with the issue of dormitory security. The issue was cast in the college as a tension between security and liberty: Should the dormitories be locked at night so that students would have either to enter by key or be admitted by security? Or would this change limit student freedom too much? College personnel and students were divided; but more important, no one wished to take responsibility for a decision because consensus was impossible. College personnel for student life waited for the incident to be forgotten instead of addressing it and denied their obligations by insisting that students ought to solve such problems. That anyone in a position of authority *should* face the problem and make a decision was taken as insensitive to governance procedures. In the end, the gridlock had to be broken by a decisive administrative step. The same problems often arise for admissions procedures, financial aid policies, the content of catalogs, drug and alcohol policies, and student social life generally. Such gridlock obstructs educational purposes; it also betrays explicit promises of conscientious performance made to students and their parents.

As Beach puts it:

> There is an endless wheel of governance at most academic institutions involving faculty, students, administrators, trustees, and alumni. Each of these five constituencies tends to have its own predisposition on the three grand questions: What is a university? What should it do? Who shall decide? . . . As to management decisions (as distinct from academic and research matters comprising what I have described as the essence of the university) I suggest that faculty either cannot or will not make decisions. The 60's and 70's presented elaborate schemes and structures for faculty governance, and analysts are still writing books attempting to quantify myriad factors and balance them all out like an equation. It will not work. The real institution has real human beings to deal with, usually with a faculty characterized by a multiplicity of views, doctrinaire style, and inevitable defense in depth into data-gathering and endless committee review—with everything suspended, of course, between May and September. The net result is governance gridlock on the part of faculty.[26]

Beach is convinced that faculty must have the central part in deliberations about curriculum, research, and other academic work; but their work must be distinguished from the work of trustees and administrators in the overall governance and leadership of the institution.

Beach insists that everywhere in educational institutions there must be personal virtue, and he emphasizes the need for personal courage. He rightly claims that if governors, visitors, administrators, and faculty lack courage even the most basic ideals of education are beyond our reach:

> There is a great need for more courage in academic governance and management. Courage, for example, to replace some of the hypocrisy in peer review with candor. . . . Courage, for another example,

for an administrator to do something risky or controversial, rather than avoiding the risk or the controversy by endlessly seeking consensus.

Courage, for example, to recognize and deal with sex between faculty and the students they teach as inherently coercive and unprofessional.

Courage, for yet another example, to recognize and deal with grade inflation where it is blatant to the point of undermining the institution's mission.

Intercollegiate athletics provide a vivid challenge to the courage of all segments of the governance structures of many institutions. . . .

There are plentiful examples; suffice to say that individual courage will do more to improve college and university governance and management than a hundred more books or a thousand more essays on the structures of governance or the techniques of management or the theory of either.[27]

Hypocrisy, lack of candor, sexual involvement, grade inflation, athletic misconduct—all are well known in academic life. Some faculty groups in higher education have refused even to accede that sexual relations between faculty and students are unprofessional or professionally unethical. Faculty members at the University of California "rejected an amendment to the Faculty Code of Conduct that would have declared it unethical for professors to engage in romantic or sexual liaisons with students 'under circumstances which compromise the student-faculty relationship.' A similar statement, which would have declared romantic relationships a breach of professional ethics, was defeated at the University of Texas at Arlington."[28]

At Arlington, faculty members argued that such relationships were none of the university's business. They thereby implied that Justice Frankfurter was wrong to stress the freedom of a university "to determine for itself on academic grounds who may teach" and "what may be taught"; their position implies that individual faculty members have license to conduct themselves however they want, no matter what their behavior teaches students. If, of course, an educational institution acquiesces in these circumstances, it forfeits all responsibility for the well-being of the students it was chartered, funded, and empowered to teach. Such a course is incompatible with fidelity to the public trust and further indicates the importance of John Beach's emphasis on courage.

Such attitudes are most necessary in college and university

presidents and school superintendents and principals. These are the people who must speak for the purposes of their institutions and ensure that policies and practices advance those purposes. They must lead their institutions in devotion to the fulfillment of mission above the accommodation of any group. As Secretary of Education William J. Bennett explains:

> Recently, educational researchers sought to determine those factors that make some elementary and secondary schools more successful than others. Among the most important was strong leadership from the school principal. Although colleges and universities are more complex institutions than secondary schools, with far stronger fragmenting tendencies, leadership plays the same crucial role. . . . A president should be the chief academic officer of the institution, not just the chief administrative, recruitment, or fund-raising officer.[29]

Bennett describes research showing that "only 2 percent of the more than seven hundred college and university presidents interviewed described themselves as playing a major role in academic affairs."[30] This amounts to the divorce of institutional leadership from the central purposes of the institution; because the presidents are the primary spokesmen to trustees, this trend also separates trustees from academic and policy questions. Thus, those who are ultimately responsible for fulfilling the public trust are diverted from the central questions of institutional effectiveness. Institutions must counter these trends.

For educational institutions to do their rightful work, they must succeed in attracting and keeping personnel with such virtues as courage and justice. The institutions themselves must be committed uncompromisingly to purposes that make the investment of such people worthwhile. Specifically, in all questions of institutional policy and performance, as Lloyd H. Elliott, president of George Washington University, explained twenty-five years ago:

> The objective of university reform and restructuring is clearly the improvement of the educational program. The objective must not be identified with or allowed to become placation of one group over another, a compromise with student power, or a preservation of the *statua quo*. The overriding objective must be a more effective educational program for all concerned. No other motive can be allowed to intrude.[31]

The fundamental question of policy thus becomes what kind of individuals will allow "no other motive to intrude."

We must not, of course, be naïve in supposing a universal beneficence and dedication in faculty and administrators. But we *can* insist upon certain essential features of intellect and character.

Some of us have such features. They are achievements—not given to us as are the capacities to see or hear, but brought to realization by thought and will. They rest on personal effort to civilize intelligence through the fullest respect for ideals and motives that transcend the mere gratification of an uncultivated self.

No achievement by any individual or institution is sufficient to lead us to "that happy empire of perfect wisdom and perfect virtue" which Hamilton rightly believed to be a chimera. But if we are to stretch ourselves and our institutions to attain the greatest enlightenment and degrees of service, we must be able to rely on ourselves as well as our arrangements. To bear faithfully the trust of others, we must be able to trust ourselves.

The activity that most advances the possibility of common purposes with liberty is generous understanding. It is indispensable to civilization, so it is indispensable in education.

3

Generous Understanding

What, then, is our neighbor? Thou hast regarded his thought, his feeling, as somehow different from thine. Thou hast said, "A pain in him is not like a pain in me, but something far easier to bear." He seems to thee a little less living than thou; his life is dim, it is cold, it is a pale fire beside thy own burning desires. . . . . So, dimly and by instinct hast thou lived with thy neighbor, and hast known him not, being blind. Thou hast made [of him] a thing, no Self at all. Have done with this illusion, and simply try to learn the truth. Pain is pain, joy is joy, everywhere, even as in thee. In all the songs of the forest birds; in all the cries of the wounded and dying, struggling in the captor's power; in the boundless sea where the myriads of water creatures strive and die; amid all the countless hordes of savage men; in all sickness and sorrow; in all exultation and hope, everywhere, from the lowest to the noblest, the same conscious, burning, wilful life is found, endlessly manifold as the forms of the living creatures, unquenchable as the fires of the sun, real as these impulses that even now throb in thine own little selfish heart. Lift up thy eyes, behold that life, and then turn away, and forget it as thou canst; but, if thou hast *known* that, thou hast begun to know thy duty.[1]

—Josiah Royce

JOSIAH ROYCE UNDERSTANDS that others are as we are, that one's own dear self is not unique in its capacity for exultation and for agony. He also suggests that even when we understand this, when we behold another's life, we may still turn away and forget; he sees that we can acknowledge that others are as we are and still be indifferent to them.

Understanding the likenesses between ourselves and others is a major step in human maturation, a mark of progress beyond childish preoccupation with our own putative uniqueness. Even greater maturation may be required to overcome the self-absorption that makes specific individuals and the significance of their judgments and feelings invisible or inconsequential to us. It is one thing to understand likenesses, another to care that we are, by virtue of our common humanity, kindred. Recognition of such likeness explains why the Eighth Amendment to the Constitution prohibits cruel and unusual punishment of everyone, including violent criminals, no matter how monstrous their crime. Recognizing fundamental likenesses is not, however, enough. Seeing others as we see ourselves is not enough either. We must care. To take our neighbors seriously, we must love them as we love ourselves.

When understanding is conjoined with such concern, it becomes generous understanding. John Dewey speaks of it as "the formation of a sympathetic imagination for human relations in action."[2] It is not difficult to get a sense of the activity of generous understanding in our daily, even mundane, circumstances. It begins at a rudimentary level with simply caring enough about other people to try to understand and act in light of how things look from their point of view.

Experiences in professional life are instructive about the powerful effects of generous understanding. Once, as a college president, I was asked by a student to reverse a ruling dismissing him for drug use and dealing. I refused, on the grounds that the use of drugs violated institutional policy, affronted the law, and flouted the educational mission of the college.

A few hours later, the student's father called me. He informed me that he had willingly paid very high tuition to the college because he believed that the college was educationally serious and would not tolerate behavior that thwarted its educational programs. He said that he was sorry his son had run into trouble, but our action confirmed his judgment that the college was worth what he paid for his son's enrollment in it.

This was not the conversation I expected; the parent's aims for his son and appreciation of the responsibilities of the college were unusual. He not only understood with generosity; he insisted that he would have done the same thing. As he sensed, no one devoted to the teaching and learning of the young can dismiss a student without sadness, and he went out of his way to support me, not only in my action but in my hope that his son would go on to better things.

Trying to understand generously enhances our ability to live and work with others. It can help us to take seriously our obligations to students. Conscious awareness of kinship is a wellspring of human qualities that "deserve esteem and confidence." It is fundamental to maturing personally beyond selfishness and its boundless passion to gratify petty desires.

Devotion to purposes beyond oneself, as in teaching, is obviously not sufficient to eliminate frustration in daily life. Many people in education no doubt feel that their institutions are like the universe as Stephen Crane described it in "War Is Kind":

> A man said to the universe: "Sir, I exist!"
> "However," replied the universe, "the fact has not created in me a sense of obligation."[3]

But awareness that there are purposes worth the investment of our lives, and that those purposes come alive when we see and care that others are as we, can reduce or eliminate the kinds of frustration that derive from inordinate self-love and the futility of a life limited to it.

Some of the most inspiring stories in the human heritage tell of the power of generous understanding even in the cruelest adversity. The Martyrdom of Eleazar is such a story. Eleazar, a Maccabean sage, was threatened with agonizing death if he would not forsake his religion; even his friends encouraged him to pretend to do so. He refused:

> Such pretense is unworthy of my advanced age. My pretense for the sake of a brief transitory span of life would cause many of the younger generation to think that Eleazar had gone over to the gentile way of life, and so they, too, would go astray because of me, and I would earn the defilement and besmirching of my old age.[4]

Eleazar was whipped to death. "So he died, leaving his death as an example of nobility and as a precedent of valor to be remembered not only by the young but by the multitudes of his nation."[5] Even *in extremis,* Eleazar looked toward the young with understanding and a generous regard for their learning and their lives. This is the kind of maturity, of intellectual and moral character, most needed in anyone who is expected to bear the public trust and therefore to be qualified to serve in education. If we all cannot reach the heights of an Eleazar, we can at least look to him as an ideal.

This may seem wildly unrealistic at a time when many states are determining whether teachers can even read, write, and spell. It is also difficult to identify qualities of intellectual and moral maturity in candidates for faculty and administrative positions. How high can we set our expectations when compensation levels are low? How, under such conditions, can anyone speak seriously of looking for the qualities of a Royce or an Eleazar in every teacher and administrator?

These are serious objections, and they can be met only by acknowledging that understanding generously in daily life is a matter of degree. But if we take a careful look at generous understanding, we may get a sense of its necessity in education.

Those who are entrusted to teach and administer ought to understand that others are like themselves, and they ought to care, for this reason, how they treat them. But even if we do so in the respects that Royce emphasizes, we must be equally struck by the obvious fact that we are profoundly different in our perceptions, judgments, and convictions, Some of us are thoughtful, contemplative, and deliberate, while others are impulsive and thoughtless. Yet, even when we are alike in habits of thoughtful reflection and deliberation, we differ in our assessments, our conclusions, and our courses of action. This makes generous understanding imperative in any institution, any way of life, that aspires to common purposes and liberty.

ACCOUNTING FOR DIFFERENCES

Our differences of judgment about right and wrong, good and evil, beauty and ugliness are neither astonishing nor endless. Reasonable people of good will—people who take evidence seriously and are morally conscientious—can and do disagree, especially about matters of great complexity. Sometimes we can account for differences of opinion by examining relevant facts in specific instances. But some of our accounts of disagreement involve broad themes about human nature, about knowledge, objectivity, subjectivity, and the limits to knowledge.

If, for example, two thoughtful people disagree about the best course of action in specific circumstances, they may discover that one knows things the other does not and that mutual learning leads to agreement. One might be indignant about the misconduct of a colleague only to learn from the other that the colleague was at the time greatly worried about the health of a family member. Both may then conclude that the misbehavior should be excused, and that indignation is the wrong response. Or, two people may seem to disagree because they use key words in slightly different ways. Thus, one may be opposed to "affirmative action"—meaning by it always hiring a minority member if qualifications of the person and a nonminority individual are equal, while the other favors "affirmative action"—meaning by it always advertising positions in a variety of publications read by diverse groups. If the two use the words unambiguously, they may reach agreement.

Two people may also discover that they espouse the same principles but disagree in specific cases about their applications. Both may stand, for example, for justice, but disagree about how justice can be achieved. This is not a disagreement about ends, but rather about means—the kind of disagreement we have seen over the question of whether justice can better be achieved in South Africa by divestiture and economic sanctions. Recognizing that the disagreement is over means rather than ends can sometimes temper the hostility of adversaries. Even if they never reach agreement, they may learn to behave civilly. People may also disagree because the detailed content of their principles is different as a result of religious conviction, experience, background, and upbringing. They may, for example, agree that justice calls for retribution and punishment, but disagree about what forms of punishment are fair for specific crimes or misconduct.

In all such disagreements, most of which derive from the complexity of human life, reasonable people of good will—people who try to reach conclusions by using evidence, and who try to discover by careful deliberation what their duty is and to do it—always have some common ground. They at least agree about the importance of evidence and of good faith effort to discover duty and to fulfill its requirements.

But disagreement, including basic disagreement about principles, is sometimes accounted for by the theory that morality is fundamentally subjective and relative. This theory holds that nothing is really right or wrong, or good or evil, except insofar as an individual, group, society, or culture believes it to be. On this explanation of differences, no universal standards identifiable by reason can overcome individual or cultural differences. We are, finally, it holds, individually or culturally idiosyncratic.

Generous understanding belies this account of our nature and limits. It demonstrates that we are sufficiently alike in thought and feeling to enter a public domain of reasoned discourse, to penetrate and grasp the perceptions and concerns of others, and to take them into account in our deliberations and conduct.

Even relativistic accounts of disagreement about moral questions do not deny that reasoned discourse is possible for us in other subjects, such as mathematics and science; often relativism draws a distinction between facts and values and concludes that, while knowledge of facts is possible, and while reasoning about factual matters can lead to objectivity, moral judgment is subjective and not, finally, a matter of reason.

Drawing a hard distinction between facts and values is not a particularly useful way of accounting for disagreement, because mathematicians and scientists also disagree; indeed, all of us sometimes disagree about the facts of a specific case. That we are reasonable and objective—impartial in our methods of inquiry and discovery—is no guarantee that we will always agree. The inadequacy of the fact-value distinction as a means of identifying the limits of human knowledge is further suggested by philosopher Jon Moline who explains: "It is a fact" that the rape of an innocent victim "is an outrageous wrong."[6]

The fact-value distinction and its supposed explanatory power founder when confronted with judgments that are at once normative and determinate. A judgment such as "This argument is valid," or "That is a grade AAA egg" ascribes value and is determinate; the rightness or wrongness of the judgment is discovered by applying criteria as specific as those for verifying such judgments as "That brick weighs three pounds" or "This book has a thickness of 2.5 inches." In many disagreements, the problem is not that there is a difference between facts and values, but rather that the judgments do not admit of such precise application of fixed criteria. Thus, "This argument is persuasive" invites the questions, "How persuasive, and to whom?'' while the validity of an argument is not a matter of degree.

For these reasons, we need more subtle and fruitful accounts of disagreement. In any complex case, we virtually never have the complete story; not all the evidence is in, and sometimes it never will be because of limited time or limited technology. There is the fact of complexity itself. As John Silber observes, ours is a world of such complexity that it does not admit of "simple moral answers and moral certainty."[7] He explains that we can be morally conscientious only by "demonstrating anew the fallibility of conscience and the importance of respecting the moral integrity of those with whom we may disagree."[8] In addition to such facts of the human condition, sometimes we do not know enough about how to reason well, how to be objective, or how to understand generously. All these take effort and practice.

When we encounter disagreement in the spirit of Josiah Royce, when we see that others are as we are in their humanity and yet differ from us, we try to identify a domain of standards in reason, standards of inquiry and discovery, that is publicly accessible. We aspire to grasp and apply such standards to see whether we can be impartial and fair-minded in assessing the claims and convictions of those who initially disagree with us. The conviction that some degree of objectivity is possible is basic to formal education, since formal education is inseparable from the study of reasoned inquiry and discovery. At its fullest, the aspiration to objectivity includes the application of the same standards of criticism to our own beliefs as to the beliefs of others. At this level, we achieve intellectual honesty.

In some of us, observing the combinations of likeness and difference can generate a yearning to understand as another does. If the aspiration to objectivity consists in concerted effort to escape the confines of idiosyncrasy and to enter a public domain by means of systematic observation and thought, the yearning to understand generously consists of concerted effort to enter in thought and feeling the place and point of view of other people. It is the effort to perceive the world as another sees it, grasps it, and understands it—an effort motivated by recognition of our common nature.

These aspirations—to be objective and to understand gener-ously—are forms of our natural desire to know. When the two aspirations are conjoined they become an impetus to learn, a singularly powerful motive for systematic study. For they give direction and method to the desire to know; they give it concreteness.

Learning standards of objectivity, standards of reasoned inquiry and discovery, is essential to learning generally. This helps to explain why Euclid became the paradigm of and for learning in Western culture. Learning to understand generously is not indispensable to learning, but it dramatically expands what we can learn from each other. It is the most ennobling response to differences among us.

We must, however, be clear that generous understanding is profoundly different from intellectual promiscuity. Trying to grasp how others think and feel does not mean accepting their views or passions, does not mean accommodating them, does not mean tolerating the intolerable. In personal and professional life, we must finally make decisions on the basis of our best lights. Certainly, we want to avoid being the kind of person who simply does not care what anyone else feels or thinks; but we must be equally diligent to avoid collapsing into indecision, irresoluteness, and intellectual and moral impotence.

The experience of most teachers and administrators, for example, is sufficient to show that there is no substitute for listening carefully to students to grasp all you can of their perspectives. But once you have done so, it does not follow that you must acquiesce in their ideas and desires. For instance, I recall a conversation at St. John's with leaders of the student government about college policy on underage drinking. Some of the students thought the college should leave the matter alone, and allow students and their organizations to do as they saw fit in both public and private. I wanted to understand as much as possible about why, as leaders, they thought this—not why students *wanted* to be free to do as they pleased, but why they *believed* the college could responsibly indulge illegal behavior by student organizations selling drinks to minors and by the minors themselves.

One of the most mature and thoughtful students said, "Look, Mr. Delattre, very few students in America study the things we do. All of us read Plato and learn about Socrates." He continued that Socrates was a hero to many students, a man who refused to be pushed around by the state. His conclusion was that Socrates had made his own decisions about how to live and had flown in the face of institutional pressure; accordingly, students should emulate Socrates, and the college should take Socrates' conduct as a reason to avoid interfering with student life.

As a philosopher, I found the Socrates he described hard to recognize. At the same time, I was convinced that the student was not being sophistical or intellectually perverse. The sincerity of his views was not in question for me. I asked him to explain how Socrates defended himself against accusations of lawbreaking in the *Apology*. He said that Socrates denied that he had broken the law. I asked why Socrates refused in the *Crito* to flee from jail when his friends had arranged for his escape. He replied that Socrates had refused to flee because of his respect for the laws—Socrates would not commit this illegal act. I then asked him how, if we respect Socrates, we can be indifferent to his regard for the law.

The student, with the honesty I expected, looked me in the eye and said that we could not. He did not point out that Socrates had insisted he would not obey an unjust law, and he did not argue that laws against underage drinking were laws we should not obey. In a way, I was disappointed that he did not, as his doing so could have made the discussion of conscientious judgment in the establishment of institutional policy more comprehensive. It would have engaged us in a more thorough discussion of civic obligation. In the end, the college took a firm position against underage drinking in public and student organizations that permitted it. Although many students were disappointed, to my knowledge no one in the student government opposed the policies because of any judgment that the college was indifferent to the ideals of Socrates.

Best of all, students and administrators were not blind to the feelings and thoughts of others. Among us all, there was evidence of generous understanding and of regard for shared purposes.

BLINDNESS TOWARD OTHERS

Understanding generously is described with eloquence by William James in a penetrating talk to students called "On a Certain Blindness in Human Beings." At the outset, he says:

Now the blindness in human beings, of which this discourse will treat, is the blindness with which we are all afflicted in regard to the feelings of creatures and peoples different from ourselves.[9]

In seeking to illustrate what it means to see through the eyes of another, James points out that it is forever inexplicable to your dog, despite the bonds of affection between you, why you sit in a chair spending hours with pieces of paper which hold none of the joys or smells of bones, hedges, and lamp posts, and none of the ecstasy of chasing sticks and balls. Literature is forever lost on the dog, but we need not suppose that human beings are forever so impenetrable to one another.

He then tells a story of Africans unfamiliar with writing who gathered in great curiosity around an American visitor who was avidly reading a New York newspaper he had somehow obtained. James writes, "When he got through, they offered him a high price for the mysterious object; and being asked for what they wanted it, they said: 'For an eye medicine'—that being the only reason they could conceive of for the protracted bath which he had given his eyes upon its surface."[10]

This is a perfectly intelligible explanation of the high price offered for the newspaper—once you grasp it. The local people are not different from the American visitor in the way they reason, but rather in the facts they know. It is imperative to recognize in them habits of reasoning like our own, and to see that they could come to understand as the visitor does. How? By learning to read and thereby to enter a public domain of which he is already a part. Then, by grasping that his interest in the events of home is akin to their own interests, they can understand the appeal of the newspaper: they can enter the domain of his thoughts and feelings.

But without such learning, they are limited to being spectators. James speaks of the differences between spectator and beholder:

> The spectator's judgment is sure to miss the root of the matter, and to possess no truth. The subject judged knows a part of the world which the judging spectator fails to see, knows more while the spectator knows less; and, wherever there is conflict of opinion and difference of vision, we are bound to believe that the truer side is the side that feels the more, and not the side that feels the less.[11]

We are not bound to conclude that greater feeling demonstrates greater purchase on the truth. Sometimes just the opposite. But it would be a fine thing if we would normally take seriously the feelings and judgments of people who are directly involved in an enterprise we only observe. It would make generous understanding easier to learn if we were disposed to believe that others are sometimes more qualified to judge. But, in fact, we tend as we outgrow childhood to be more as Descartes described us than as James does—satisfied with our own good sense.

Worse, if we think we are not qualified, often we deny that qualifications matter. Our tendency to safeguard ourselves from admitting that somebody else may know better or that we may be incompetent to judge is clear in such clichés as, "I don't know anything about art, but I know what I like" and, "Beauty is in the eye of the beholder." These clichés spare us the arduous task of making our vision as powerful as the eyes of others who know how to look and what to look for. Such dodges are, of course, deadly to objectivity, to learning, and to generous understanding.

This kind of dodge comes naturally to us. Hobbes observes that:

> Such is the nature of men, that howsoever they may acknowledge many others to be more witty, or more eloquent, or more learned; Yet they will hardly believe there be many so wise as themselves: for they see their own wit at hand, and other men's at a distance.[12]

Understanding generously bridges the gap between ourselves and others. Martin Luther King appeals to our ability to bridge this gap in his "Letter from Birmingham Jail." There, after appealing to objective grounds—factual evidence of 340 years of discrimination and injustice toward black people in America—he asks readers to think and feel as he does. Human endurance and willingness to wait passively for improvement "run over . . . when you suddenly find your tongue twisted and your speech stammering as you seek to explain to your six year old daughter why she can't go to the public amusement park that has just been advertised on television, and see tears welling up in her eyes when she is told that Funtown is closed to colored children, and see ominous clouds of inferiority beginning to form in her little mental sky."[13]

James also offers a moving illustration which suggests that if we believe beauty is in the eyes of the beholder, then we ought to try to become qualified beholders.

James describes a visit to North Carolina where he sees the valleys, called coves, the settlers have cleared to build cabins and plant crops. He finds the cabins and small fields with tree stumps and zig-zag fences dreadfully ugly. He feels depressed by the rudeness of the places and concludes that nobody should have to live in such crude settings without the advantages of all "the best spoils of culture woven in." But, as he explains:

> Then I said to the mountaineer who was driving me, "What sort of people are they who would have to make these new clearings?" "All of us," he replied. "Why, we ain't happy here unless we are getting one of these coves under cultivation." I instantly felt that I had been losing the whole inward significance of the situation. Because to me the clearings spoke of naught but denudation, I thought that to those whose sturdy arms and obedient axes had made them they could tell no other story. But, when *they* looked on the hideous stumps, what they thought of was personal victory. The chips, the girdled trees, and the vile split rails spoke of honest sweat, persistent toil and final reward. The cabin was a warrant of safety for self and wife and babes. In short, the clearing, which to me was a mere ugly picture on the retictory, was to them a symbol redolent with moral memories and sang a very paean of duty, struggle, and success.
>
> I had been as blind to the peculiar ideality of their condition as they certainly would also have been to the ideality of mine, had they had a peep at my strange indoor academic ways of life at Cambridge.[14]

How apt the tense in which James casts the last words: "I *had been* as blind. . . ." Blind no more is James, either to the principle of seeing with the eyes of another who may be more able to see, or to the particular beauty perceptible to those who have made those coves into places where love, common purposes, and security can flourish. Surely, in some sense, James's initial reaction to ugliness is appropriate. But it is not the whole story, and it is through understanding generously that James learns the rest. Likewise, it is through understanding generously as parents, as people who ever loved *any* child, that we can grasp the horror of injustice as Martin Luther King did.

The first dimension of generous understanding—recognizing the moral status of others as equal to one's own—is essential to the achievement of common purposes because it is human decency that neither tyranny nor procedures and forms can duplicate or replace. The second dimension—overcoming our natural blindness, provinciality, and narrowness of perspective—is the most durable base of common purpose with others *as an achievement of genuine individuals.*

It is not the only possible base of joint action, because without any generosity of understanding a person may become part of a mob driven by blood lust. A person may likewise be joined with others by mutual subjection to a tyrant, or collapse into the brutish fanaticism of a herd. We can in some measure work together by trade-off, compromise, and mutual tolerance even without generous understanding. But it is the strongest component in durable, shared purpose among genuine individuals.

This is so for three reasons. First, generous understanding enables full intellectual liberty. For this reason, it helps to construct durable individuality. Second, generous understanding often makes disagreement instructive rather than sterile. And third, it is one wellspring of the conviction that institutions can face their hardest problems. That is, generous understanding is a basis of courage.

INTELLECTUAL LIBERTY

We often say that we have a right to our opinion, meaning that we have a right to think whatever we want to think. But the right to think whatever we want is only as powerful as our capacity to think, reason, and imagine. We can hold opinions only to the extent that *we are able to think of them.* The difference between what we want to think and what we are able to think can be vast. What we want, surely, is to believe things that are true, to have opinions that are reliable. But nobody is free to think anything he or she cannot think of, and so we are often kept from thinking what we want, not by external constraints, but by the internal limitations in all of us—limitations of intelligence, time, imagination, vocabulary, vision, or knowledge. A person who does not know American history cannot appeal to it in deliberation or teach it to a child; a person who will not learn mathematics cannot see the elegance and power of great theorems; a person who cannot grasp a painting is at a loss in a museum; and a person who lacks the words to state a problem of injustice cannot understand it fully.

Trying to be objective and to understand generously resolves these internal, personal constraints to full intellectual liberty. To achieve objectivity and generous understanding is not sufficient to overcome all external constraints to intellectual liberty such as political or cultural tyranny. It is the alternative to the limits of freedom that constrain every person who is isolated in purely personal perception and who cannot profit by grasping the thought of another.

Objectivity, intellectual honesty, skillful reason are essential to reading a book with any hope of grasping its argumentative and descriptive points. Learning them is the means of access to the public domain of which the book is a part. Generous understanding is essential to grasping the place and point of view of the author so far as his writing embodies the personal, that is, the initially private.

These points also apply to entering a conversation with any hope of sharing the thoughts of the participants. Objectivity and generous understanding are even necessary to the private dialogue of the single soul in solitude if self-criticism is not to be easily rationalized away. Together they are the most powerful motive for learning the languages of other people, for recreating the experiments of those who have persistently sought to understand natural phenomena, or for imagining the feelings of others in circumstances they have suffered or enjoyed. These activities of objectivity of mind and generous understanding are the gateways to literature, language, philosophy, religion, the sciences, and history, and also to the minds that have made them what they are. They are irreplaceable means of taking possession of our heritage, of cultivating our own intelligence, and of understanding the ideas of our friends.

These are the very activities by which people become rigorous in thought and abundant in imagination. They are the touchstones of intellectual exercise and the alternatives to mere idiosyncracy. A person engaged in them enjoys both productive solitude and instructive companionship. A person without them faces only solitary confinement; being limited to one's own uninformed and lonely devices is a shackle on intellectual liberty and therefore an obstacle to the achievement of durable individuality.

No measure of objectivity or generosity is a guarantee of agreement among us. Even at our most rigorous and insightful, we may still disagree. But when we reason and understand well, we can at least be sure of apprehending the views we reject, and we can be reasonably confident that our disagreements are based on the fullest knowledge we can achieve under the circumstances. Informed disagreement includes our sense of the other; this discloses commonality of purposes where it exists and reveals us as truly alien to one another when we actually are.

INSTRUCTIVE DISAGREEMENT

Because a generous understanding of others entails our taking their views and feelings seriously, it underlies as well our notions of common decency and civility, and opposes our tendencies toward intemperance and cruelty. To take others' convictions seriously is to seek to understand them before assessing them. We can disagree with them, yet hope for an eventual reconciliation for the sake of purposes we share. We can give constructive criticism and encouragement in the midst of disagreement, thereby summoning the intellectual best in all of us, rather than allowing disagreement to descend into contentiousness or even contempt.

Not all disagreement is fertile, and some of it may be unavoidably deadly—but understanding generously is the surest measure for discerning the nature of our disputes and ascertaining the limits to the possible. Such understanding, more than any other human achievement, equips us to face questions about our potential relations with individuals and groups of people. These are questions of immense moment: whether we can be friends, cooperative colleagues, or at least acquaintances who can avoid enmity; or whether we must be enemies, and finally whether we must resolve to restrain or even to kill one another.

The collapse of what is humanly possible into violence is described succinctly by St. Exupéry. In his October 18, 1939, radio broadcast on "The Propaganda of Pan-Germanism," he explained that German propaganda had worked brilliantly, just like Hollywood special effects. He described the problem the propagandists faced:

> Germany, in order to expand, must absorb a given territory. How could they present this new demand to the world in such a way as to disturb its common sense and confuse its conscience? So the teams launched slogans.
> For a long time we were fooled. We seriously discussed the

justification of their motives; we tried not to denigrate the adversary's line of argument, but to appeal to his good faith and make him ashamed of his contradictions. We used words where words were not appropriate.

We believed that if human beings were ready to fight and die for a cause, it must be because this cause appealed to their idealism. We had forgotten that some motives for action have nothing to do with idealism and that a country may tend to expand as any blind organism does.

We had forgotten this because for us civilization represented the conquest of mind over elementary urges. But over there, the mind was only a lackey charged with justifying the urges of the organism. . . . And so we know now that laying down our arms would mean confirming Germany's appetite. . . . Those who have left their farms, their shops, their factories, fight in order not to become mere fertilizer for German prosperity. They have gone out to gain the right to live and to live in peace.[15]

St. Exupéry had come to see what the world looks like to utter ruthlessness. He did not conclude that values and morals are merely relative or idiosyncratic or basically impenetrable. Instead, having been generous, he understood the point of view of the ruthless leadership of a foreign nation. He rightly concluded that their attitudes were evil, immoral, unreasonable, and filled with bad faith rather than good will. Perhaps such perception is not possible for most of us, even in imagination. Still, we can *try* to see things as they are seen by ruthless people and then seek suitable means for dealing with them. This is the message that Mr. Duff Cooper, first lord of the Admiralty, tried to convey to his countrymen a full year before St. Exupery's broadcast. In resigning his position as minister to protest the policies of his government, Cooper appealed to Hitler's violation of the Treaty of Versailles and the Treaty of Locarno, and his broken promise not to interfere with Czechoslovakia, and Cooper said, "The Prime Minister has believed in addressing Herr Hitler through the language of sweet reasonableness. I have believed that he was more open to the language of the mailed fist."[16]

It is dismaying to realize that not all disagreement, tension, and strife can be ameliorated by sensitive communication. Yet we fail to acknowledge this fact at our peril, for such failure gives rise to false hopes, imprudent actions, and lack of resolve. Lack of resolve can lead, in turn, to shameful behavior. As Churchill confided to a friend on September 11, 1938, "Owing to the neglect of our defenses and the mishandling of the German problem in the last five years, we seem to be very near the bleak choice between War and Shame. My feeling is that we shall choose Shame, and then have War . . ."[17]

No human being and no human institution deserves the public trust without the will to learn these lessons. The lessons are best learned through generous understanding. Because generous understanding is inseparable from giving consideration to others, it is a bulwark of moral humility. Because it enables us to grasp the nature of others' ideas and feelings, it is a bulwark of intellectual humility. These qualities are fundamental to the ideals of education and are therefore the prerequisites of excellence in the teacher or administrator. There are no substitutes for them.

Properly understood, generous understanding cannot be confused with any of the popular and vicious forms of voyeurism and vicariousness. It is hardly generous understanding when, for example, an interviewer on television jams a microphone in the face of the victim of some disaster and asks "How do you feel?" The interviewer seeks a spectacle—nothing finer—because everyone of the slightest sensibility already knows how the victim feels. The interviewer insults everyone concerned, and exhibits almost total indifference to the likenesses among us—the farthest thing from generous understanding.

COURAGE

Generous understanding also gives us courage. Nothing is more tempting in the life of institutions than for their members to deny or evade hard problems on the grounds that alone they are impotent to solve them. Easing ourselves into this comfortable justification for inaction is tempting because sometimes it is true that alone we can accomplish little or nothing; some problems are too big and too complicated.

But there is no need to despair of the achievement of common purposes, unless generous understanding is universally absent. Nothing makes this so clear as the experience of understanding another or of being understood oneself in this way. This experience gives life to community because it reveals what is humanly possible. It is the fundamental experience that puts the lie to the dogmas of cynicism and to the cowardice about conducting our lives together as individuals that always attends those dogmas.

Perhaps no more touching example of a generous understanding can be found than Abraham Lincoln, in both his public and private life. He set a tone for our deliberations about common purposes and individual liberty in general and especially in education.

In 1858, Lincoln corresponded with Captain James N. Brown of Kentucky who had inquired about the meaning of some of Lincoln's speeches. Lincoln wrote him:

> Before proceeding, let me say I think I have no prejudice against the Southern people. They are just what we would be in their situation. If slavery did not now exist among them, they would not introduce it. If it did now exist among us, we should not instantly give it up.[18]

Lincoln saw that we are joined by our common humanity; we must recognize those who disagree with us as kindred in the sense that we must ask whether we would behave any differently in their circumstances. This is not entirely an act of generosity toward others; it is also the act of imposing the most exacting standards on ourselves, of assessing truthfully how we would behave in the skin of another person. It is notable that Lincoln's depth of generous understanding did not prevent his taking his country to war in defense of the Constitution and the Union. Generous understanding does not suggest or imply indecision, cowardice, or incapacity for the hard duties of adulthood.

Lincoln's understanding is vividly displayed in his friendship with Mentor Graham, whose epitaph reads simply: "The Teacher of Abraham Lincoln." Graham helped Lincoln through the reading of Euclid to achieve the sense of self-discipline and of an ordered universe that ultimately led him to the presidency. But at the time, that study restored Lincoln from near suicidal despondency and encouraged him to carry on.

When Graham's young son Septimus later died, it was Lincoln who helped him lower the child into the grave. When Lincoln left "late at night, he could muster no farewell words or any syllable of comfort when Graham followed him out, watching him saddle up. Lincoln started to mount, threw down the reins, folded both arms around his friend in a brief embrace, swung up quickly into the saddle, and rode off without a word."[19] This kind of kinship—perhaps most easily recognizable and reachable in genuine friendship—is realized in generous understanding.

We have achieved means of living and working together with civility and respect for individuality that do not require generous understanding. We have formed and brought to life alternatives to tyranny and to universal impotence: law, checks and balances, civil rights and liberties, institutional and personal accountability. Some of us have become skilled in the arts of compromise and mutual tolerance.

These are magnificent human advances. They are indispensable to peaceful coexistence. But purposeful, deliberate union of individuals for the sake of worthy ends calls for more from us. It calls for generous understanding. Nowhere is that need greater than in education. Generous understanding is essential to a faculty and administration working toward a coherent institution, and also to students who want to know. Without this achievement, formal education will leave us deeply dissatisfied. Institutions cannot take the place of individuals or provide adequate substitutes for personal virtue in fulfilling any purpose.

EXPECTATIONS IN EDUCATION

There is no novelty in the idea that generous understanding must be achieved by teachers and administrators, and aspired to by students. Forty years ago Jacques Barzun observed that "communication is just what teaching is. Its ideal aim is to have two minds share one thought."[20] Shortly thereafter Gilbert Highet explained that one principle of effective teaching is clarity; he told teachers and parents, managers and politicans that to achieve this with students and colleagues:

> You must think, not what you know, but what they do not know; not what you find hard, but what they will find hard; then, *after putting yourself in their minds,* obstinate or puzzled, groping or mistaken as they are, explain what they need to learn [emphasis added].[21]

Yet, even if this must be accomplished to fulfill the public trust, is it realistic to expect it, demand it, or, for that matter, even to hope for it in our schools, colleges, and universities? Is the embodiment of such an intellectual and moral ideal too much to ask?

Of course it is. But these facts do not justify despair. The highest ideals deserve our effort even if they are beyond us. We must come as close as we can, knowing that our institutions can be no better than we are and that our children cannot progress except by working from the standards we manage to meet. Asking for some measure of objectivity and generous understanding is no more—and no less—than Martin Luther King asked of his readers.

Moreover, we seldom even approach our limits; we do not ask all that we can realistically expect of ourselves. This is as true in education as elsewhere and it is clear in its effects on public schools. One of the great unfulfilled needs of American education is that teaching be a seamless profession, that there be mutual respect and sharing of information among teachers and administrators at all levels. But faculty members and administrators in higher education and advantaged private schools are often far removed from their public school counterparts. This separation may be traceable to a time when the American professoriat was exclusively male and many schoolteachers were women who did not have opportunity for advanced scholarship.

Whatever the reasons, the teachers' backgrounds and working conditions are profoundly different. In higher education, advanced degrees are expected. Though a sophisticated academic preparation is no guarantee of generous understanding, it provides an opportunity to recognize its importance. Schoolteachers are not always exposed to such opportunity before they enter teaching, even though by the spring of 1983, 51.9 per cent had master's degrees.[22]

In some schools, conditions make thinking about anything beyond discipline and survival difficult; in 1978 the National Institute of Education reported that 250,000 secondary students were assaulted and that more than one thousand schoolteachers required medical attention due to physical attacks every month in our schools. Such strife is largely unknown in higher education.

There is, of course, no other remedy for such damage to our schools than resolute administrative leadership and board governance that refuse to tolerate such conditions. This requires resolve that personal and institutional conduct will place a premium on the intellectual and moral progress of students and insure that means to this end are implemented.

Naturally, disagreement about how to address disciplinary problems runs deep. Some school officials in Florida, Delaware, and Maryland, for example, opt for alternative schools with rigid discipline, remediation, and no extracurricular activities. Others fear that such special institutions will have the unintended effect of removing black students from the mainstream. These officials therefore opt for centers staffed by social workers and psychological aides who help suspended students. In Maryland's Prince George's County near Washington, D.C., John R. Rosser, chairman of the Education Committee for the Black Democratic Council, insists that the problem of disruptive black students calls not for ostracism, but for "human relations officers" and the training of teachers and administrators "in human relations and positive discipline."[23]

So long as schools temporize about such issues or fail to assess the effectiveness of their methods, the likelihood of progress is small. The likelihood is diminished when schools alone are expected to address such problems. Traditional forms of school discipline have been most effective when they are supported by parents who also teach discipline at home.[24] Many schools simply cannot rely on such support from the parents of students who behave worst at school. They may have to turn for support to the parents of the students who are the victims.

At the same time, offering the best to students requires that standards of teacher preparation, appointment, and tenure will enable this mission to be fruitfully pursued. Trends since 1973 in the characteristics of students preparing to become teachers show how difficult this is likely to be:

> Since 1973, college-bound seniors taking the Scholastic Aptitude Test (SAT) have been asked to choose from a list "the field that would be your first choice for your college curriculum." Data show that the SAT scores in 1973 of intended education majors were lower than those of all college-bound seniors, and by 1981, the gap in test performance had widened further.[25]

By 1981, "the SAT verbal mean score for college-bound seniors whose first choice was education declined from 418 in 1973 to 391"; in mathematics, "from 449 to 418."[26] SAT scores are not, of course, the only indicators of aptitude or potential, but students with the scores cited above could not gain admission to any selective college in America. This makes it imperative that we do everything possible to see that students' educational opportunities make the most of their talents; their teaching and academic programs must be exceptionally good—a difficult challenge in itself. Attracting better candidates to the applicant pool will not be any easier.

Mary Futrell, president of the National Education Association, insists:

> *Every* child deserves a fully prepared, fully qualified teacher in every class; . . . our nation's children deserve teachers whose formal training includes extensive study of cognitive theory, developmental psychology, and pedagogical technique.[27]

If these subjects are taught and studied well, they will emphasize the indispensability in teaching of objectivity and of the will to understand the point of view of others, as Barzun, Highet, and others have pointed out. If they are not so taught, they will do little to advance educational opportunity in America.

Administrators and faculty involved in selection of personnel must themselves appreciate and recognize such virtues in prospective colleagues. Significant and expensive inservice programs of faculty and administration development will be essential as well, just as they are in higher education.

Whatever the contribution that money, intelligence, and resolve can make to excellence in instruction and companionship for students, the largest contribution comes only by looking for and nurturing within the teaching profession objectivity and generous understanding—intellectual and moral maturity. Failure here will mean disarray and confusion of educational institutions about their purposes and the means to realize them.

As Gerald Grant explains, a school lacking a strong sense of shared purposes and serious learning "implicitly teaches students to think, 'How can I manipulate this rule system to maximize my self-interest?'" By contrast, a properly directed school is "a community that would teach [students] to ask, 'What is expected of me, and what do I owe to others?'" In such a school:

> all must commit themselves to the goals of the community and to loyalty to each other. Since education . . . is both intellectual and humane, the students and faculty derive mutual support from sharing of themselves and their ideals. Yet the happiness of everyone in the community depends on consideration and awareness, restraint and candor, discretion and shared joy. Collaboration toward these imprecise but worthwhile ends is an expectation which all in the academy hold.[28]

How can this expectation be brought to life?

4

Attitudes About Reality

The pleasures of the intellect are notoriously less vivid than either the pleasures of sense or the pleasures of the affections; and therefore, especially in the season of youth, the pursuit of knowledge is likely enough to be neglected and lightly esteemed in comparison with other pursuits offering much stronger immediate attractions.[1]

—*A. E. Housman*

TWO UNCRITICAL ATTITUDES about reality prevail in America. The first is that the classroom is entirely distinct from "the real world." The second is that values are not "real." Both misconceptions encourage students to disdain intellect and knowledge in favor of more immediate pleasures. They are, therefore, inimical to formal education and to respect for teaching and learning.

THE CLASSROOM AND 'THE REAL WORLD'

We speak thoughtlessly of the classroom and "the real world" as separate places. We thus encourage students to believe that they are not in the real world and therefore that their actions have no more than transient consequences; that the work and lives of students are not so important as what people do in "the real world"; and that what happens in classrooms is significant only in relation to what happens when students have later entered "the real world." This attitude has become so ingrained that the University of Bridgeport in Connecticut has adopted as its motto "Educating for the Real World." Many other institutions also acquiesce in the dichotomy as if it were harmless.

But it is not harmless. We have long reserved the word *real*, as Thoreau observed, for things we believe important. The most popular soft drink in the world is promoted as "the real thing," and we Americans call good things "the real McCoy." *Reality* is what matters to us.

When we teach the young that life as a student is less than real we explicitly encourage them to view study as relatively unimportant and as worthwhile only insofar as it is training for life after school. We thereby destroy their seriousness of purpose, and we diminish their chances to learn of the pleasures of the intellect.

Small wonder that when parents, employers, media figures, and even teachers and administrators demean their work, students believe that grades and diplomas which can be used as credentials are important, while learning, information, and reliable study habits are not important of themselves. Small wonder, then, that students taught that today is inconsequential compared to tomorrow are overly lax and self-indulgent, dedicated neither to learning nor to decency of conduct.

Students deserve instead to learn of the differences between the classroom and the *rest* of the real world. Unless they learn that life in school is as real as life in the rest of the world, they will never properly participate in any educational mission that concentrates on the kinds of people they become *as* students, *in* school. They must learn that thinking well, and studying well, have irreplaceable power in all activities, or else they will be dangerously limited in the reliability of their judgments, their objectivity, and the generosity of their understanding.

Equally important, students deserve to learn that good classrooms, while different from most of the rest of the world, are not any less real. Students are unlikely to have many opportunities later in life to concentrate exclusively on becoming rigorous in thought and abundant in imagination—the basic purposes of the classroom. But differences of purpose do not mean less real.

Yet the supposed distinction between the classroom and reality, even if attacked head-on, will die hard if it dies at all. We have too many motives for demeaning formal study. The greatest is to spare ourselves the hard work of disciplining our minds. In the short run, it is always easier and more comfortable to avoid discipline of any kind, and intellectual discipline is no exception.

If study is demeaned, then anyone can forego it with feelings of impunity. There is no reason to grapple with hard ideas, to study books, or to try to take the place and point of view of a difficult thinker if these activities are less significant than what is real. The obligation to aspire to generous understanding, and to become qualified judges of the true, the good, the right, and the beautiful, is often thwarted by the denigration of learning. The false distinction between the classroom and the real world thus provides an excuse for disdaining the intellect and the refinement of its sensibilities. It allows ignorance and the helplessness of ignorance to persist in self-satisfaction.

This is an old ploy in the human condition, an old way of justifying ignorance. It was common, for example, in the Athens of Socrates and Plato. In the *Gorgias,* Socrates talks with Callicles, a man of considerable political and financial power. Callicles is no fool and he despises indecision and cowardice, as he understands them. But when he tries to persuade Socrates that might makes right, their conversation ends in a confrontation. Callicles insists that a life of persistent intellectual effort promises nothing but hard knocks and public contempt, and that these are exactly what such a life deserves:

> It's an excellent thing to grasp as much philosophy as one needs for an education, and it's no disgrace to play the philosopher while you're young; but if one grows up and becomes a man and still continues in the subject, why, the whole thing becomes ridiculous, Socrates. My own feeling toward its practitioners is very much the same as the way I feel toward men who lisp and prattle like a child. . . . Such a fellow must spend the rest of his life skulking in corners, whispering with two or three little lads, never pronouncing any large, liberal, or meaningful utterance. . . . Such a man, if I may use a vulgar phrase, is one you can slap in the face with impunity! Now, my dear friend, take my advice: stop your refutations, take up the Fine Art of Business, and cultivate something that will give you a reputation for good sense.[2]

Callicles' contempt for intellectuals in general and teachers in particular as people not skillful in "the real world" is familiar to all of us. America is not alone in having anti-intellectualism as part of its history. But this does not excuse the people who care about the young—parents, prospective employers, political representatives, media spokesmen, or teachers—who encourage the belief that the academy is not as important as the marketplace.

At least some of the disposition throughout history to treat the marketplace as more real than the academy stems from the conviction that nothing is quite so real as money. There is nothing wrong, of course, with recognizing the reality of money; it is wrong, however, to allow that reality to exclude all others.

Money, as the song says, can't buy happiness, but it can certainly buy pleasure, release from backbreaking toil, exemption from many sanctions of the law, access to the best medical care, the opportunity for charitable giving; it can also buy political influence and financial security for loved ones. It cannot buy leisure, however, because leisure is the activity of self-improvement, and no one can engage in that except by knowing how to become better. Money can buy free time and comfort. In a world without much sense either of happiness or well-being, what money can buy may exhaust what is appreciated and therefore treated as real.

This phenomenon is not unique to us. It appears throughout history. Seneca said in the first century that "a sound mind can neither be bought nor borrowed. And if it were for sale, I doubt whether it would find a buyer. And yet unsound ones are being purchased every day."[3] He objected specifically to those who undertook liberal studies merely for the sake of making money—then, as now, a popular justification for education. The Bible (I Timothy 6:10) cautions against lust for money as the root of all evil—not money, but obsession with it. Kierkegaard observed in 1848 that, among his fellow Danes, "the greatest danger, that of losing one's own self, may pass off as quietly as if it were nothing; every other loss, that of . . . five dollars . . . is sure to be noticed."[4] The lives of Chinese mandarins, Mideastern potentates, and Soviet *nomenklatura* confirm the universal appeal of money as the most obvious reality for those who make no effort to perceive any other.

For the young, who are usually terrified of missing anything, the appeal of money is enormous. There is no use trying to deny them their dreams in this respect, but there is every reason to deny that only the world of those dreams is real. Failure to do so renders education useless for anything else.

Remarkably, America invests more money in formal education than in any other single dimension of domestic life; our expenditures dwarf medical and retirement programs. And for all that, many of us consider classrooms as less than real. Since

we are willing to pay such a price, we ought at least to insist that
what is purchased is something real.

Popular clichés we use to spare ourselves the demanding
project of learning by study show how we buttress this attitude:
sayings such as "Experience is the best teacher," or "That may
be true in theory, but it won't work in practice." Neither is in
any way new, and, in America, both are very much alive.

Perhaps the most extreme advocate of experience as the best
teacher was Benito Mussolini, who said in his *Autobiography:*

> During my life, I believe, neither my school friends, my war friends,
> nor my political friends ever had the slightest influence upon me. . . .
> I do not believe in the supposed influence of books. I do not believe
> in the influence which comes from perusing the books about the lives
> and characters of men. . . . For myself, I have had only one great
> teacher. . . . The teacher is day-by-day experience.[5]

Whatever experience taught Mussolini, it was not enough. It
certainly did not teach him how to undertake, in John Dewey's
words, the "reconstruction or reorganization of experience
which adds to the meaning of experience, and which increases
ability to direct the course of subsequent experience."[6] It did not
teach him Cicero's principle that "there is no way friendship can
exist without virtue,"[7] nor Cicero's explanation that in the life of
the tyrant "everything is always suspicion and flattery, there is
no place for friendship."[8] It did not teach him that most wonderful experience of learning from friends in the course of daily life.
It did not teach him how to avoid repeating mistakes or how to
avoid a disgraceful life and a shameful death.

We do well to remember the entire couplet of which Mussolini
remembered only half:

> Experience is a great teacher;
> A fool can learn from no other.

Because the full couplet is seldom taught the young, often
they are not aware that fools must learn everything by themselves, the hard way, cannot learn by study which saves time,
and cannot possibly experience enough to learn very much in
one lifetime.

Students are seldom reminded that learning by study is every
bit as real as any other kind of experience. They therefore do
not realize that it makes no sense to distinguish study from the

realm of experience. Instead, they believe that study is not as real, or as effective, as learning by other kinds of experience—the kinds one gets in "the real world." Yet study is the only possible kind of experience for understanding literature, history, science, mathematics, philosophy, and other methods of inquiry that have advanced civilization since the dawn of human intelligence. That is the reality everyone faces, despite our still fashionable clichés.

Even fairly young students learn to disdain thinking and say, "That may be true in theory, but it won't work in practice." This old saw first became popular in the eighteenth century. Men and women were then trying to envision how constitutions might establish a stable social order that respected individual liberty. Those who believed that human beings could not be trusted with liberty said that constitutions might be fine in theory but would never work in practice.

The widespread dismissal of thinking about a humanly practicable governmental structure led Immanuel Kant to write a short book *On the Old Saw: That May Be Right in Theory, But It Won't Work in Practice*. Kant proved that the sentence is self-contradictory and necessarily false. His argument is not complex: The sentence "This theory is true" *means* "This theory works in practice." Thus, when we say that a theory is true, we can mean nothing else than that it works in practice, under the test of experiment. If a theory that is true does not work in practice, either the theory is incomplete or it has been wrongly, perhaps foolishly, applied.

Theories and the activity of theorizing cannot be dispensed with by casually declaring that truth in theory has nothing to do with practice or reality. This, too, most students never learn, and so they fall victim to the thoughtless old saws by which we demean intellectual activity and defeat the very purposes we expect of education.

What happens in classrooms is as real as what happens everywhere else, but this is *not* to say that whatever happens in classrooms is good. Teaching can be bad or ill-planned, students can fail, lessons can be trivial, objectivity and generous understanding can be absent, facts and evidence can be ignored, and decency can be violated. All of these malpractices find their way into education. But because classrooms and their consequences are real, we are obliged to make them good.

John Dewey once identified the "most needed of all reforms in the spirit of education. 'Cease conceiving of education as mere preparation for later life, and make of it the full meaning of the present life. And to add that only in this case does it become truly a preparation for after life is not the paradox it seems. An activity which does not have worth enough to be carried on for its own sake cannot be very effective as a preparation for something else.'"[9] We believe that our children, our students matter. We cannot denigrate educational activities and environments.

THE UNREALITY OF VALUES

Self-destructive attitudes about the unreality of classrooms are conjoined with another bit of conventional wisdom that is even more crippling for education: the attitude that values and ideals are not real.

The study of ethics and the study of values in other fields, including aesthetics, political theory, and the philosophy of science, raise fundamental questions about human knowledge and its limits. Questions about morals and conduct, art, political structure, and methods of discovery lead to basic issues in epistemology, semantics, and logic. These questions are not only intellectually respectable but necessary in the sense that they arise from efforts to plumb the nature of truth and falsity, objectivity and subjectivity, right and wrong, good and evil, beauty and ugliness.

Because these are fundamental questions—that is, questions about the foundations of meaning and knowledge—they are not questions for beginners. They presuppose a student literate in morals, aesthetics, religion, and science. Thus, such study becomes appropriate only after a person has learned what morality calls for in normal daily life, how scientific inquiry is actually conducted, and so on. Philosophers and other scholars of great learning do not entirely agree on answers to these questions. Some hold that value judgments cannot be rationally justified; others say they can. There is even disagreement over the logical status of sentences like "This form of conduct is right" or "This painting is beautiful." In issues of such complexity, disagreement is hardly surprising.

The view that values are not real, which currently enjoys popularity in America and in many of its educational institutions, does not emerge from careful study of such questions. It assumes, without considering evidence, that value judgments cannot be rationally justified and are therefore merely subjective or relative. This attitude is dogmatically visited on many students at all levels; it takes a number of forms, but all of them have the effect of teaching students that there is one simple, final answer about the nature and logical status of value judgments. Many learn to take this for granted before they have the slightest understanding of how to reason well, how to deliberate in morals, how to look at a painting, how to conduct a scientific experiment, or how to study the history of a political institution. The question of whether values are relative does not in itself endanger their intellectual development—so long as the question is not put to them before they have any hope of understanding it. It is the dogmatic answer that cuts off subtle and mature inquiry.

The notion that values are not real takes both a primitive and a more sophisticated form. The primitive form is that reality includes only the tangible—what can be touched or held or possessed. A slightly more refined version contends that reality is limited to what can be perceived by the senses—what can be touched, seen, heard, smelled, or tasted. Both versions are materialist. This is a very old view. Plato described its advocates as people who "drag everything to earth out of the sky and the invisible, and simply (artlessly) get their hands on rocks and oaks, for in clinging to all things of the sort they insist on this: only that is which affords the possibility of some kind of application and touching, and if anyone will say of anything else that it is . . . they altogether despise him."[10] Since values cannot be touched like rocks and oaks, they are not real, true, or important.

Most people who say they hold this belief belie it in their behavior. They are resentful when they are treated badly. They suffer visibly when their feelings are hurt. And they are offended when people are inattentive to their ideas. Thus they indicate their belief that at least their own rights, feelings, and ideas are real enough to be taken seriously even though they are not perceptible to the senses.

Students are quick to see the inconsistency of the primitive materialist critique of the reality of values with the conduct of the very people who espouse it. For this reason, the primitive version of the attitude is relatively harmless.

The more sophisticated account of the unreality of values is not harmless. This is relativism as uncritical dogma, namely, absolute relativism. This view holds that ideals are not real and that no principle, no form of conduct, and no virtue or vice is genuinely good or evil, right or wrong. Consequently, it maintains that no statement about good, bad, right, wrong, beauty, ugliness, or any other value is either true or false. There are absolutely no *reasons* for adopting one value rather than another, no rational justification of any commitment to any ideal. Values and ideals are relative to the particular individual or group that happens, by whatever circumstances, to espouse them simply according to their tastes and preferences. The values have no standing in reality, no kind of objectivity, and no basis in reason. Values are real only in the sense that what a person believes affects the way he or she behaves, but no ideal of life or conduct is held to be better than any other.

The most popular and widespread instrument for the inculcation of this dogmatic position is known as "values clarification." Values clarification intends to enable students to recognize what they value. Spokesmen for this method, Louis Raths, Merrill Harmin, and Sydney B. Simon write: "Clarifying responses operate in situations in which there are no 'right' answers, such as in situations involving feelings, attitudes, beliefs, or purposes."[11] These and other proponents of values clarification deny that educational institutions can legitimately stand in favor of traditional values which, they claim, are really no more than platitudes and therefore a type of hypocrisy. Not surprisingly, values clarification advocates impress on students and parents that moral judgment is no more than learning what we want and then deciding how to get it. Because we differ about what we want, "Values statements may be seen as alternatives rather than correct answers."[12] Parents and teachers are repeatedly advised that the most precious legacy they can leave to youngsters is the ability to identify wants.

The implications of this dogma are clear enough: No virtue is really a virtue, no vice a vice; no action is really wrong, none right; no human achievement is really important, no failure is of consequence. Nothing matters except insofar as individuals or groups believe it matters, and whatever anyone believes to matter is no more than an idiosyncratic preference with no reality to it. No purpose is genuinely good, none really evil; having a purpose is no better than being without one; betrayal of purpose is not wrong except for people who happen to believe it is wrong. Courage is no better than cowardice, wisdom than foolishness, temperance than intemperance, justice than injustice. Generous understanding of other people is no more right than manipulating them to your own advantage. And there is no point to generous understanding, since all you will discover is illusion. These are the most obvious implications of the simplistic attitude that ideals are not real.

Oddly, the relativism of values is offered as a reason for us to be tolerant of each other's differences. But the dogma implies that tolerance is no better than intolerance, and that respect for difference is no better than contempt.

When this dogma is visited on students from the time they are quite young, it stifles the crucial inquiry into the foundations of the dogma: Are there ways of reasoning, thinking, and deliberating that can show some things to be right and good and others to be wrong and evil? Students are, therefore, not likely to learn through formal education anything of virtue and vice, let alone how to tell whether a particular characteristic is good or evil. The ideals of learning and knowing collapse, along with all other ideals, into unreality. Minds are closed, often early; life is reduced to learning how to get what you want, whatever it happens to be.

Students indoctrinated in uncritical relativism find it difficult to question the dogma at even the most elementary conceptual level. But: If actions are right or wrong only insofar as one believes them to be so, what of a person who is torn between two courses of action? Is being of two minds on an issue only silly, since whatever one decides to be right is right because he or she decides it? If actions are right or wrong only insofar as one's social group or culture or nation believes them to be so, what if one is a member of two social groups whose beliefs are contradictory? What if one's culture or nation is divided? These questions suggest even more subtle questions about relativism, such as: What if a group insists that all facts are irrelevant to moral judgment? What if an individual disagrees with the others in his group? Is all disagreement wrong if relativism is right? But how can disagreement be wrong if *nothing* is wrong? Doctrinaire relativism of the sort students are normally exposed to ignores all such questions, to the students' intellectual disadvantage.

The closing of minds by dogma is nowhere more apparent than in the frequent invocation by students of the question "Who's to say?" Given the supposition that values are relative, this question is a show-stopper. As Hans Oberdieck explains in "Who Is To Judge?":

> The question is not so much *who* shall judge, but *how* should anyone judge. That is, what principles and criteria are morally relevant. . . . Once we determine how any of us is to judge, that is, once we determine correct or justifiable standards of judgment, then the question of who is to judge will fade in importance.[13]

Students who do not learn the uses of reason in establishing criteria and principles of judgment, whether in morals, science, literature, or art, will be stultified. Neither will they achieve the beginning of wisdom which, as Oberdieck states, "lies in recognizing that in the end the question 'Who Is To Judge?' admits of but one answer: each and every one of us must judge. The end of wisdom, of course, lies in establishing and applying moral principles that will aid us in determining how we are to judge."[14] Dogmatic relativism invites dismissal or utter neglect of principles and their rational application to our conduct. It prepares students badly for thinking well *or* living well.

No one of intellectual subtlety lightly dismisses questions about the limits to human knowledge and objectivity. But the dogma of relativism as typically conveyed to students is not subtle. It ignores the difficulty of these serious questions and teaches the young only to dismiss them. Like all simplistic dogmas, it subverts seriousness in teaching. As William Arrowsmith explains:

What matters is the kind of context we can create for teaching and the largeness of the demands made upon the teacher. Certainly he will have no function or honor worthy of the name until we are prepared to make the purpose of education what it always was—the molding of men rather than the production of knowledge.[15]

If teachers and administrators have no conception of what men and women ought to be or ought to have a chance to become, there are no models to emulate, no ideals to pursue. And, not suprisingly, life is not expanded into fertile possibilities; instead it is dramatically and terribly reduced.

HUMAN LIMITS

If nothing is really right or wrong, and values are but individual or societal illusions, then nothing we do matters. Relativism disdains aspiration, loyalty, and respect; it leaves no guide to conduct except our wants. It implies that we cannot be united in common purposes by reasoned conviction because convictions are deemed arbitrary, not reasonable. Thus, we can be joined and can live together only by accidents of affection which pass with time or by rights which are guaranteed by law. Finally, because the dogma leaves us with nothing imperative except getting what we want, we are bound to think of ourselves as individual or group constituents whose principal human standing is displayed in terms of rights. The doctrine of constituent rights enforceable by law is the sole alternative to anarchy and barbarity. And even this is scant refuge because, under the influence of relativism, one's duty to respect or enforce the law has no robust support.

This renders the world of human intercourse barren. No institution, no way of life, can truly have worth or merit. When we behave as though it did, we exhibit naïveté. To this characterization, a relativist may reply, "It implies precisely that, and this is the truth we should teach our students." But the relativist cannot argue consistently that we *should* or *should not* do anything. In this sense, the dogma is self-refuting. But perhaps its self-refuting quality helps to explain why it is more fashionable in education than elsewhere. In education, it is commonplace to take rights for granted and expect respectful treatment, factors which make the consquences of relativism less evident.

For the relativist, intellectual sophistication necessarily leads to cynicism. In this view, we lose all rationale for aspiring to civility and liberty. We lose sight of what Jacques Maritain saw so clearly:

> The essence of education does not consist in adapting a potential citizen to the conditions and interactions of social life, but first in *making a man,* and by this very fact in preparing a citizen.[16]

The great experiments of history that have grown out of respect for human beings could never have been undertaken under such a dogma as relativism. Madison could not have addressed the problem of ordered liberty without believing human depravity and "other qualities of human nature which justify a certain portion of esteem and confidence" to be real. If depravity and virtue alike are illusory, there could be no reason to undertake an experiment in liberty and justice.

In addition, relativism eliminates the grounds for self-criticism and self-respect. The cowardly desire not to become involved when someone is being murdered before our eyes is licensed because cowardice is not wrong. *Nothing* is wrong. Reflective and wise application of principles is no more praiseworthy than fanaticism or apathy. There is no reason for a self-controlled life instead of a life of drug addiction and violent crime to pay for it. In effect, there is nothing worth living for, nothing worth living up to, and nothing about living worth learning.

This is the emptiness to which the dogma of relativism invites our children, both inside and outside formal education. Because the dogma denies that it is wrong to betray a trust, it is the ultimate betrayal of all trust, specifically of the public trust of teachers and administrators.

Generous understanding stands in direct oppostion to this cynical conception: it reveals how much our ideals and conduct matter. In conduct, it amounts to taking responsibility for ourselves.

The principle of generous understanding helps us to answer questions about the teaching of values in formal education and in our homes. Whether the values are intellectual, moral, civic, or aesthetic, we cannot expect schools, colleges, and universities to bear the public trust faithfully unless they face these questions.

5

Education and Values

It is impossible to have children without teaching them. Beat
them, coddle them, ignore them, force-feed them, shun them
or worry about them, love them or hate them, you are still
teaching them something, all the time.[1]

—*Gilbert Highet*

BECAUSE OUR CONDUCT inevitably teaches students what matters to us, the place of values in education is a compulsory
question. Tension over what to do about values in formal education seems to be felt by many Americans. Articles and editorials
on the subject in popular publications suggest as much, as does
the proliferation of books. Litigation about curricula and textbooks often reveals persistent tension.

For example, *Washington Post* columnist Richard Cohen
makes a typical point:

My generation was taught values—values we still cherish. We want
to stay married, but many of us don't. We want to supervise our
kids, but often we can't. We want a drug-free environment, but we
create one in which a white powder sometimes provides the only
high. A society that talks one way and acts another is obligated to
answer a question from the very kids we want to be taught values:
What exactly are our own?[2]

Newsweek once described the question of teaching values in
schools as a "morals mine field."[3] The 1986 case of *Mozert* v.
Hawkins County Public Schools pitted parents against school
officials over textbooks and teachers' guides used to teach
reading. The trial brief of the plaintiffs insisted that "the use of
these textbooks involves the direction or manipulation of what
children believe" and "the school will not let the children
receive another view other than the official school position."
Specifically, plaintiffs objected that the texts did not "accommodate" their religious beliefs.[4]

83

The main questions of the debate are: Should values be taught? Is it possible *not* to teach values? If not, what values should be taught? And what methods should be used if values are taught? Public debate offers dramatic and extreme alternative answers to these questions. Some people say that all teaching of values infringes on the freedom of children to think for themselves and therefore is wrong. Others insist that it is appropriate to use the means necessary to impart specific beliefs they personally espouse.

As noted in chapter 1, this is not new. In 1837, in his first *Annual Report to the Massachusetts Board of Higher Education,* Horace Mann emphasized the problem:

> When such teachers as we employ are introduced into the schools, they address themselves to the culture of the intellect mainly. The fact that children have moral natures and social affections, then in the most rapid state of development, is scarcely recognized.[5]

Mann concluded that schools were neglecting a most important part of education at the expense of the young:

> Is it a matter of surprise that we see lads and young men thickly springing up in the midst of us who startle at the mispronounciation of a word as though they were personally injured, but can hear volleys of profanity unmoved; who put on airs of superior breeding, or sneer with contempt at a case of false spelling or grammar, but can witness spectacles of drunkenness in the streets with entire composure?[6]

What, then are we to do? Are we hypocrites if we try to teach any values at all, given our behavior as adults? Or are we being cruel if we cast our children into the world with nothing to rely on but their own devices? What are we doing to students if we neither exhibit nor encourage objectivity and generous understanding?

The extremes of public debate offer us no resolution. The idea that we should not teach values ignores the simple fact that children are always learning what the adults around them consider right and wrong, no matter what their teachers say or do not say about values. Value-free education is impossible. Our only real choice is whether the teaching and learning of values is to be done well or badly. Thus, anyone who would be a good parent or teacher simply must resolve not to need to be a hypocrite. Since hypocrisy is a kind of homage that weakness and vice pay to strength and virtue, we feel the need to be hypocritical when we are ashamed of our conduct. Resolve not to need to be hypocritical is resolve to behave in ways we are willing for our children and students to know about and to imitate. This much—that we try to make our behavior worthy of imitation—our children and students should be able to take for granted.

INTELLECTUAL HONESTY AND IDEOLOGY

Schemes to *make* the young accept the values of some or other group always lead to manipulation and intellectual dishonesty. They encourage the intellectual corruption of the young, ostensibly for their own good.

An eighth grade textbook, *Science,* now in use in some schools, shows what happens when textbook authors believe that ends justify means. In it, the theory of evolution is presented as both false and evil. The text reads:

> "You see," responded the judge, "people really believe what they want to believe. Because you want to be right with God, you find it easy to believe and accept the facts. A person who is not right with God must find reason, or justification, for not believing. So he readily accepts an indefensible theory like evolution—even if it will not hold water. That is his academic justification for unbelief. In fact, that is what all the many theories of evolution are—a mental justification for unbelief."[7]

But children exposed to such textbooks may someday learn that you cannot prove a theory false by attacking the people who hold it. If they do so learn, they are likely to become cynical about what they had been taught. If they do not so learn, they will be vulnerable to all the political demagogues who will gladly take advantage of their ignorance. In either case, they will be victims of manipulation, no matter how well-intentioned. Manipulative treatment will drive them away from objectivity, intellectual honesty, and generosity of understanding.

This sort of ideological manipulation exists in higher education as well. Stephen Balch and Herbert London, for example, claim that:

> The American campus is now the nesting place for a significant population of political extremists. . . . Whereas twenty years ago the campus Left was largely confined to registering its presence through vocal demonstrations and protest, today it is more comfortably ensconced within a network of journals and professional organizations, university departments and academic programs.[8]

Balch and London argue that the radical political Left on campus has succeeded in increasing the "number of one-sided, question-begging, or highly partisan course descriptions now to be found in college catalogues," and has established politicized journals that provide publication opportunities leading to tenure.[9] They quote Michael Parenti, a Marxist political scientist at Brooklyn College, on the ideological purpose of the Left in academe:

> Our job in academia is not only to reach out to working people but also to remind students that they're workers . . . that their struggle is also a labor struggle, [and] that labor struggle is the most profound democratic struggle in our society.[10]

Edward Shils comments on the emergence of ideological influence from the Left in academic institutions:

> One manifestation of the vigour of political partisanship in the universities has been the movement in the social sciences and in the humanities to make appointments with fairly explicit references to political criteria. The view that a department should have representation of "the Marxist view" or "the radical view" is put forward not infrequently. . . . This argument is apparently seldom adduced when the appointment of non-Marxists is being discussed.[11]

Obviously, many school textbooks are much better than *Science*. And many teachers at all levels are neither religious nor political ideologues. Many faculty and administrators at all levels object strenuously to ideologues masquerading as teachers. They rightly insist that there is no room in schools, colleges, or universities for manipulation or proselytizing that portray themselves as objective and impartial.

But what of objectivity and impartiality themselves? Are these not ideals and values, and, if so, is it right to teach them? And, if so, how are they to be taught? These questions suggest that it is imperative at the outset of the debate to distinguish the values for which a school stands, and the ideals it considers indispensable to the fulfillment of its mission, from the issue of whether student belief about values is being manipulated or warped by dishonesty.

First, when a school, college, or university adopts standards of discipline, class performance, and expectations of student behavior and makes them known to students, there need be no manipulation. The institution should declare itself straightforwardly, and be consistently fair and decent in applying its standards. To insist that standards will apply and, if necessary, be enforced so that study is not disturbed is obligatory.

Many students will not have learned at home or in prior schooling that educational institutions have such obligations, and they may feel imposed upon. Institutions should therefore try to teach students how official policies and purposes are related. Candor in catalogs and orientation programs is imperative to this end, and wherever possible should be conjoined with clarity about the best reasons for standards and their enforcement. As students mature sufficiently, they deserve to learn of the great historical tensions between liberty and authority and to study, for example, the observation of John Stuart Mill in *On Liberty:*

> All that makes existence valuable to anyone, depends on the enforcement of restraints upon the actions of other people. Some rules of conduct, therefore, must be imposed.[12]

By candid instruction, students may learn that standards are not by nature manipulative, but point, on the one hand, to the incompatibility of chaos and license, and on the other hand to instruction and systematic learning. Furthermore, when administrators, faculty members, and trustees think in such terms, they may be better able to distinguish legitimate and necessary standards from those which are arbitrary and unjustified.

Second, learning and being taught to reason well—to be objective and impartial—inculcate specific ideals. These are the ideals of reason itself, and any student who does not learn them is forever in thrall to his or her own ignorance. It is no arbitrarily imposed standard to teach a student to identify valid and fallacious formal and informal arguments; to measure probability; to apply relevant criteria; to verify and falsify propositions; and to confirm or disconfirm hypotheses. In fact, it is irresponsible to teach less.

Teaching ideals of rationality is sometimes said to be teaching only how to think. Teaching students *how* to think, it is claimed, is no imposition of values, while teaching them *what* to think imposes, is ideological and manipulative. But the distinction is not entirely useful, because how we think inevitably influences what we think. Logical form cannot be separated in the practice of thinking from implications for the substance of what is thought.

For example, a student who learns how to think and who thinks well will regard *Science* as a bad textbook. The book claims that a position is false because the people who advocate it are bad. On this principle, if Caligula holds that the earth is round or that $2 + 2 = 4$, we have reason to conclude that these statements are false. Any textbook that teaches children to reason this way is a bad textbook. Learning to reason well, therefore, has consequences for *what* students think and do. Learning to reason well from true premises is clearly not an imposition on freedom.

Teaching that there are right and wrong kinds of arguments is no imposition either; indeed, what else could we truthfully teach students? To teach them anything else is to lie to them.

Third, learning how to be objective and to apply reason to questions takes students from initial training toward understanding. This is the alternative to subjection to ideology in education and the rest of life. If learning to reason reliably is not one of the educational purposes of a school, college, or university, then the institution is not committed to intellectual progress and may be explicitly opposed to it.

Allowing religious or political ideology to dictate to education is as bad as the barrenness of uncritical and equally dogmatic relativism. How are we to avoid all such dogmatism? How are we to impart ideals of decency—the ideals of objectivity and generous understanding—and avoid, as C. S. Lewis puts it, gelding our young and them absurdly bidding them to be fruitful?[13]

The answer is that we must be clear that all manipulation for the sake of conversion, whether political or religious, is tyrannical. It is rooted in contempt for human beings and their capacity to discover the truth. It denies that anyone who is given a genuine chance to learn rather than being manipulated, can be trusted. The ideologue as manipulator is as cynical as any other tyrant.

Believing that ends justify means is beneath our dignity as human beings. We can steer a course between the dangers on all sides by paying attention to what we know.

We send our children to school to overcome the ignorance in which we are born. As parents, we teach them what we can. We expect schools to concentrate on subjects we lack the time or experience to handle.

Schools should teach our children the three Rs. We want students to learn to use words and numbers well, to read, write, and translate with understanding, to do calculations, and to conduct experiments. We want them to learn how the past is related to the present, and to be able to look at a painting or listen to a symphony intelligently. Many of us expect our children to study English, mathematics, languages, science, literature, history, and the fine arts.

We want our children to achieve reliable study habits and self-discipline through the curriculum, the classroom, homework, and extracurricular activities. When we successfully teach, learning is no longer mere drudgery.

Education cannot be neutral to the difference between good and bad habits. The work of schoolchildren is to become good learners. Teachers must design their courses and assignments so that good habits of learning and success—even the appearance of success—are not separated.

A good learner can learn things on purpose, rather than by accident or luck. Working hard is not enough, because the student must know how to work, what to concentrate on, and which skills to use. Good learning depends on one value above all others: the value of intellectual honesty. Children who never learn this have slim chance of significant benefit from school.

Intellectual honesty takes evidence seriously in deciding what is true and what is false. It means not hiding from the facts when they run counter to our wishes. It is a much greater and more important achievement than sincerity. A person can sincerely believe something and refuse to listen to any question of the truth of the belief. Not so with intellectual honesty, which requires the hard work of *continuing* to think about important matters. An intellectually honest person makes up his or her mind on the basis of the best available evidence, all the while acknowledging that new evidence may become available tomorrow.

Conversations in classrooms and in homes provide abundant illustrations of the emergence of intellectual honesty. I once spoke, for example, with public high school students who were discussing fair housing practices. Some claimed that they had a right to choose their neighbors and that, for this reason, property owners should be able to exclude minorities from consideration when offering houses for sale. Others objected, and the discussion became heated. Opinions on all sides seemed quite firm, so I asked the first group of students whether they thought minority members, too, had a right to choose their neighbors. They quickly answered yes, but qualified their response by insisting that minorities should want to choose "their own kind" as neighbors. (I might have forced the issue about what "their own kind" means, but I did not.) I asked whether these students were willing to be told whom *they* should want as their neighbors.

They were not, and I could sense the tension between their desire and intellect. They had begun to see that what they wanted—their own homogeneous neighborhoods—and what they had already accorded themselves—the right to choose their neighbors—were in conflict unless they also denied others the right to choose their neighbors. But they understood such a denial to be unfair. They could not bring themselves to admit in so many words that they assigned their rights precedence over other peoples'.

They were not perplexed as a person is perplexed when two incompatible arguments seem to warrant assent. They were perplexed in the way of a person who is trying to get what he wants and cannot quite figure out how to do so. Unable to justify the satisfaction of their desires by compelling reasons, several of them said they merely guessed that everybody has a right to choose neighbors when moving into a neighborhood, irrespective of race.

They were not necessarily happy with this conclusion. Their understanding of others may have been no more generous than when they started. Their passion to keep minorities from their neighborhoods was scarcely reduced because human proclivities and passions are not so easily exhausted. But they were intellectually honest enough to concede that they could not live complacently with their original position. This intellectual honesty is a good example of the connection between methods and content in reasoning, and it shows how compelling such honesty can be without imposing values.

If we and our children could not trust teachers, textbook authors, and administrators to be intellectually honest, then the hope of promoting objectivity and generous understanding would be futile. Our children might otherwise be given neo-Nazi publications that claim there were no death camps and that the holocaust is a Jewish fabrication. Students might actually be deprived of the chance to read *Huckleberry Finn* by censors who are so afraid that students are tempted by racism that they are incapable of intellectual honesty. There are actually those who cannot read *Huckleberry Finn* with enough open-mindedness to see that, over and again, Mark Twain pokes fun—and not so subtly either—at the illogical arguments of racism. These censors prefer to visit their cynicism on our children, depriving them of opportunity to become intellectually honest, and make education propaganda that leads only to bondage and to ignorance. There is no limit to the perils for our children posed by such self-righteous purveyors of ideology and special interest.

When our children are learning to respect intellectual honesty, they may absorb a number of related lessons about values—that intellectual honesty means trying not to be prejudiced, reserving judgment until at least some facts can be considered. Trying not to be prejudiced takes patience, one of the ideals of maturity. It takes courage to listen to things that may disturb complacency, courage to try to have an open mind instead of an empty head. It takes fairness to be willing to listen. These qualities of mind are opposites of prejudice, favoritism, and self-indulgence. They are values our children must learn if they are to achieve good habits of learning. To be successful, schools must respect these ideals.

Honesty, patience, courage, and fairness do not apply only to the way we treat ideas. They apply also to the way we treat each other. A student who learns intellectual honesty in study learns also about decency and civility in conduct. It could hardly be otherwise. Education can no more be isolated from such values than can the rest of our lives. To suppose otherwise is to make education itself impossible.

VALUES AND ACADEMIC FREEDOM

A college or university should enable students to make their minds their own. Classes ought to deal primarily in questions of substance, and nurture reflection, contemplation, speculation, and deliberation about such questions. These activities establish a reasoned independence of mind. They are elements of objectivity and generous understanding.

This is one fundamental trust that every teacher bears. Every teacher—every institution itself—has the responsibility to be faithful to this trust. Academic freedom is the guarantee that makes it possible to accept such a trust; academic freedom guarantees that teachers and their students will enjoy the liberty to follow questions wherever they may lead, to assess and to disagree, and to raise doubt wherever it is intelligible. Fidelity to this trust is central to the calling of teaching.

Do all teachers bear the trust faithfully? Of course not. Some teachers come to class ill-prepared, some teach what interests them rather than what is worthy of being taught, some treat student assignments cavalierly, and some inject political ideology into their work. Teachers who have a political agenda are, like most ideologues, remarkably naïve about abuse of power, often not recognizing this vice in themselves. Thus, they are able to violate their professional trust, sometimes self-righteously.

The problem is not new. In 1939, Judge Learned Hand was awarded an honorary degree by Columbia University. In his acceptance speech, he cautioned against confusing teaching with propagandizing, objectivity with ideology:

> You may take Martin Luther or Erasmus for your model, but you cannot play both roles at once; you may not carry a sword beneath a scholar's gown, or lead flaming causes from a cloister. You cannot raise the standard against oppression or leap into the breach to relieve injustice, and still keep an open mind to every disconcerting fact, or an open ear to the cold voice of doubt. I am satisfied that a

scholar who tries to combine these parts sells his birthright for a mess of pottage; that, when the final count is made, it will be found that the impairment of his powers far outweighs any possible contribution to the causes he has espoused. If he is fit to serve in his calling at all, it is only because he has learned not to serve in any other, for his singleness of mind quickly evaporates in the fires of passions, however holy.[14]

Teachers who carry the sword of ideology beneath their gowns treat academic freedom as a license to carry a concealed weapon. They wish to live by the sword but not to die by it. They are a threat to academia because they wage war on freedom of inquiry and on principles of impartiality from within ivied walls. They treat the university as a battleground for possession of the minds of students; they betray, however shrewdly, the fundamental goal of all teaching—that students should come to possess their own minds. They implicitly deny that teaching is a means to intellectual maturation and self-knowledge.

Yet, however compelling Learned Hand's insight is, misleading conclusions may be drawn from it. He cautions against trying to assume mutually exclusive roles and in this he is surely right. Are we to infer, however, that the only legitimate voice of the classroom is the cold voice of doubt, that teachers should be indecisive in their lives, that open-mindedness means never reaching a conclusion and never staking anything on a judgment, and even that teachers should lie to students rather than reveal their convictions?

I think Learned Hand did not intend these conclusions. But how are we to make the necessary distinctions between candor and proselytizing, between inquiry that reaches conclusions and ideology that begs questions and betrays intellectual honesty?

It is too easy to suggest that students should be invited to consider diverse and conflicting positions. Surely they should, but it is not intellectually honest for a teacher to imply that all positions are equally logical, factual, and reliable. Open-mindedness cannot entail indifference to quality and evidence; quite the opposite. Teachers should help students learn to be dubious when there is reasonable ground for doubt, and to be decisive when evidence warrants resolution. The goal is not a mind that is independent in the sense of promiscuous or indiscriminate, but a mind that is independent in the sense that it can rely on its own judgment—not infallible, but rigorous.

A teacher sees students as people working toward a condition of intellectual maturity and self-reliance; the ideologue sees students as prospective followers or disciples. Thus, the teacher will consciously seek to advance intellectual honesty and the independence it sustains; the ideologue will not. All who aspire to teach students might therefore do well to recall these words of the Danish philosopher Justus Hartnack:

> A disciple's spiritual dependence on his master at best hinders independent thought, and, at worst, prevents it. And a thought which is not independent is a thought only half-understood. It contains no personal truth.
>
> This is the dilemma of anyone who wishes to transmit knowledge and learning to others. On the one hand, to teach is to pass your own knowledge to the pupil, to introject your knowledge into him. On the other hand, learning is not mere receiving. For knowledge is not knowledge if it is without insight and understanding; both must be there if anything is learned, and neither can be received like a gift. . . . To teach is not to instill a true idea in the pupil, but to help him to think it himself.[15]

To try to help a student achieve knowledge for himself clearly requires the conviction that knowledge is possible. The teacher who listens to the cold voice of doubt understands that it is not to be heard at all times and about everything. We can see this in the conversations with students described above. It would have been irresponsible to allow the inconsistencies of reasoning in the conversation about fair housing to pass unnoticed, uncriticized. It would have been equally irresponsible to ignore the facts of Socrates' defense in the discussion of college policies on underage drinking. *Reasonable* doubt rests on respect for standards of reasoning and evidence that apply in all work with students. By these standards, some knowledge about any subject is possible. Thus, responsible teaching is not by nature tentative and inconclusive; accordingly, the teacher does not become an ideologue by forcing an issue so that students can penetrate the faults or recognize the strengths of a position. And he does not become a good teacher by conveying the lesson that every position is as faithful to reason and evidence as every other.

The distinction between teaching and propagandizing became

especially important to me when I was teaching philosophy at the University of Toledo in the early 1970s. Many of my students were the first members of their families to go to college; a large number worked for their tuition and commuted to school. They saw education as a means to better jobs. In introductory philosophy courses, many of my students disliked Socrates intensely. They were impatient with questions and wanted quick answers; they wanted to get on with their lives and their ambitions, so they saw philosophizing as delay and inaction. A significant number thought Socrates a bully, a would-be destroyer of perfectly good ideas about how to live and what to try to get out of life. Some agreed with Callicles that grown people who continue to ask philosophical questions are foolish. They did admit that Socrates had integrity, but they found this unimpressive because they believed that, as an old man, he had little to lose in dying.

I had a good deal of respect for most of these students. They took on backbreaking workloads, were prompt in completing assignments, and were remarkably forthright in conversation. They made sacrifices every day, as they put it, "to better themselves."

Even though I agreed that Socrates was sometimes a bully, I did not want them to miss out on the power of philosophical inquiry and the virtues of men and women who will not betray principle for personal gain. My opportunity as a teacher was the fact that Socrates made them angry; he did not bore them or leave them indifferent.

I could have portrayed Socrates in a more favorable light and altered his position so he would gain their approval. By manipulating the students, I could have brought them to admire Socrates—or at least a sugar-coated Socrates. But this would have been dishonest.

Instead, we took the positions expressed by the people Socrates questioned and applied them line by line to the daily lives of students. What would actually happen to us if we behaved as they said we should behave? The impatient students agreed with Callicles that "might makes right," yet still resented it when, as they told me, their bosses were unfair to them. Why? The young man Polus laughed at Socrates' ideas, and the students laughed with him. Why, then, did they get angry when other students laughed at things they said seriously? Why did they say that

Socrates should have listened to his friends and broken the law to save his life? They themselves strongly supported "law and order" politics and became indignant when outsiders parked illegally in student parking spaces. Long and thorough discussions of details became our daily work. Most of the students were much more interested by detail than by general claims. And like the rest of us, when they paid attention to detail, they tended to offer more plausible and considered generalizations.

Sometimes they became impatient with me or with each other, but for the most part they brought good humor and generous disposition to the work. And if some left the courses believing that integrity can cost more than a prudent person should be willing to pay, few dismissed considerations of personal honor and consistency as trivial. I think, for the most part, they were more thoughtful about their ambitions; at least some of them came back to talk with me and asked for reading lists after they had graduated.

In such matters, the attitudes of teachers and ideologues are fundamentally opposed. The ideologue has a calling different from and incompatible with the calling of the teacher. It does not matter whether the rallying cry of the ideologue is justice, peace, human rights, or what have you. The ideologue betrays the trust of students. He is single-minded and treats students as instruments of his passion.

Ideologues do not, of course, believe this. All ideologues are convinced that any reasonable person of good will must reach their conclusions. Ideologues believe that they possess the whole truth and luxuriate in the self-satisfying view that, by manipulating others—students in particular—they give them the truth. Teachers, by contrast, seek to empower students intellectually so that they can think for themselves. Because ideas cannot merely be given as a gift, a genuine teacher knows that academic freedom is rightly indispensable. He or she pursues truth, a pursuit possible only for those with humility and respect for human intelligence and ready to admit a degree of ignorance and fallibility. These qualities the ideologue does not affirm and therefore does not have.

Ideologues cannot bear the trust of education because they do not themselves trust independence of mind. Teachers work in the faith that human intelligence has a future, even a bright future, and they will bring illumination to classroom inquiry in the expectation that students are thereby acquiring lights of their own. Ideologues believe that, other than their own light, there is only darkness; students to them are no more than potential carriers of the torch of ideology. To teachers, by contrast, students are heirs to a future which they may enlighten one day with torches of their own.

I never felt more aware of this true calling of the teacher than when I went into Toledo Hospital for surgery. By chance, most of the personnel in the operating room had been my students. I had confidence in their qualities of mind and judgment and in their conscientiousness as professionals. I felt safe in their hands. Finding yourself totally dependent on your own former students is a wonderfully powerful reminder of what you hope, as a teacher, they have become.

It is not always easy to identify ideologues in education because their effectiveness consists in appearing not to be ideologues; they can seduce students because they can deliver the rhetoric of independence of mind as persuasively as the truest of teachers. Alexander Meiklejohn rightly explained fifty years ago in *What Does America Mean?* that ideologues tell many a lie that is factually true. The lie consists in the context in which it is conveyed, and in giving the impression that the fact is being taught for the sake of the students when it is actually being taught in order to manipulate.[16] As William Blake put it, "A truth that is told with bad intent, beats all the lies you can invent."

All of us are familiar with people and institutions that tell truths with bad intent. When an oil company proves in commercials that cars get better mileage using its gasoline with performance additives than they do using *its own* gasoline without additives, it tells the truth. But the intent is to convince viewers that its gasoline is superior to *other* brands of gasoline; the demonstration is logically irrelevant to that suggestion, however, and anyone who draws the intended conclusion has been successfully misled. Similarly, a lawyer who tells a jury that premeditated murder is a terrible crime tells the truth. But when the lawyer uses the jury's hatred of the crime to lead them to the idea that the defendant committed it, the truth is told with bad intent. This example recalls the story of a lawyer who pleaded for mercy for his client—a boy who murdered his parents—on the grounds that the boy was an orphan.

Similar episodes occur in classrooms. While I was teaching at a maximum security prison in Mansfield, Ohio, I watched another teacher incite racial hatred by clever manipulation of the fact that most of the inmates were black. From this fact about the prison population, the teacher coaxed the students to the conclusion that white people are racists who want as many blacks as possible to be incarcerated. Likewise, I have seen classroom teachers in educational institutions use the unrelated facts that the United States has bombed other countries and that terrorists use bombs to lead students to the conclusion that the public officials of the United States are terrorists.

Ideologues are not always obvious in their betrayal of educational trust. This is because the success of ideological manipulation depends on shrewdness and on the vulnerability of the innocent. For this reason, schools, colleges, and universities must be vigilant about the nature and quality of work done with students. No institution can fulfill the duties of academic freedom unless the individuals who work in it understand and are committed to them.

External watchdogs, such as groups outside academia, are not likely to accomplish very much in this regard. If teachers, administrators, and trustees do not take their trust seriously, there is little hope of sustained, conscientious educational performance. Some have the courage this trust calls for and are unwilling to bequeath to the future less than we have inherited.

Is there a conscientious way to prevent the betrayal of students?

The sole remedy for abuse of liberty without the destruction of liberty itself is for colleges and universities to display courage in defense of the trust they bear. They must exhibit the courage to be restrained in borderline cases because excess of certitude jeopardizes academic freedom. And they must have the courage to be decisive in cases that are not borderline—whether the failings consist in laziness, incompetence, or ideology.

In my experience as a teacher and administrator of educational programs for children, youths, and adults, I have seen all the effects of failing in the situations I have described. I have, for example, seen ideologues who believe many things I believe myself. They are not unfit to teach because everything they passionately believe is untrue, but because they will go to great lengths to make students believe what *they* believe. I have also seen ideologues shocked to be told by colleagues that they are ideologues and seen them become trustworthy teachers as a result of critical self-examination. I have seen others who will never change. And I have seen incompetence and laziness persist because to rid an institution of them is painful and demanding. To my knowledge, however, the only way to bear the public trust is to conscientiously undergo the ordeal such a situation presents and act conclusively where there is compelling evidence of inadequacies or improprieties.

Generous understanding reveals that as human beings we deserve to be conceived as equals by virtue of our humanity. Perhaps its simplest prescriptive formulation is in the Golden Rule—that we should do unto others as we would be done to. The ideologue does not understand others generously, and so does not recognize the samenesses in us that give vitality to what is humanly possible. As in all of human life, our fate in education lies not in the stars but in ourselves. So, too, the fate of our students.

The question, then, is *how* schools, colleges, and universities are to find and keep administrators and teachers who will stand this ground, and who will bring to their work objectivity and generous understanding. For in the end institutions are what the people within them make them, and so what we achieve will be no greater than what we aspire to achieve.

6

Building Faculty and Administration

A man may in theory own the most prodigious mountain of learning that mortal man ever amassed and still be, in every fundamental sense, stupid, unenlightened, and irrational. . . . None of the enterprises of the human spirit is carried on in a vacuum. . . . If one cannot enter into the ideas of the *Inferno* or *The Wasteland,* one cannot properly respond to it. . . . Human beings never merely think, and never merely feel; all the main sides of their nature are at work in everything they do. Adequate criticism, therefore, cannot be offered from a single point of view. It must surround and enfold the work with a comprehensive knowledge and a generous understanding of comparative value. It must be able to say of a play, for example, that its wit is refreshing, its plot original, its dialogue clever, its construction weak, its morals confused, its characterization sound, its theme important, its sense of dramatic development feeble. A wholly adequate criticism could be offered only by a mind to which nothing human was alien.[1]

—*Brand Blanshard*

THE POWER OF mind described by Brand Blanshard in the preceding citation is a rare achievement in a single person. More often, we must learn from one another in order to offer a wholly adequate criticism of any work of art. This is one reason for building the best faculties and administrations we can in schools, colleges, and universities—that together they may develop such a power and expose students to it.

The question of how to build the best faculties and administrations has at least three parts: What can the academic profession do? What can institutions that educate prospective faculty and administrators do? What can individual schools, colleges, and universities do with and for their own personnel?

A SEAMLESS PROFESSION

Schoolteachers and administrators are seldom considered members of the academic profession. Even speech reveals this: we speak generally of *schoolteachers* but specifically of university *faculty* members or college *professors*. Higher education offers greater opportunity for scholarship and research and greater prestige than schoolteaching, and it normally expects a more extensive educational background of its faculty members. Usually, though not always, college and university faculty are better paid than schoolteachers.

This division makes schoolteaching seem less important, less crucial, and less attractive as a career. It would be valuable to the elevation of standards if this perception could be corrected. Communication and cooperation between schoolteachers and college and university teachers are often fruitful for both; experience in teaching and scholarship cuts across levels of education when communication is established and when alliances are formed between schools and colleges.

Yet there are enormous barriers to gaining an acknowledgement by the professoriat that schoolteachers and administrators are fellow professionals. The exclusion reflects attitudes within the general public and within academe itself. As John Palmer, dean of the College of Education at the University of Wisconsin at Madison, explains:

> Only the public demand for a supply of well-educated teachers prevented many public universities from relegating teacher education entirely to less prestigious state colleges and normal schools. The low status of teacher training in state universities was established early, and it has persisted. It continues to be a primary factor in determining the resources, the faculty, and the student body available to students and colleges of education. It is a paradox that universities in this country have often treated with disdain the preparation of individuals to assist the young in their intellectual development.[2]

However paradoxical this phenomenon, the explanations for it are not terribly complicated.

First, we tend to think of a professional as a person who is particularly mature and has achieved knowledge and judgment from advanced and extended study. The personnel of our schools are often young; nearly half of them have only an undergraduate education.

Second, we tend to think of members of professions as people who will invest much of their adult life in their chosen career, such as a doctor, lawyer, minister, architect, or military officer. But school personnel are frequently in the field for only a few years; often they are women who leave to raise families. Prejudices against women *as* professionals may figure in this attitude as well.

Third, we tend to think of intellectual development as a high human accomplishment, something that occurs after childhood. When we speak of intellectuals, either disparagingly or otherwise, we normally do not speak of children; the learning and teaching of the young supposedly fall in some other category than *intellectual* development.

Fourth, most of us become parents without any particular knowledge about being parents, and we normally trust in our own competence—having once been children—to raise our own offspring. If we lack confidence, we can always read such "experts" as Dr. Spock. We tend to think we are peers of schoolteachers in offering instruction; after all, we help with homework, already know much of what our children study in textbooks, and have been students ourselves. These facts, too, tend to diminish the professional standing we accord schoolteachers and administrators.

Fifth, within the academic institutions of America, there is greater respect for the classical disciplines and the natural sciences than for the study of teaching or administration of institutions. The traditional disciplines are associated with research and scholarship, rather than practical application of the sort to which colleges of education must attend. This tends to reduce the status of teacher education in academia.

Finally, though few of us serve as our own doctor or lawyer, we are in some ways our own teacher. Moreover, virtually everyone is cast into teaching others whether at work, at church, at home, or even in casually giving directions to strangers. We tend, therefore, to think of teaching as something everyone can do.

Perhaps these attitudes are also buttressed by our memories of our own schoolteachers. Some of us have had influential teachers, but all of us have also had schoolteachers whose performance is best forgotten. The same is true of the teachers we had in higher education, but for some reason we seem not to blame them as much as we do our schoolteachers.

The applicant pool of prospective teachers and administrators cannot be dramatically improved without some significant effort to make the profession seamless. Avoiding the burn-out of school personnel will be difficult, too, unless we come to think of the obligations, as well as the rightful oportunities, of school personnel by analogy to those in higher education.

The power of such analogy may be seen in a summary of the professional obligations of college and university teachers. In *The Academic Ethic,* Edward Shils offers the following account:

> All the particular obligations of university teachers to students, to colleagues, to their universities and to their respective societies derive their binding force fundamentally from their obligations to ascertain what is true in their research, study and teaching, to assess scrupulously what has been handed down as true and to cultivate and propagate an active quest for truth as an ideal. . . . Teaching and research are about the pursuit and transmission of truths, the methods of distinguishing between truth and error, so far as that is humanly possible, and the distinction between fallacious and valid evidence and argument. . . . The service of knowledge entails not only the discovery of new knowledge but also the transmission of the best of established knowledge to students. No teacher should allow himself to go on teaching as if the body of knowledge in his field has remained constant. . . . Teaching . . . must aim at conveying understanding of the fundamental truths in the subject and the methods of enquiry and testing characteristic of their subject. . . . A teacher cannot hope to arouse the spirit of enquiry in his students or to get them to see the need for care or imagination if his teaching is desultory. . . . [T]eachers should try to make their students extend themselves intellectually. . . . The students must be pressed to attain the highest level of knowledge which their immaturity, their capacities and their previous acquisition permit. . . . The matter comes down therefore to each teacher's own sense of obligation and his

voluntary submission to it. The bearing of a conscientious teacher affects the attitude of his colleagues towards their own teaching. The sense of obligation of a teacher is strengthened by the awareness of the strength of that sense of obligation in his colleagues. This is not a tautology; it is a self-closing circle of reciprocal influences.[3]

Should respect for truth, for reasoned inquiry, for humility, for continued learning, for extending students intellectually, and for obligations to students and colleagues be any less central in the lives of schoolteachers and administrators? Is reciprocal influence less a fact of life in schools than everywhere else? Surely not.

But by excluding professors of prospective teachers as well as schoolteachers and administrators themselves from the professional mainstream, we have left them to devices that are destined to disaster. And we subtly suggest that their obligations are somehow fundamentally different from "real" academic duties.

This condescension concerning schoolteachers and administrators will reap sorrowful consequences for us and our children. We can predict these consequences with confidence because, in several ways, they have already come to pass.

Specifically, the isolation of schoolteachers and administrators and their professors from the mainstream of academic life has resulted in the idea that schools are not places of respect for truth, for reason, for striving, and for intellectual and moral accomplishment.

Strangely, this idea took root within the education colleges themselves. As Andrew Oldenquist explains in *The Non-Suicidal Society,* from the 1960s until today "within the education colleges self-esteem became the chief good to be achieved by schooling and its perceived enemies were grading, competition, and standards of any sort that implied that someone might fail to meet them. These included ethical standards with their threats of guilt and shame."[4] The self-esteem movement explicitly denied any kinship between the obligations of teachers in schools and those in higher education. It assumed that healthy feelings could be nurtured only by dismissing rationality and respect for truth from education; and it has therefore denigrated nurturing the intelligence of children.

When this divorce of feeling from reason inevitably threatened the quality of our schools, efforts were made to compensate for it by a new conception of intellectual development. Oldenquist continues:

> Here the new idea was that real education is learning how to think, to question, and to integrate experiences; it is not just learning "dead facts." Noble as this sounds, what it usually meant in practice is sneering at acquiring facts and substituting sessions devoted to discussion and self-expression. For it is not as though the professors had in mind "live" facts to replace dead ones; all factual knowledge is "dead" and its replacements are self-esteem pumping, "hands-on experiences," and self-expression. What was forgotten was that learning how to think—how to appraise, to reason, and to research facts—supplements and cannot replace learning lots of facts. Unfortunately, the teachers who were supposed to teach children how to think were not themselves taught how to think nor were *their* teachers (the education professors). No one in this chain was taught the necessary logic and scientific method, for that would require a rigorous and sometimes technical training that was contrary to the relativist and self-expressive spirit of the times.[5]

As usual, we have reaped as we have sown. Deny that schoolteachers, administrators, and their teachers are part of the academic profession, and they will naturally be uninformed or uninfluenced by the obligations of that profession. Prospective teachers and administrators will respect the ideals of the profession *only* if we eagerly welcome them into it and not if we show contempt for their talents and estrange them from the intellectual and moral standards of the profession at its best.

All prospective teachers should learn that teaching children, youths, and adults is intended to lead to the maturation of human beings, and that what happens to children has consequences. Teaching a child is every bit as important as teaching a Ph.D. candidate. Teachers should learn that, without common purposes and ideals of the kind Shils describes, the levels of education are not only not mutually supportive, but perhaps even in conflict. Making this clear to those who plan to teach is essential to their recognizing each other as colleagues in a common enterprise. Furthermore, professors must regard teachers as fellow professionals doing equally noble and important work if there is to be change in public attitudes toward school personnel.

Many objections can be offered to the idea of a seamless

profession of education. Most of these are rooted in the differences between the background and work of schoolteachers and administrators and their counterparts in higher education. The dignity of the profession, it may be argued, can be maintained only by restricting its membership to highly educated academics involved in research and scholarship or at least in continued study of their disciplines. School personnel almost never undertake research in the scholarly and scientific disciplines and seldom contribute to scholarly publications. Furthermore, to require of school personnel the advanced study normally expected of college and university professors would virtually eliminate the applicant pool. Who would submit to the labor and expense of a Ph.D. to obtain the schoolteacher's average annual salary of $22,019?[6] And how are schoolteachers and administrators to find time for scholarly research? Their daily responsibilities are usually much more time-consuming than a professor's.

Nonetheless, many administrators in higher education are able to advance knowledge and quality of research and teaching by wise investment of resources. Their school counterparts ought to do the same. And many professors advance knowledge primarily by excellent teaching based on continuing, rigorous study of their discipline whether or not they publish much. Their school counterparts ought to be able to do the same. We must draw their respective responsibilities closer, rather than accepting the current differences as immutable.

Schools, colleges, and universities and those who teach and administer in them share similar purposes. We should seek ways of joining their efforts for the sake of students everywhere. Jon Moline suggests in "Teachers and Professionalism" that "the distinctive character of the professional in the honorific sense" may be found in "the particular type of service relationship he or she has with clients. This is not simply a service relationship; it is fiduciary. This means, of course, that it involves trust. . . . We demand of paradigm professionals that they take their trust seriously, believing themselves bound to act in equity, good conscience, and good faith, 'with due regard for the interests of the one reposing the confidence.'"[7] Moline argues that, in order to bear such a trust, the professional must be able to distinguish the needs of those served from their wants, the good for them from what is harmful. As education cannot do its work except by instruction in the disciplines of inquiry and discovery, teachers must themselves have a powerful grasp of subject matter in order to do their students good. Thus, standards must be understood and respected by all teachers and administrators at *all* levels, else the distinction between teaching and quackery is lost.

Such standards are not impossible; they can be reached if we unite the efforts of school and higher education personnel to realize them at all levels. As Chester Finn and Diane Ravitch explain, "Nicholas Muray Butler spoke in 1925 of 'the close and intimate association of the secondary schools and colleges in dealing with a common interest and a common task.' More recently, that association has seldom been either close or intimate. It needs to become so again."[8]

Several efforts in this direction are already well established and could be expanded. The Summer Seminars for School Teachers program of the National Endowment for the Humanities brings hundreds of schoolteachers and administrators into seminars led by distinguished scholars. From the late 1960s to the early 1980s, the National Humanities Faculty brought school, college, and university personnel together in schools to study the humanities and curriculum development; it conducted programs in all fifty states. Similar work is being done by its successor institution at Emory University, the National Faculty of Humanities, Arts, and Sciences.

Also, over two hundred alliances among schools, colleges, and universities, involving more than five thousand educators, were initially supported by the National Endowment for the Humanities, the Rockefeller Foundation, and the Exxon Education Foundation. The Carnegie Foundation for the Advancement of Teaching has said such partnerships are the way to build a "seamless web" in education. Through such partnerships, as *The Chronicle of Higher Education* reports,

> School and university educators who have eyed each other warily in the past often find they have a lot in common. Members reported a renewed sense of interest in their work and a greater understanding of the links between school and college curricula.[9]

Through such projects, schoolteachers and school administrators are able to sustain intellectual development whether in physics, foreign languages, history, literature, geography, mathematics, or other disciplines. And their gain is matched by that of teachers in higher eduction. As Robert M. Williamson, a professor of physics at Oakland University, who participates in an alliance, observes: "Those of us who teach introductory classes find we have more in common with high-school teachers than with senior colleagues in our departments."[10]

To build a seamless profession, we need to recognize that opportunities cut both ways. We should not suppose that teachers and administrators in schools must invariably be drawn closer to the standards of higher education. School personnel may often be able to improve professional standards for professors and administrators in higher education.

For example, Dr. Steven L. Dubovsky of the University of Colorado Medical Center writes that many experts are becoming increasingly concerned about problems among physicians such as "emotional ill health, declining humanitarianism, dishonesty, greed, cynicism, and lack of independent thinking."[11] He suggests that medical schools encourage an attitude he calls "entitlement," which is "a sense of being entitled to attention, care taking, love, success, income, or other benefits without having to give anything in return."[12] Included are the notions that "knowledge is a 'right' that should be delivered with a minimum of exertion and discomfort on the part of the 'consumer'; the expectation that others will provide all the education that is necessary; the feeling that problems in learning are due to the inadequacies of the teacher, the course, or the system, rather than to the student's own shortcomings; the belief that everyone should receive equal recognition and reward, regardless of individual effort and ability"; and the feeling that "discussion of the student's own behavior . . . is thought to create undue stress."[13]

Dubovsky counters this conception of entitlement:

> Experience in public education has demonstrated painfully that lowering expectations in response to complaints that course work is too difficult leads only to inadequate learning. Students then come to expect less of themselves, further decreasing their ability to master even basic material. In work arenas, people tend to rise or sink to the level that is expected of them.[14]

Indeed they do. Thus schoolteachers and school administrators who expect much of themselves and their students—who show by example that they study hard to expand their knowledge and insist that nobody is entitled to achievement because no one can be given achievement—have important counsel to offer their counterparts at even the most sophisticated graduate and professional levels.

The opportunities that lie before us in such mutual exchange do not require great sums of money. Communication and mutual reliance can be established easily; in most cases, a telephone call is sufficient for a beginning. There is no reason why teachers at different levels of education should be strangers, and there is every reason for the continuing intellectual development of all teachers and administrators at every level, especially in the schools where it has been most neglected.

Finn and Ravitch rightly insist that five elements of professionalism must be emphasized in schools: acknowledgement of good teaching through increased status, compensation, and authority; greater self-regulation at all levels of education, including refusal to tolerate incompetence, sloth, and malpractice; greater teacher involvement in staff and curriculum decisions; comprehensive examination in subject matter for certification; and expanded opportunities for intellectual maturation.[15]

EDUCATION AND TRAINING OF PROSPECTIVE FACULTY MEMBERS AND ADMINISTRATORS

When many of today's educators were children, Jacques Barzun wrote:

> Happily, there is something stable and clear and useful behind this phantasmagoria of education—the nature of subject matter and the practice of teaching.
>
> The word helps us again to the idea. The advantage of "teaching" is that in using it you must recognize—if you are in your sober senses—that practical limits exist. You know by instinct that it is impossible to "teach" democracy, or citizenship or a happy married life. I do not say that these virtues are not somehow connected with good teaching. They are, but they occur as by-products. They come, not from a course, but from a teacher; not from a curriculum, but from a human soul . . . [E]ducation is the hope of the world only in the sense that there is something better than trickery, lies, and violence for righting the world's ways. If this better thing is education, then education is not merely schooling. It is lifelong discipline of the individual by himself.[16]

Lifelong self-discipline, intellectual and moral discipline, fidelity to the principles of reason and the sensibilities of generous understanding—these should be central ideals for all students, certainly for all who are to bear trust as professionals.

They cannot, of course, become ideals for anyone who does not learn of them. No aspiring teacher can appreciate the difference between being an educated person and being "stupid, unenlightened, and irrational" unless he or she can learn to recognize the distinction. The ultimately unavoidable question about the education of teachers and administrators is, therefore, how to make this distinction familiar.

The answer is regressive. Students need guides—people living or dead who can help them to find their way. Thus, the question becomes, who are their teachers and whom do they study? Who are their educational companions in person, in books, in laboratories, in drama, and so on? The issue is the human content of their own education. If that content is shallow and pale, they will be fortunate to overcome it. If it is deep and vivid, they will at least be exposed to the fullness of what is possible. Exposure is no guarantee of aspiration or achievement, but it is the best way human beings have found for drawing each generation toward adult responsibilities.

John Palmer observes that "an educational program cannot rise above the quality of the individuals who staff it."[17] Not surprisingly, neither can an institution, even though the best people in it may draw it to higher quality than it could achieve without them. For the intellectual and moral virtues that make people worthy to teach and administer, and to bear the public trust, are the same that enable them to pursue common purposes in a spirit of liberty. Students should be presented with the best that adults bring to all of daily life. Here is the most profound and simple sense in which the classroom is indivisible from the rest of reality.

Because this is so, institutions that educate those who are to teach and administer must try to instill in them the ideals of objectivity and generous understanding. Each institution should try to appoint and retain faculty members and administrators who embody such civilized intelligence as Blanshard describes—"comprehensive knowledge and a generous understanding of comparative values." To do so, the institutions will need the courage to insist that they will not hire, reappoint, or grant tenure to anyone in whom these qualities are not evident. They will have to deny that anyone is entitled to work in education who does not embody these ideals. Fitness to bear the public trust, and to keep company with students, cannot safely be dismissed as a consideration in staffing institutions.

Institutions have to contend with varying limits of money, talent, and time. Strength in one area may not guarantee strength in others. Not every rich institution is sound, and not every poor one is short on talent.

Unfortunately, public discourse about the financing of education usually discounts these local differences and treats the issues as entirely national. Surely national investment in the education of the public matters profoundly. But knowing that, "in real terms, appropriations for federal student aid have increased 62 percent since 1975, and public and private college tuition and fees have gone up 14.5 percent and 29.3 percent, respectively," or that "some 64.2 million Americans . . . were studying, teaching, or otherwise occupied in schools and colleges in the fall of 1986" at a cost of "about 7 percent of GNP,"[18] is largely uninstructive about the condition of specific institutions. "American education" is nothing apart from the vitality of individual institutions, and it will not do to form our attitudes about each one on the basis of facts about the nation as a whole.

Specifically, the education of faculty and administrators for all levels has a preservice element—preparation—and an inservice component—educational opportunity while working in the field. Much more attention has traditionally been paid to the preservice education and training of schoolteachers than of prospective college and university faculty, while as part of their regular work professors have much more time for study than schoolteachers. At times, we seem to believe that if schoolteachers know enough about pedagogy, their grasp of subject matter will take care of itself; and, if faculty in higher education know enough about subject matter, their teaching will take care of itself. Neither is true.

No one can teach who is not thoroughly qualified in at least one of the scholarly and scientific disciplines. A person may have greater or lesser natural gifts as a teacher; what is more likely is that a person will have more or less charm, style, personal appeal—and that students will gravitate toward these as much as toward real excellence in a teacher. Neither scholarship nor teaching can, therefore, be left to take care of itself in preservice education.

Within these general boundaries, though, it is folly to prescribe some universal curriculum, or how many years it should take to study it. Neither are universal certification requirements sufficient. Regulations help to keep out manifest incompetence, but regulations can neither attract nor keep the best people.

Faculty members and administrators of institutions that prepare teachers need to decide what they believe their students must learn in order to bring objectivity and generous understanding to their work. How much depth and breadth must their students achieve to be fit to teach? Those who teach prospective teachers must ask what *they* themselves need to know and to be. If they believe that the education of children is as important and as demanding as that of youths and adults, then they ought to insist on high standards of preparation for schoolteachers. It may be useful to ask, "What kinds of schoolteachers and administrators would I want for the formal education of my own children?"

How an institution should achieve standards at least this high can be answered only in light of local circumstances. The quality of faculty publications, of student work, and of performance by graduates working in schools should be considered. External evaluation is essential to objectivity. But this is meaningful only against the background of explicit standards for students both before and after they enter the profession of education. Good thinking about such standards has to be specific.

The Goldilocks Case

In the spring of 1983, an elementary school in Santa Fe, New Mexico, gained national attention when on "Law Day" its fifth-grade class conducted a mock trial of Goldilocks for criminal trespass, criminal damage to property, larceny, and burglary. A federal judge presided, teachers played parts in the drama, students served as jurors. Goldilocks was convicted of the first two charges and acquitted of the other two.

After the conviction, the judge explained to the students that he could, but would not, sentence Goldilocks to eighteen months in jail; rather, he sentenced her to give twenty hours of work at an animal shelter, to sell pine cones to pay for Baby Bear's chair, and to try to make friends with Baby Bear. He then instructed the children that service on a jury is the most important act of citizenship. Children interviewed by the press said they had learned how difficult it was to be a lawyer and "never to do anything wrong."[19]

All this was well-intentioned, an attempt by means of a simulated courtroom trial to give the youngsters a sense of due process and governments of laws rather than of men. But even though this was a mock trial of a fictional person, the teachers risked conveying pernicious lessons. The risks could have been avoided by the reflections of a knowledgeable community of teachers. What was risked in this simulation?

First, the students' conclusion that prosecution is a proper response to an eleven-year-old child who is lost, cold, hungry, lonely, and afraid and seeks shelter in the only dwelling she can find. Second, that parents such as the Bears care more about their rights and their property than they do about the Golden Rule. Third, that day-to-day conduct as a citizen—treating one's fellows with kindness, generosity, and civility—is not as important as service on a jury. Fourth, that litigation is better than candid, patient conversation among interested parents and guardians. And fifth, that media celebration of the trial and conviction of a child, even though only in simulation, is no invasion of privacy. The simulation portrayed a bleak vision of parenthood, a shallow vision of citizenship, a crude vision of problem solving, and an uncritical vision of the powers of the press.

For all these flaws, the teachers and administrators in this school give hope: they are trying to engage students in learning that emphasizes accepting responsibility, that treats evidence as relevant to judgment, and that requires homework and reading. All this is to the good, and it encourages further questions about avoiding the flaws in the design of the lessons.

The flaws arise from a conspicious absence of effort to understand from the point of view of the child Goldilocks. The trial is rendered less than fair because no one asked, "Who speaks for Goldilocks?"

There is nothing exceptional in suggesting that the professors of prospective teachers should give greater thought to simulations of this kind. At the preservice level, better thinking elevates the quality of classroom teaching in the schools. All that is required is thought and planning by professors, not some massive curricular or institutional reform.

If the professors plan thoughtfully, they will be setting standards for teaching and for inservice programs that their graduates will later design for themselves. If the graduates of the college or university already know something about how to achieve a morally generous understanding, their inservice programs will reflect it by being intellectually rigorous.

How might a professor teach these lessons to prospective teachers and administrators?

A class devoted to John Adams's insistence on a proper defense for the British soldiers involved in the Boston massacre might be sufficient to avoid insensitivity to the point of view of the accused. Attention in class to a powerful refutation of criticism by an individual whose circumstances are different from our own might be used to illuminate understanding of the intended victim. Perhaps Sojourner Truth's response to a critic at the Women's Rights Convention in Akron, Ohio, in 1851 is as instructive as any.

Sojourner Truth's circumstances were different from most of ours, at least in degree. She was born a slave in 1797, freed when New York state liberated slaves in 1827, and became an eloquent spokeswoman for human rights even though she never learned to read.

At the Akron convention, a man "ridiculed the weakness and helplessness of women" and concluded that they "should, therefore, not be entrusted with the vote." Sojourner Truth replied:

> That man over there says that women need to be helped into carriages and lifted over ditches, and to have the best places everywhere. Nobody ever helps me into carriages or over mud puddles, or gives me any best place. And ain't I a woman? Look at my arms! I have ploughed and planted and gathered into barns, and no man could best me! And ain't I a woman? I could work as much and eat as much as man—when I could get it—and bear the lash as well! And ain't I a woman? I have born thirteen children, and seen them most all sold off to slavery, and when I cried out with my mother's grief, none but Jesus heard me! And ain't I a woman?[20]

The simple logic of her reply is apparent even to the dullest students and teachers, provided they are not irretrievably prejudiced. Reasonability and generous understanding do not have to be built on grand texts of great complexity. They can shine through in the passionate eloquence of an individual who brings them to life. Every school and college library in America stores many such examples and every faculty has access to them. What is required is educational focus by conscientious faculty—not more money or better students or dramatic institutional reform. We need to pay attention to doing our best with ample available resources.

Does this involve teaching values? Certainly. The values of logical consistency, relevant evidence, succinct speech, and freedom of expression; the value of listening to what others say (as Sojourner Truth listened), and of learning from the point of view of another person. Anyone of normal ability can learn and teach these values in the same spirit as Royce or James or Socrates. In practice, the cultivation of the mind of a prospective teacher is not impossibly complicated.

If a prospective teacher is unimpressed by such examples, then teaching is not his or her line of work. This, too, should be recognized by a professor who can give encouragement in other directions. And, if the professor has spine, he can caution prospective employers about the teaching limits of this student.

Every institution has hundreds of stories like the Goldilocks case. They show the strengths and needs of the institution. Each institution must then proceed from *its own condition* to a better one.

The Confucius Case

In the spring of 1981, I watched a high school sophomore English class read and discuss a story about a group of shipwreck victims: stranded on an island, some castaways build a raft hoping to return to civilization; one of the group is a black man, and he is subjected to the others' racial prejudices.

Class discussion of racism is desultory, although the students are critical of racism in regions of America whose history and current features are obviously hazy to them. Many enter the discussion even after they acknowledge that they have not read the assignment. Their teacher acts as though it is perfectly all right to take the stance, "I don't know the story, but I know what I like."

One student who has been attentive but silent adds during a pause in the conversation, "Before he died, my father told me that you can tell a lot about people by how they treat other people who can't do them any good or any harm." The class is momentarily suspended by her observation. She has invited the others to take the conversation seriously. She asks too much. Another student begins to clap and say, "Thank you, Confucius." All laugh, including the teacher. The girl returns to her silence and the class returns to recrimination of distant people of whom they know nothing, with no further reference to the story under discussion. No one notices that the treatment of their classmate is every bit as cruel as the treatment of the black man in the story. The class ends with the teacher assigning the next reading. Understandably, few students pay attention as they gather their books and rush away.

Like the case of Goldilocks, this episode is not unusual. There is less to celebrate and work with here, although it can at least be said that the class was not disruptive and attendance was good. The downside is that there was nothing of significance to disrupt.

The teacher and the students were afraid of taking their work seriously. It is not difficult to teach prospective teachers how deadly this fear is; in fact, a description of the opportunities lost in this class alone should be sufficient to make any aspiring teacher resolve never to let such a situation occur; and never to allow self-righteousness about the faults of others far away to obscure how abysmal our own conduct has been. Any professor of prospective teachers can teach by example that no one is welcome in discussion who has not read an assignment. The slightest consideration of those who *have* done the homework makes clear what an imposition it is to waste their time with uninformed opinions.

All this can be routinely taught and learned. Average students easily learn such standards. Most people readily see that certain kinds of fear make their work impossible. Again, it is not a question of attracting different people to teaching, or of addressing some profoundly difficult issue, or of investing great sums of money. It is a matter of doing our best in ways that are within virtually everyone's reach.

Are values taught by such lessons? Certainly: the values of asking as much of ourselves as we ask of others, of working to develop informed opinions, of treating time as something not to be wasted. It is futile to expect classrooms to be effective without them.

It is equally pointless to expect colleagues who lack respect for such values to serve common purposes within a stand for liberty. What applies to classroom behavior and standards applies to the rest of institutional life.

The Technology Case

Many institutions are now trying to bring their students to some awareness of advancing technology and related problems. For the most part, they are more concerned about problems—in nuclear energy, production of toxic chemicals, genetic engineering, modern warfare—than they are about benefits and blessings—in medicine, transportation, information usage, and the like. But worse, they do not teach their students to ask very good questions, largely because they expect students to address topical questions without much grasp of science, mathematics, and history, and worst of all, without much grasp of human proclivities and institutions. Topical questions, however, must have a context if they are to train the intellectual and moral powers of students. How might this be done at the preservice and inservice levels?

One way is to show students that the issues of technology as part of the human condition are far from novel, that they have been with us for generations, and that they involve not only what the technology is and can do, but also who we are, how we anticipate the future, and how we control ourselves. Of course, what we *are* includes patterns of impulsiveness without planning, carelessness about the consequences, and self-indulgence.

One approach to this set of problems might be a careful reading of *Romeo and Juliet*. One of that drama's central figures is Friar Laurance—consummate medical technologist and pharmacist, an accurately self-described master of his art, and a maker and dispenser of medicinal potions. Friar Laurance is the man whose potions do *exactly* what they are intended to do.

But the people Friar Laurance seeks to help all die; his good intentions result not in marriage and happiness but in anguish and death. Why? Not because of any flaw in the technology. The fatal error is in Friar Laurance's simple failure to stop, think, and inquire: what happens if the "technology" of dispatch service breaks down and my letter to Romeo is not delivered?

He is so captivated by the youthful impulsiveness of Romeo and Juliet that he partly loses the thoughtfulness of maturity. He is human as we are; the disaster occurs because of what he is, which is what we all are; the heartache derives from *that,* not from the technology. Teachers may use such a drama to teach students to think well and to ask the right questions about technology.

Indeed, if teachers wished to engender consideration of conceptual questions about human nature, and the nature of human institutions, human progress, and human backsliding, they might want to explore with their students other broad visions of who and what we are. They might, for example, articulate some of the problems of power—whether political, economic, military, or technological. Perhaps they would want students to read Madison and Hamilton. Having put human nature before the students as neither beast nor angel, but a combination of the two, they might want to examine D. H. Lawrence's position about Americans in writing of Fenimore Cooper's Leatherstocking novels:

> True myth concerns itself centrally with the onward adventure of the integral soul. And this, for America, is Deerslayer. A man who turns his back on white society. A man who keeps his moral integrity hard and intact. An isolate, almost selfless, stoic, enduring man who lives by death, by killing. . . . You have here the myth of the essential white America. All the other stuff, the love, the democracy, the floundering into lust, is a sort of by-play. The essential American soul is hard, isolate, stoic, and a killer.[21]

Is *this* what we are? *Who are we* that make technology and possess power—from Shakespeare to the Federalists to the Deerslayer, the Deer Hunter, and Rambo?

In this sort of fertile imagining and rigorous thinking teachers take students seriously. There is no substitute for such an approach. Such work is well within the ability of most secondary and college students, and most prospective teachers and administrators at all levels. Thoughtful attention to materials available everywhere in American education can result in profound lessons without massive, expensive overhaul.

Topical questions may then show that classrooms and the rest of the real world are indivisible. These lessons about technology apply directly to the Gander crash in which many members of the 101st Airborne died needlessly in 1985, and to the explosion in 1986 of our spacecraft Challenger. For many of us in education, the death in the Challenger explosion of Christa McAuliffe, a teacher at Concord High School in New Hampshire, strikes especially close.

Students who have looked at technology in the context of human proclivities have a chance to assess disasters realistically. The Gander crash, for example, did not occur because technology is always dangerous or because technological frontiers involve risk. It happened because of human willingness to put unfit airplanes into the sky, airplanes with scores of uncorrected mechanical faults identified in inspection reports. American servicemen and women died because of administrators who were callous as well as careless. The crash of Challenger is a more complicated case, since the craft is nearer to technological frontiers. But in spite of the unavoidable risks at any frontier, there were people on the ground who knew—and others who knew they knew—the needless peril of launching the shuttle at low temperature. Thus, the Challenger crash can also be attributed to a human failure.

On any frontier, there will be heartbreak and death, but this does not warrant indifference to avoidable death. All normal administrators, teachers, and students are entirely capable of learning this. We can reach this standard of intellectual and moral seriousness without recasting educational institutions, applicant pools, curricula, or salary scales from scratch.

Concord High School has addressed these issues with intellectual seriousness and a generous understanding. Principal Charles Foley has explained to me that the National Aeronautics and Space Administration (NASA) and school personnel emphasized in advance some of the risks of a shuttle flight; in fact, students admired Christa McAuliffe's courage because they understood that she was facing real danger.

Christa McAuliffe's death came a scant month after a Concord student was killed in the hallways in a confrontation with police. The Challenger crash was a second harsh blow to the school community. The immediate problem for teachers and administrators after the crash was that many students felt guilt in addition to grief. They had watched the Challenger launch and, not recognizing the explosion as anything out of the ordinary, had continued to cheer at the unforgettable image of separating contrails. When they learned that they had cheered during their teacher's death, they felt guilty.

Concord's teachers and administrators did not follow the pattern criticized by Oldenquist of teaching that no one should ever feel guilty or ashamed. They did not try to promote self-respect by destroying its conditions. Instead they helped students to understand that when you celebrate a thing you believe to be good, and you have no way of knowing that it is not, you have no *reason* to feel guilty. They taught the students that they were blaming themselves when they deserved no blame. They understood the students generously and so could help them to grasp the relevant facts more accurately, thereby guiding them to an appropriate assessment of their own conduct. They helped the students to be fair to themselves.

School personnel have offered students comfort and instruction in their grief as well. They are trying to help students to learn, in their grief, to live in a world that is less without Christa McAuliffe.

This attentiveness to the facts that cause grief is essential. The students deserve to learn that when death takes someone you love, there is nothing to do but grieve with all your heart. You must learn to live with the facts that occasion your grief. How different such lessons are from strategies for "coping with grief." The notion of "coping with grief" suggests that it is the grief that deserves attention—not the facts that cause it. Students ought never to be taught that we should make our own psychological states, such as guilt or grief, the principal objects of our attention. They deserve to learn how to tell whether their feelings are appropriate to the facts. Their guilt at Concord High School was not. But their grief is a measure of the inescapability of the fact that Christa McAuliffe is dead. And it is the *fact,* not their grief, that they must bear.

Teachers who achieve even the rudiments of a generous understanding can offer students comfort and teaching worthy of them. This is within our reach through preservice education that takes the maturation of intellect and character seriously. These are grand themes, but in practice they do not call for more than we are able to give if we pay attention to what matters.

INSERVICE EDUCATION OF FACULTY MEMBERS AND ADMINISTRATORS

A school, college, or university that achieves clarity about its educational purposes is best equipped to ask what investments it must make in the inservice education of its own faculty and administration. What ongoing learning is essential for teachers and administrators to be lively, active members of the intellectual life the institution desires for itself and its students? How is the institution to sustain such learning with its available resources? On what should programs concentrate? These questions must be answered in light of local circumstances, educational purposes, current strengths and weaknesses. But some general observations apply for all except the most tireless teachers and administrators, who always perform far above reasonable expectations.

First, inservice study in the scholarly and scientific disciplines takes time, if teachers and administrators are to be intellectually fertile throughout their professional careers. There are no shortcuts and no alternatives. Most schools and many colleges and universities will have to reorder some budget priorities to provide this time.

In schools, especially, the teaching load of most teachers must be reduced if they are to have a chance to study. In most colleges and universities there is considerably more time provided for faculty study, research, and scholarship, although frequently not enough.

Presently, schoolteachers often teach five or six periods a day, with different classes to prepare, all followed by supervision of extracurricular activities, preparation of lesson plans, review of examinations and other assignments, and participation in departmental or school committees. The general public supposes that teacher workloads are light—fewer hours in school per day than many businesses demand, extended holidays, and three months of summer vacation. This popular impression would be laughable if it did not do so much harm. Conscientious teachers give their evenings, weekends, and holidays to preparing for class and grading assignments and take other jobs in summer to supplement low income. For most, there is little time for hard or serious study in the disciplines they teach, let alone the other disciplines their students are expected to learn. Conscientious administrators, of whom there are not enough, often spend sixteen-hour days in school and in other community meetings, summer months included.

In higher education, six to twelve class hours per week is normal, in addition to a few office hours for students. The low end of this range allows substantial time for scholarship and research. In a typical school, the norm is closer to thirty or more class hours a week, with more students, more papers to grade, and so on. This discrepancy must be reduced if we are to reach professional standards throughout education.

Even a 20 per cent reduction in the teaching responsibilities of schoolteachers would make a difference; it would provide six or more hours a week for serious study, privately and with other teachers and scholars, supplemented by the hours available as a result of reduced out-of-class duties. If teachers and administrators were able to devote ten hours a week to their own intellectual maturation, the consequences could be awesome. Many would not necessarily know how to design programs for themselves, but with the help of colleagues in school and scholars and teachers from colleges and universities they could learn. This could help break the back of the "teacher-proof" curriculum and textbook mentality, and it might help to restore curriculum design responsibilities to teachers, taking it out of the hands of putative "curriculum specialists" who are part of most school administrations.

The principal obstacle to this improvement is the impression that such a step would be terribly expensive—increasing personnel costs by 20 per cent. It would appear to have no immediate results and its long-term results are uncertain. Furthermore, the time available for study might be misused. Misuse of time is not an issue for most teachers, and a school should not employ the few it cannot trust.

Released time for teachers and administrators increases the total budget only insofar as every other expenditure must be continued at its present level. Budgetary fat, waste, and nonessential costs could be eliminated to provide some relief. But if the budget is tight and well-managed, the reduction in teaching hours will indeed be a major additional expense—not so great, though, as the cost to our students of refusing to invest in the intellectual growth of teachers and administrators.

What of immediate and long-term results? As anyone who has worked with teachers and administrators knows, most inservice programs are episodic, with a certain number of inservice days each year. These are days normally devoted to pedagogical and curricular questions, not to subject matter. Often they include lectures by visiting stars who vaunt one gimmick or another. The standard criterion of such days is whether they provide new methods that can be employed immediately in the classroom without training or study.

This criterion reduces practicality to immediate usefulness; it reduces the long-run to the extremely short-run. Its adoption is a symptom of deep-seated belief that pedagogical gimmicks can take the place of a knowledge of subject matter.

The first message of sustained, nonepisodic inservice programs, therefore, is that the leadership of the school cares about the long-term. Caring about the long-term *means* investing in the intellectual growth of all who work in the school so that they may become more professional. This is the greatest evidence of belief in its own people that a school, college, or university can offer. Because it also displays patience, it points toward a future that promises not to be just more of the same routines. There is probably no greater remedy for teacher burn-out than this promise. For nothing can cause burn-out more surely than the belief that all tomorrows will be mere repetitions of yesterdays.

But the principal result to be sought in sound inservice programs is improved grasp of subject matter itself. Here there is no short-term payoff. For intellectual advancement, as Tocqueville insisted, takes time.

If a school, college, or university cannot provide inservice opportunities for all its personnel simultaneously, then it ought to allow professional time for some of them each year on a rotating basis. Even this arrangement can elevate expectation of self and improve habits of study, inspire plans for individual study over time, and enrich communication among colleagues.

In Portland and Falmouth, Maine, for example, system-level administrators of the public schools have created the Portland-Falmouth Teachers Academy. The academy is a three-week summer program for elementary and secondary schoolteachers in which administrators also participate. It is designed to study the content in the academic disciplines and methods of teaching; often it ties them together. Plato's *Meno* is read, for example, and the nature of dialogue and its place in classrooms is discussed, but the fundamental questions *Meno* raises about virtue and knowledge are addressed as well. Other dialogues and classical texts are also studied and discussed: *Gorgias, Apology, Crito, Phaedo, Nicomachean Ethics, The Federalist Papers,* and selections from the Bible. Over forty members of the Portland and Falmouth staffs participate each year. Funds are provided by Unum Charitable Foundation, the school boards, Casco Northern, Hannaford Brothers, and Shaw's Supermarkets, and, for 1986 and 1987, by the National Endowment for the Humanities. During the summer and in follow-up seminars and meetings during the school year, emphasis is placed on good thinking, listening, speaking, and writing, all in the context of reading significant books. Participants describe the experience as involving good fellowship, increased discussion of substantive issues, extension of their own reading and study during the school year, and renewed enthusiasm for learning and teaching. Nationally recognized scholars join the participants during the summer and make visits during the school year. Local press coverage and community support are excellent.[22]

In higher education, at St. John's College in Annapolis, Maryland, and Santa Fe, New Mexico, permanent supplemental endowment funds were secured by 1986 to release a portion of the faculty from one-third of their teaching duties each year to allow for study together. Nearly all members of the faculty receive sabbatical leave at full salary every seventh year, after an initial sabbatical in the eighth year. This means that, on average, one-seventh of the faculty members annually devote all of their time to study. Between sabbaticals, several faculty members are released each year to participate in seminars and study groups devoted to subject matter and academic program review. The faculty are supported by the college principally for the sake of their intellectual development, beyond the natural benefits of good teaching and sustained dialogue with students.

During 1986–87, for example, ten members of the faculty were on sabbatical, five were released from a portion of their teaching for study of political theory and other disciplines, and one was free to review and rewrite student laboratory manuals. Total cost is $411,804 in an education and general budget of $11,992,804.[23] Because the normal teaching responsibility is nine credit hours, several other faculty had time to participate in study groups without release. Costs, higher in some years than in others, are a small price to pay to ensure, for instance, that as a lifelong student of the works of Newton nears retirement, a significant number of faculty will be able to study those works with him. By this means, the greatest strengths of the college are transmitted from one generation to the next and an intellectual community is sustained over time. Few schools, colleges, or universities are so financially strapped that they can do absolutely nothing of this sort.

Whatever the specific local needs and interests, questions of program content should be asked with Whitehead's counsel in mind: "Education is a patient process of the mastery of details, minute by minute, hour by hour, day by day. There is no royal road to learning through an airy path of brilliant generalizations."[24] This is one reason that institutions should try to build permanent programs for the intellectual maturation of faculty and administrators. It is also worth reminding teachers that what applies to them applies to students as well.

Furthermore, as Oldenquist argues and experience confirms, many teachers and administrators are weakly prepared in standards of rigorous thought. Inservice study in logic and scientific method are thus indispensable. Learning how to reason well can elevate discourse among colleagues more than any other single achievement. Informal logic has broad daily applications, and the principles of deductive and inductive logic, the hypothetico-deductive method in science, and probability theory are essential to good thinking and therefore to good teaching.

The study of rigorous thinking is complemented well by the

study of writing. Oral discourse permits imprecision that the written word will not tolerate; any study of logic should therefore include writing essays as well as evaluating arguments written by others. This practice also advances generous understanding, because the difficulty of writing well generates appreciation of the efforts of others. Writing well often involves a fair amount of conscientious reading of good books and articles. The field is limitless, and actual choices can be made to reflect local concerns and interests. Wise choice of texts as part of the study of reasoning itself can draw faculty and administrators together across specializations and thereby enhance their interest in subjects other than their own.

Building a coherent faculty by such means can highlight common purposes and reduce indifference to the overall learning of students. It can prompt science teachers to remind students that quality of writing is of general consequence and not solely the province of English teachers, and it can do the same for humanities teachers concerning mathematical and scientific evidence. Students may learn that a powerful intellect can bring knowledge from all disciplines to bear on any question, and that it is narrow-minded to aspire to less. With their teachers they may even get a glimpse of Blanshard's ideal—a "mind to which nothing human is alien."

The need for this kind of faculty development was brought home to me initially in high school, but more strikingly in 1961 when I was an undergraduate. I was concentrating that year on philosophy, including logic, and American history. The courses were very good; in one history course, I had a chance to write an extended paper on John Calhoun's *Disquisition on Government,* an important set of arguments intended to justify secession. I wrote that the arguments of the text were valid but unsound; that is, that the reasoning was logical but the premises were not all true. Although the conclusions of the book followed from the premises, their truth remained in doubt. The distinction is simple: validity is a property of the form of an argument, while soundness is a property of both form and content. Thus, the argument, "All frogs are turtles, and all turtles are elephants, so all frogs are elephants" is valid—the conclusion follows from the premises—but unsound, for the premises are untrue, and, in this case, so is the conclusion. To my surprise, the history professor denied that any such distinction was known to him or mattered in the analysis of texts. His position might have relegated my work in logic to inconsequence in my study of history. Fortunately, I was not put off by his obvious error, and I continued to apply my learning in one discipline to the other. I would have learned much more about Calhoun's book, however, if the teacher had known the distinction, granted its application to the book, and then criticized my paper on substantive grounds. An error so fundamental and elementary should not be committed in education; a modest level of communication among faculty across disciplinary lines might prevent it.

In each school, college, and university, the basic questions concern the intellectual growth that faculty and administration need to advance the educational mission of the institution. These questions should be asked by teachers and administrators together. When they are answered, a list of priorities for inservice programs can be established. Colleagues at home and scholars from other institutions may be called upon for bibliographic guidance and to lead study groups, lectures, and projects. Librarians may participate as well.

As the programs develop, assemblies and PTA meetings may be the occasion to present subject matter. For example, in the 1970s, at Langley High, an exceptional public high school in Virginia, William J. Bennett, now U.S. secretary of education, worked extensively with teachers and administrators on issues of law and morality. A widely attended PTA meeting included a presentation by Bennett, participation by school faculty, and a formal reply by the fathers of two students—William Rehnquist, now chief justice of the Supreme Court, and appelate court Judge Robert Bork. The cost for the overall program of study, lasting for eighteen months and involving some two dozen teachers and administrators in regular sessions and seminars, was borne principally by the National Endowment for the Humanities, and services and visiting scholars were provided by the National Humanities Faculty. Expense to the school for the entire program was small—a few thousand dollars—and many participants contributed their services. Every school and community has in it a wealth of people who can be drawn upon, who will be happy to participate and will do so conscientiously.

These activities also tend to draw the members of a school toward common purposes and shared high standards.

The PTA meeting in Virginia was only one event in a program of extended study for teachers and administrators. Working together and with faculty from universities in the area, they read, wrote, and talked about matters of consequence, using such texts as *The Moral Point of View* by Kurt Baier, *The Abolition of Man* by C.S. Lewis, *A Man For All Seasons* by Robert Bolt, "Quandary Ethics" by Edmund Pincoffs, and "On Guilt, Relativism, and Black-White Relations" by Orlando Patterson.

As a result, they were able to lead students to more penetrating reading and discussion of texts in their own courses. Using Ibsen's play *Enemy of the People,* one teacher wrote later:

[We] were impressed with the possibilities of taking our students beyond the point of their accepting of Dr. Stockman as a hero, a moral 'shining light,' simply because he stood up for his beliefs and seemingly martyred himself. Stockman's stand seemed to them a rallying point; they offered him automatic and enthusiastic support because he did what he thought was right. . . . What we did was to use the comments that some of the kids had made and gently turn the discussion to the examination of the following:
1. What were Dr. Stockman's motives for doing as he did?
2. What were his responsibilities as a citizen, doctor, father?
3. Is sincerity enough to warrant our view of Dr. Stockman as a good moral agent?
4. What exactly is good character?
5. What are the responsibilities of a leader?
6. How admirable is innocence?
7. What makes a hero?[25]

At New Trier High School in Winnetka, Illinois, a school of well-established reputation, teachers studying together across disciplinary lines were able to build a powerful humanities program for students in their junior year. The eleventh grade normally includes the study of American history. The faculty concentrated on American identity and values, and therefore highlighted the opportunities of a free people for independence of mind and responsible judgment. In order to teach what these opportunities mean in practice, the teachers posed problems for their students to solve.

Many so-called interdisciplinary programs are only a hodge-podge of subjects. They lack intellectual discipline because their treatment of subjects is shallow. In such programs, faculty learn little from each other, and students make little if any worthwhile intellectual progress. Ninth graders in one Eastern high school are required, for example, to take an interdisciplinary course in the cultures of the world. It is quite evident from the course materials and conversation that students are not learning even the most elementary meanings of the word *culture*. In such instances, students would be much better served by courses within specific disciplines.

In the program at New Trier, however, the faculty, because of their own studies, were not reduced to leaving students to their own devices to solve problems. English and mathematics teachers cooperated to teach logic and language; history and science teachers taught how to organize data and formulate hypotheses and experiments for testing them while enabling students to practice in laboratory work; fine arts teachers contributed to students' ability to explain the nature and results of their inquiries and problems.

Throughout, teachers and students alike confronted serious texts and authors: Puritan sermons, the Army-McCarthy hearings, Nathaniel Hawthorne, Jonathan Edwards, Ralph Waldo Emerson, Herman Melville, W. E. B. Dubois, Ralph Ellison, and Arthur Miller. Works of Winslow Homer were studied, the aesthetics of mathematics received attention, and a noted local architect helped teachers and students to grasp fundamental problems of creating an environment.

This is inservice study and professional teaching at its best. In practice, at all levels of education, successful inservice programs depend above all on two things. As Nettie Silver, a distinguished teacher at Richmond Hill High School in New York City, explains:

> The teacher must be passionately in love with the subject—for content is the bedrock. . . . A highly supportive administration and program chairperson are essential.[26]

Thus, if our schools, colleges, and universities are to become great, they will need faculty and administrators who are resolute builders, who love the life of the mind, and will invest themselves and their institutional resources in that life, for colleagues and students alike.

Obviously, inservice education at all levels is not the cure for all the weaknesses of education. Institutions will have to face with equal resolve standards for appointment and tenure. The profession will have to overhaul standards of certification and attract graduates of our finest colleges and universities.

All this will take time. Partisan interests will make some of it difficult. But if we face up to the needs and opportunities, we will find allies and colleagues, sometimes from unexpected places.

We may take heart in remembering a man like William Syphax, who is eloquently described by Thomas Sowell as

> the man who spearheaded the drive that led to the founding of the school which ultimately became Dunbar High School. William Syphax was a "free person of color," born in 1826 and active in civic affairs and civil rights issues, "fearing no man regardless of position or color." As a trustee of the Negro schools in Washington, Syphax preferred to hire black teachers, but only when their qualifications were equal to those of white teachers—for the trustees "deem it a violation of our official oath to employ inferior teachers when superior teachers can be had for the same money." He addressed demands not only to whites in power, but also to his own people, exhorting them to send their children to school with discipline, respect, and a willingness to work hard. These became hallmarks of Dunbar High School, as did the academic success that flowed from them. . . . Dunbar meant business.[27]

If we remember the lives of those who have for centuries ennobled the profession of education, our students will also learn of them.

Money matters, of course. Levels of compensation matter. All parents would prefer to send their children to the finest schools. If Gandhi had been prevented by lack of funds from attending school in England, his genius might never have matured; poverty might even have prevented him from buying the glasses that enabled him to read.

The problems of compensation in education will have to be faced. Not one cent should be paid to anyone who says he will do a better job for more money—if a person is not doing his or her very best, his fitness to teach at all is questionable. But compensation commensurate with the importance of the work is long overdue.

Still, the most profound issue is not money but vision and the will to bring it to fulfillment. And, for vision, we and our successors may stand on the shoulders of giants like William Syphax.

7

Curriculum

I am under no illusion as to the limited importance of curricula
and the greater importance of faculty and students capable of
creating an intellectual community among themselves. But if
any particular curriculum is not so important, the existence or
the lack of existence of a viable and responsible community in
which membership signifies pressure, duties, responsibilities,
and the excitement obtained from a certain coherence seems
to me to be of major significance.[1]

—Edward Levi

THE AMERICAN COUNCIL on Education reported in *Campus
Trends: 1985* that "curricular change continues to occupy
center stage on the nation's campuses. More than 80 percent of
responding colleges were currently reviewing the curriculum or
had recently done so."[2] The report noted widespread concern
about curricular matters in colleges and universities, including
identification of proper competencies to be taught students;
attention to mathematical or computer skills, writing, reasoning,
and foreign languages; and emphasis on values or ethics, multi-
cultural understanding, and international relations.

Undergraduate curriculum reform has been catapulted into
the limelight again by recent events. From 1973 until 1979,
Harvard University undertook an extensive internal review of
its curriculum. From 1979 to 1983, it implemented a core curriculum that has been widely publicized and debated.

Since that time, national reports have lamented the incoherence and mediocrity of undergraduate studies. The National
Institute of Education says that "the bachelor's degree has lost
its potential to foster the shared values and knowledge that bind
us together as a society."[3] The Association of American Col-

leges reports that "evidence of devaluation in college curriculums is everywhere."[4] And as chairman of the National Endowment for the Humanities, William J. Bennett said in *To Reclaim a Legacy,* "A student can obtain a bachelor's degree from 75 percent of all American colleges and universities without having studied European history, from 72 percent without having studied American literature or history, and from 86 percent without having studied the civilizations of classical Greece or Rome."[5]

Many institutions are drawing more part-time and adult students, and more students who need remedial courses, than ever before. In the face of demographic trends, some view these shifts in student composition as essential to survival. Motives for curriculum reform range from financial fears and concern for educational soundness to dismay about the ability of the United States to compete with other highly developed countries.

Bennett's report is particularly instructive because it gives evidence that access to education is meaningful only if institutions have a clear sense of worthy purposes—and if their teachers and programs of study take these purposes seriously.

Access to colleges and universities means little if what is offered is aimless. Bennett argues specifically that many institutions have lost their sense of purposes because they no longer understand what constitutes an educated person. The phenomenon is reflected by decline in the study of English, foreign languages, history, philosophy, literature, mathematics, and the natural sciences. This leaves all too many students ignorant of their heritage, in a vacuum, without access to the educated men and women throughout history.

As Bennett shows, concern for curriculum soundness is essential to the well-being of every school, college, and university. But preoccupation with it is not a thing to be celebrated. A curriculum is only one means of bringing the ideals of an institution to life. By itself, it cannot give an institution common purposes or integrity, nor can it produce a top quality faculty or administration. A curriculum is not self-executing. Its educational power depends on the fabric of institutional life into which it is woven and on the people who weave it.

In 1979, in *The Great Core Curriculum Debate,* George W. Bonham, executive director of the Council on Learning, wrote of colleges and universities that "by their very exercise of deliberating curricular options, their sense of institutional purpose will be inevitably revitalized. And so will the undergraduate experience."[6] Unfortunately, nothing is inevitable in human institutions, including educational ones, and certainly not with regard to revitalization. Curriculum debate is sometimes more a reflection of battles and compromises about enrollment, academic turf, economic power, and departmental and institutional prestige than of an educational mission. Even when curriculum discussion is motivated by concern for quality, it can be derailed by timidity and failure of nerve. As Harvard Dean Henry Rosovsky and Associate Dean Phyllis Keller observe, "The problem of collegiate education today derives from much longer-term social and intellectual trends. By and large, faculties abolished requirements because they themselves were no longer sure of the rationale for them."[7] Debate among those who have lost faith in the possibility of identifying and cultivating civilized intelligence cannot vitalize or revitalize institutions.

James Q. Wilson served as chairman of Harvard's task force on the core curriculum. His account of the difficulties of reform explains why institutional revitalization does not necessarily follow from curriculum review. David Riesman and Christopher Jencks in their book *The Academic Revolution* described the academic revolution that occurred in the shift of faculty loyalty from their institutions to their professions. Wilson claims that a second academic revolution has occurred in "the transfer of power within universities from trustees and administrators to the faculty. As a result, we have a paradox: The faculty is supposed to govern collegially, but it is not a collegium. . . . The chief impediment to change is beliefs, some of which happen to correspond to departmental or professional loyalties, but others of which are highly individualistic, and all of which are deeply held."[8]

Revitalization hinges on the extent to which these beliefs include belief in the institution itself, in the seriousness of the duties of every teacher and administrator, and in the common educational purposes that are the ground of institutional integrity and student opportunity. Vitality depends on what administrators and teachers in each institution invest of themselves in students and in each other. As Bennett explains:

> Revitalizing an educational institution is not easy. Usually it requires uncommon courage and discernment on the part of a few and a shared vision of what can and ought to be on the part of many.[9]

For this reason, Bennett concludes, "curricular reform must begin with the president."[10]

The challenge of revitalizing institutions is perennial. Over a century ago, John Stuart Mill described the difficulty:

> Reforms, worthy of the name, are always slow, and reform of governments and churches is not so slow as that of schools, for there is the great preliminary difficulty of fashioning the instruments; of teaching the teachers.[11]

Teachers and administrators at all levels need to learn the importance of common purposes, of institutional coherence, of personal loyalty to specific institutions, and of the courage to present students with intellectual and moral ideals. If each faculty is to bear the responsibility that John Beach says it ought to have, and that James Wilson says it does have, then its members must resolve to give the best in themselves to the institution and its students. The leadership of the institution is obliged to draw faculty to this resolve. When this happens, quality of teaching will do more to revitalize institutions than any reform of curriculum. As Barry O'Connell, associate professor of American Studies and English at Amherst College, insists in the debate about Harvard, "What we need is what we have always needed, and it is rare: great teachers among us."[12]

NATIONAL DEBATE

Building such a community is the work of each institution, to be done in light of local traditions and obligations. According to the Carnegie Foundation for the Advancement of Teaching in its *College: The Undergraduate Experience in America,* "What we urgently need today is a constructive debate about the meaning of the undergraduate college. . . . "[13] But in America we do not have "the" undergraduate college. We have specific schools, colleges, and universities, and no national debate can do their work for them.

As the Yale University faculty insisted in 1828, when it was called to decide whether "dead" languages were essential studies in the liberal arts, the question for them applied *only* to Yale:

> What then is the appropriate object of a college? It is not necessary here to determine what it is which, in every case, entitles an

institution to the *name* of a college. But if we have not greatly misapprehended the design of the patrons and guardians of this college, its object is to LAY THE FOUNDATION of a SUPERIOR EDUCATION.[14]

Yale's faculty went on to argue that "the two great points to be gained in intellectual culture, are the *discipline* and *furniture* of the mind; expanding its powers and storing it with knowledge."[15] They argued that the former is perhaps more important than the latter, and that the study of Latin and Greek contributes profoundly to it. This was their answer *for Yale,* in light of Yale's history and purposes, Yale's reasons for being.

National debate about institutional purposes cannot attend to local facts and details; it cannot take the place of local leadership, dialogue, resolve, and planning. Neither can it respond to questions about curriculum: What should be the curriculum *here,* in this school, college, university? Why should *we* and *our* students study this curriculum?

Many national pronouncements about curriculum are simplistic overstatements that do not encourage clear discussion, open disagreement, and resolution of issues at the local level. For example, in December 1986, college presidents in the United States, the Soviet Union, Japan, and China "endorsed a 'worldwide curriculum for peace.'"[16] These presidents viewed informed public opinion "that sees arms control as an element of national security" as "the best chance to stop the arms race." Jean Mayer, president of Tufts University, said that "if people knew enough of what was going on, this would help to cut down the arms race."[17]

Should specific institutions implement "peace" curricula? Or should they call the proposal by its right name and ask whether to implement "arms control" curricula? Surely, the study of peace and the study of arms control are not identical. Or would it be better to ask, as Bennett suggests, what should be studied in history, literature, political theory, political science, and comparative religions—not to mention mathematics, geography, and physics—if students are to achieve the intellectual discipline and knowledge of subject matter necessary to begin to make responsible judgments about arms control or any other significant issue in foreign or domestic policy?

If local institutions proceeded by attending to the last question, in the context of their own convictions about educational purposes, their students would benefit from curriculum review. They might then learn to ask questions about peace: Should Moses have said to Pharoah, "Let us have peace" instead of "Let my people go"? Should Eleazar have taught the young to betray faith for the sake of peace? Should David have asked Goliath for peace? Should Socrates have sought peace at his trial? Should Jesus have capitulated before Calvary? Should Abraham Lincoln have settled for peace after Fort Sumter? Should Chamberlain have paid the price he paid for peace at Munich? Should Martin Luther King have stayed away from Birmingham for the sake of peace?

By studying literature and history, rather than "peace" or "arms control," students might learn to think more knowledgeably about both. They might, for example, read of the horrible peace St. Exupery foresaw for France in 1942 as he flew to Arras:

> Already as I move in the direction of Arras, peace is everywhere beginning to take shape. Not that well-defined peace which, like a new period in history, follows upon a war decorously terminated by a treaty. This is a nameless peace that stands for the end of everything. . . . The peace that is on its way is not the fruit of a decision reached by men. It spreads apace like gray leprosy.[18]

What St. Exupéry saw is not learned by studying peace, but by studying literature and history.

Students concerned about peace should also think about more arresting concerns of the sort raised by Walter Lippmann:

> There is no mystery about why there is such a tendency for popular opinion to be wrong in judging war and peace. Strategic and diplomatic decisions call for a kind of knowledge—not to speak of an experience and a seasoned judgment—which cannot be had by glancing at newspapers, listening to snatches of radio comment, watching politicans perform on television, hearing occasional lectures, and reading a few books. It would not be enough to make a man competent to decide whether to amputate a leg, and it is not enough to qualify him to choose war or peace, to arm or not to arm, to intervene or to withdraw, to fight or to negotiate.[19]

No decent curriculum can be built by bolting fashionable topics onto it. Whitehead said, "I am certain that in education wherever you exclude specialism you destroy life."[20] Questions of policy in arms control are one instance of this principle; such specialism must be based on broad and deep study in the relevant disciplines. A conscientious development of programs of study never neglects such facts.

Students whose curricula are designed without attention to the sustained discipline and furnishing of the mind, or to questions of educational purposes, will not profit from national curricular pronouncements, including those about peace or arms control. Issues of educational purpose are too fundamental for such treatment.

Great national debates about curriculum tend to be unproductive, tendentious, and repetitive. They generate more heat than light about the ideal core curriculum, distributive requirements, and electives; about breadth versus specialization; about knowledge for its own sake versus knowledge for some social or economic purpose; about relevance, cultural narrowness, methods, and content; about great books and textbooks; the classical and the topical, and the past-looking and the future-looking; about intellectual and moral ideals; about science, technology, and the humanities; about students' expectations and society's needs.

Such debates were rehearsed by the Yale faculty in 1828. They were apparent in the course of legislation of the Morrill Acts in the last century. They surfaced again in the postbellum reconstruction of higher education in the South. These debates were undertaken with vigor and passion by the advocates of majors with electives for undergraduates and by the advocates of prescribed, nonelective curricula—at Harvard, Columbia, Chicago, and St. John's—in the 1930s. They were revived by the political activists of the 1960s on campuses throughout the country.

Why are these debates unresolved? Why do we repeat them from generation to generation? It may be argued that curriculum debates consist of philosophical questions that are ever new, ever fresh; each generation, it would follow, must come to grips with such questions for itself, and herein lies the wellspring of educational progress and improvement. Surely, in age-old questions about access to postsecondary education we have made progress concerning equality, justice, liberty, human capacity, and the well-being of society itself. It is striking, though, that these are *not* curricular questions, and they are *not* in full measure unresolved. We *have* made progress, both in our conception of justice and our achievement of it.

National curriculum debate, by contrast, seems usually to run aground on two questions: "What should be *the* curriculum?" and "What is *the* best curriculum?" Obviously, these invite the additional question, "What is the best curriculum *for what purposes?*" But even if the purposes rightly emphasize intellectual discipline and high-quality furnishing of the mind, there is no apparent reason to conclude that some specific curriculum is demonstrably superior to all others. As the Carnegie Foundation stated in 1979:

> No studies show that one undergraduate curriculum is clearly better than another. . . . The curriculum is important, but it is not the most important aspect of undergraduate education. The most important is the quality of the faculty.[21]

The pursuit of *the* ideal curriculum is as elusive as the quest for a happy empire of perfect wisdom and virtue. The challenge is for each institution to build programs of study that, in the hands of able and devoted teachers and their students, lead to intellectual discipline, knowledge of subject matter, and seriousness of purpose.

This can be done successfully in many ways with many different kinds of curricula. Alumni of schools, colleges, and universities whose curricula differ dramatically flourish in the conduct of their lives and exhibit intellectual and moral virtue. All of us meet and benefit from the friendship of people who have studied electives and a major discipline, people who have studied the liberal arts without a major or specialization, people who have done all their formal studies in structured courses, people who have undertaken extensively individualized and independent study, and so on. Every kind of curriculum also leaves some of its students in poor intellectual and moral condition. No curriculum is universally effective.

Broad, national curricular debates have tended away from considerations of effectiveness and toward a kind of curricular metaphysics or *a priorism*. One curriculum is declared superior to all others on grounds of intellectual quality, beauty, coherence, fidelity to absolute truth, responsiveness to student differences, and the like.

Arguments about curricular excellence in terms of fidelity to absolute truth typify such metaphysical approaches. Perhaps the most striking cases in this century arose in controversies over the superiority of completely prescribed, or of elective, curricula. These debates reached their greatest intensity in 1940 and 1941 during and after the initial meeting in New York City of the Conference on Science, Philosophy, and Religion in their Relations to the Democratic Way of Life. The conference addressed the question of whether adherence to sectarian metaphysical and religious dogmas is necessary to good citizenship and to the survival of democracy. The fundamental issue, then, was whether a curriculum should be tolerant, pluralistic, and committed to diversity, or, instead, rooted in specific doctrines prescribed in the curriculum and basic to its design.

At the conference, Mortimer Adler said:

I say that the most serious threat to Democracy is the positivism of the professors, which dominates every aspect of modern education and is the central corruption of modern culture. Democracy has much more to fear from the mentality of its teachers than from the nihilism of Hilter. . . . Without the truths of philosophy and religion, Democracy has no rational foundation.[22]

To this position, Arthur E. Murphy replied:

And what, more specifically, is this pernicious professorial mentality? It was clearly exemplified in the opposition of "the professors" to the educational schemes of President Hutchins of Chicago. "The glorious, Quixotic failure" of Hutchins to convert the professors is proof enough for Professor Adler that such men will not listen to reason. . . . Who can blame Professor Adler, then, when he goes on to inquire whether the tyrants of today are not perhaps "instruments of Divine justice, chastening a people who had departed from the way of truth"—that is, from the Hutchins-Adler philosophy. . . . [T]he identification of Divine wrath with the Adlerian grievance does appear to give a rather comic importance to past academic wrangles in Chicago. . . . But the attack on the right of men within the democratic community to differ on fundamental issues of philosophy and religion, while it may be ridiculous, is not funny.[23]

Murphy went on to point out that "many men of good sense and good will no more need a general proposition about the charismatic value of men as an image of the Absolute on this planet to buttress their reasonable loyalty to the government of the United States than they need a general proposition about female virtue to assure them that their wives and mothers are worth loving."[24]

Professor Murphy's observations are a useful reminder about liberty and pluralism in free countries and in their educational institutions. Even if we agree with Robert Hutchins's emphasis on the absolute need to make our educational institutions into intellectual communities, we do not have to assent to the idea of *the* definitive curriculum or to his insistence that "the heart of any course of study designed for the whole people will be, if education is rightly understood, the same at any time, in any place, under any political, social, or economic conditions."[25] Ideals, principles, and purposes must abide among us, but giving them vitality can be accomplished by many kinds of curricula.

This point was affirmed in 1977 by Earl J. McGrath of the Council for the Advancement of Small Colleges. In *Developing the College Curriculum,* McGrath stressed the importance of avoiding "the practice of the past of suggesting that the curriculum policies of one institution, however sound they may appear, are suitable for adoption in another whose student body, faculty, resources, facilities, and traditions may be quite different."[26]

COHERENCE AND QUALITY

Curriculum reform is a time-consuming activity, and sometimes it ends in more spinning of wheels than actual movement. Henry Wilkinson Bragdon observed in *Woodrow Wilson: The Academic Years* that it is an "academic truism that changing a curriculum is harder than moving a graveyard."[26] Frederick Rudolph and others have noted that curricular reform is least difficult when an institution is on the verge of oblivion, when financial and enrollment problems threaten a disaster.[28]

Nonetheless, reflection about identifiable criteria for curricular soundness can be useful. The standards most often invoked are coherence and quality; even these standards by themselves, however, are insufficient for educational merit. Taken in due proportion, and in light of efforts to make institutions *themselves* coherent and intellectually strong—given a context of the sort envisioned by Edward Levi—they may nonetheless be valuable.

Coherence cannot be an ideal in itself; a context is required. After all, "the big lie" is coherent, but it remains a lie. Curricular rather than institutional coherence can lead to worse incoherence than students are presently subjected to, for though coherent, a curriculum may have no foundation at all. Similarly, quality in itself is no remedy for these hazards. No matter how well told nor how splendid the materials used in the telling, a lie is still a lie. A curriculum isolated from institutional purposes is vulnerable to such perversions.

What is a curriculum? It is a program of study, not a mere collection of courses, whether prescribed or elective, general or specialized. A program must be ordered by some principle of unity. If that principle is to organize and refine the curriculum, it cannot be drawn from the curriculum. A faculty must decide what it considers worthy of study. This decision should be grounded in the mission—the purposes—the institution has in offering educational programs in the first place. The coherence of the curriculum must be derived from the coherence of the mission itself. Faculty members must become a collegium, a group of colleagues faithful to the institution and to its ideals. A curriculum cannot take their place.

A curriculum is in a sense an invitation for faculty and students to join in study of something worthwhile. It is not an invitation for prospective students to come and do whatever they wish. The ideals and purposes of an institution must be recognized—by students, teachers, administrators, and trustees—for the invitation to be meaningful. Without such understanding, students are adrift, teachers are isolated, administrators make their judgments about budget and operational priorities with no rational basis, and trustees oversee a thing of no substance.

The curriculum itself, and every course in it, is a selection of studies and materials drawn from many possible combinations and orderings of content, methods, exercises, and assignments. Limits of time and resources always force limits upon the curriculum. Good curricula exclude much of what is worthless; every curriculum also excludes much that is worthwhile. Reasonable decisions about what to include and what to exclude cannot, therefore, be made in isolation from a grasp of the purposes it is to serve.

A unified structure in itself is no guarantee of educational merit, for we can build a coherent curriculum that is shallow. Dorothea Brooke's education, George Eliot tells us in *Middlemarch,* consisted of "the shallows of ladies-school literature."[29] Eliot does not say, nor is there any reason to believe, that those shallows were incoherent. In totalitarian societies, special pleading, propaganda, and ideology inspire highly coherent programs. But such curricula are flawed by perversity of purpose.

Will attention to quality prevent defects of shallowness and perversity? If we focus only on the issue of quality *within* the curriculum, no. The very best of shallowness is still shallow; the very best special pleading, propaganda, and ideology are still educationally perverse. We are forced to look outside the curriculum for a guide to quality. A coherent and high-quality curriculum can be devoid of educational purpose; indeed, it can be anti-educational.

An institution can avoid the deepest of these pitfalls if its personnel resolve to exclude the shallow and trivial, and to include only that which requires intellectual rigor, truthfulness, accuracy, and independence of mind. These standards are not entirely sufficient either, though, because disagreement will persist over what they mean. After all, scholarship that some consider trivial is deemed important by others. But if administrators and faculty remember that the time available for undergraduate study is limited and precious, they may at least exclude some nonessentials. And if they truly want students to become adults who can exercise judgment in a condition of liberty, they can avoid propaganda.

At its best, a curriculum is a kind of dialogue into which students are invited by their teachers in anticipation of the future life-long dialogue they commence after they have left their teachers behind. That dialogue can be made fruitful by faculty and administrators who attend together to the purposes and instruments of their own institution. Mutual trust and dependence may then develop. Christopher Jencks and David Riesman emphasized this in 1968, suggesting the utility of faculty and teaching assistants for specific courses meeting on a regular basis "to discuss books they were reading with undergraduates, preparing seminar papers that would also be delivered as course lectures, and discussing individual lectures given in the course in both substantive and pedagogic terms."[30] Here, the idea is to expand that activity beyond individual courses.

It is difficult to imagine institutional coherence without something of this sort. Even in an institution whose faculty members are perceptibly separated requires their active support of mutual ideals to achieve institutional coherence. Suppose, for example, that a college decides that significant educational opportunity can be provided simply by exposing undergraduates to genius in action. Unlike most institutions, it builds its faculty of geniuses in various fields who teach by showing their students what their work is and how they do it. Forget temporal limits for a moment: political theory and political science are taught by Pericles, Talleyrand, Abraham Lincoln, Winston Churchill, and Margaret Thatcher; physics is taught by Newton, Einstein, Heisenberg, and Oppenheimer; philosophy by Socrates, Aristotle, Kant, and Mill; and so on. Each teacher does some of his own work in the presence of students, with no effort in class to attend to curriculum coherence; the teacher strives only to teach students how his or her work is done—how thought and judgment are undertaken, how problems are identified and addressed, how solutions are implemented.

Even in such a college—one that might be profoundly effective given sufficiently motivated undergraduates—shared ideals would be essential. Each teacher would have to be committed both to drawing students into his work and to the principle that teaching students is not an imposition. To give the undergraduate studies coherence, faculty and administrators would need to consider plenary lectures, reading lists, perhaps even joint seminars led by scientists and statesmen on applications of science in national policy. Even in this imaginary college, faculty and administrative discussion of institutional policy and institutional coherence would be indispensable. This activity would weld them together as *a* faculty and administration.

Many of us believe that much of what goes on in educational institutions is incoherent and of a level so low that it is not worth students' time and effort. We owe it to ourselves, our students, and our successors to achieve again a sense of what a faculty is and what an educational mission is because preoccupation with curriculum change ignores these roots of our disorders. How, then, in short, is the issue of educational mission to be addressed?

The worst mistakes I have made, and the worst I have seen made, about questions of mission and curriculum all resulted from seeking conclusions too quickly. If the initial effort to discuss mission immediately becomes a matter of reaching decisions and taking action, the conversation is often badly affected by several attitudes and fears. One tendency is for each person or group to defend its own turf, preserve its own economic power, maintain or increase its own student enrollment, safeguard its own faculty positions, ensure that its own interests are "represented" in the curriculum, and survive intact any institutional change. These are all conjoined with fear that any change contains greater likelihood of loss than of gain. I have witnessed discussions of this sort in which, for hours on end, students were never mentioned except in terms of numbers needed to balance various budgets. Often, discussions of mission were abrupt and vague, turning quickly to curriculum questions where the attitudes and fears are even more visible and pronounced.

Sometimes, but not always, these negative effects can be reduced by discussion—at length—whose purpose is *not* to reach decisions. Such conversations can sometimes stay on track about mission and purposes. Participants may study together the chartering and governing documents of an institution, the evolution of its programs, the explicit intentions of donors who have contributed to endowment funds, the contents of the catalog, and the promises of admissions materials and financial campaign brochures. No matter their views about personal, departmental, or group self-interest, many administrators and teachers want their institutions to tell the truth about what they stand for and what they can and cannot deliver to their students.

Mutual distrust may run deep, scepticism may be widespread, and attention to institutional purposes may be seen as a distraction from other duties. At times, faculty members believe the administration intends such conversation to keep faculty members too busy to raise questions about specific administrative agendas and priorities. Where such distrust or indifference run deep, and the institution is mired in partisan attitudes and fears, its educational prospects are dim. But every institution should try to become a community.

But suppose that faculty and administrators resolve to think through institutional purposes and their implications for the institution as a whole and for the curriculum. All documents of the institution stress its dedication to student intellectual maturation—skills, understanding, grasp of subject matter and methods in the disciplines of inquiry, discovery, and expression. In a word, the school says it stands for the achievement of intellectual self-reliance. All of us want our work, our students' opportunities, and our institution to be both coherent and of high quality; we want to be faithful to the ideals of intellectual self-reliance. What challenges do we therefore face?

First, the institutional obligation to clarify intellectual self-reliance. What do we believe enables people to rely on their own intelligence; what must their intelligence become, what habits must they acquire, what discipline must they achieve, and what must they know if they are to have trustworthy minds? What kinds of errors must they learn to avoid, of what kinds of unavoidable errors must they learn to beware, what habits of learning—reading, listening, looking, taking the place of others—must they achieve? What do they need in the way of humility, of decisiveness? What must they learn about mastery of disciplines so that they may go beyond undergraduate education, and what must they learn about unlearning and relearning?

Second, the need to envision our institution in light of our responses to these questions. What are the implications of our commitment to intellectual self-reliance beyond the curriculum? How is our commitment to be made clear to students through the policies—the *life*—of the institution? And what are the implications for curriculum itself?

As we address the first questions, we may identify exemplars of intellectual self-reliance: people who have learned enough to take responsibility for the conduct of their own lives or who have persevered in the pursuit of truth and honor despite disappointment or even vilification. Perhaps as faculty we will read and talk together about Greek philosophers and Hebrew sages, of Socrates and Eleazar, of Aristotle and his commitment to the truth, or of Montaigne, or of the American historian James

Harvey Robinson who "revolutionized the accepted idea that history could be learnt out of textbooks,"[31] or of Abraham Lincoln and Robert E. Lee, or of Sojourner Truth and Margaret Fuller, of Martin Luther King and Margaret Thatcher. Our list of heroes and heroines of intellectual self-reliance will vary, but their habits of mind and character will exhibit common traits we can identify: rigor, intellectual honesty, generous understanding, wisdom, temperance, and courage.

Our exemplars should illuminate for us a commitment that must be exhibited to students in unmistakable ways: in teaching, dormitory life, library policies, student government, student participation in institutional policy and practice, standards of honor and self-discipline, homework assignments, sports, special college functions, social life, career counseling, and alumni programs.

In all these, there can be no pandering. There must be conscientious preparation by students involved in government and in institutional questions of moment and respect for quiet places for study; there can be no spoon-feeding by teachers or counselors. Lectures cannot be a substitute for homework; assignments must require hard thinking, good thinking. However we later review our policies and practices or deliberate about particulars, we are likely to see at this stage some of the general imperatives for our institution that derive from our common purposes.

Implications for curriculum planning and course design must be spelled out, too, and they will, in turn, force upon us questions of inclusion and exclusion. Many paths offer a way to institutional coherence; at least one is to conclude that the achievement of intellectual self-reliance is advanced by study, reflection, and deliberation about the relation of the individual to the state. What should states do for individuals, and what should individuals do for themselves? What limits should apply to the conduct of individuals and of states?

It is not difficult to imagine these issues framed in a dialogue that spans centuries by which students who are invited to participate come to grips with ideas of power and subtlety. The tension between Agamemnon and Achilles or Creon and Antigone might be used to draw them into issues. These four participants speak and are spoken to by Socrates and the

Athenians who condemn him. Soon Aquinas, Hobbes, Locke, Rousseau, Kant, Jefferson, Madison, Hegel, Marx, Robert E. Lee, Lincoln, and Thoreau may enter the conversation.

In the twentieth century, the dialogue is joined by Lenin, Gandhi, Churchill, Martin Luther King, Mao-Tse Tung, and perhaps even contemporary scholars. Each belongs in the conversation and demands our attention; a coherent, high-level study may be set forth in which texts resonate and speak to one another.

But how many works by women and minorities conveniently fit? How much of what has been written and spoken, or sung and prayed, by those with few educational or civic opportunities will conveniently cohere? How will these enter the dialogue, given their relative exclusion from the mainstream? How many lives and works will not be known to us unless we are actively engaged in inquiry together, engaged because we believe such lives and works make a difference to the achievement of our mission? How will we enter the moving, if ungrammatical, eloquence of Sojourner Truth in "Ain't I a Woman?" How will we fit in the wisdom of Annie Clark Tanner in *A Mormon Mother*? How will we include people who are exemplars of intellectual self-reliance and trustworthy judgment, despite disadvantages, who are inspiring in their yearning to achieve it, and who did not despair in the face of huge obstacles? There are many who have left behind magnificent but little known texts who are being discovered but who lie in still unvisited graves. They will not be part of our curriculum unless our conception of mission leads us to their discovery. For this, teachers need each other, and need to mature together as a faculty. This is the productive form of mutual dependence.

Not everything, though, can be included, even though what is left out may fit just as coherently as what remains. Quite simply, this is unfortunate, but there must be exclusions. What, then, of colleagues or a group of students who say no, who insist that something must not be left out? How have we often responded?

The temptation is to establish some special course, or courses, to answer this "need." But succumbing to this temptation puts us on the path of curricular fragmentation by creating special studies of, say, women or minorities. Most students will never be exposed to these studies. This kind of curricular affirmative action is not a mark of vision; it is an admission that the curriculum has failed, and failed so dismally that only people willing either to specialize in an area the curriculum has otherwise excluded, or to spend electives on that area, can avoid the consequences. Yet those who so specialize or try to cover ground piecemeal do so at considerable sacrifice of equally important studies, and so the consequences of curricular failure are magnified. As research yields more that deserves our attention, the magnitude of such failure can only increase, and the pressure for fragmentation becomes greater. Increasing knowledge is our goal in research and scholarship, but doing so makes our curriculum questions harder.

The problem is not that something has to be excluded. Our finite condition dictates this, so it is useless to protest. The problem is how to think about exclusion.

In 1828 the Yale faculty recognized that, in their mission, disciplining the powers of intellect is more important than furnishing it with particular knowledge. Like them, we must be clear, and make it so to our students, that study within the curriculum is not the totality of learning. Many of the most important things we come to learn will occur outside, and for our students, *after* study in the curriculum. Because we have studied the curriculum, we will be better able to learn afterward and to continue to learn throughout our lives in ways far richer than would have otherwise been possible. Thus, we stand for intellectual self-reliance, provided that our belief is based on the genuine power of the curriculum to do what we claim it can do.

In short, we must avoid claiming for our particular studies an exclusivity that leads our students, and even ourselves, to believe that anything outside the curriculum is not worthy of attention. These studies will come to a finish. And here we see most fully why a curriculum must be seen as a means and not as an end. For while a curriculum can be completed, study and learning in the rest of our lives cannot. In the pursuit of intellectual self-reliance, we commit ourselves to that life-long study. And we dedicate ourselves to nurturing it in our students.

Other kinds of issues illustrate how the ideal of intellectual self-reliance may give direction to curriculum design. Most colleges and universities must ask how, within a curriculum, the natural sciences and mathematics ought to fit with the study of literature, history, and philosophy. At times we succumb to the false sociology of the "two cultures"; at others we exclude the study of the hard technical matters when they seem to constrain the admission or retention of students. In either case we risk teaching our students the dreadful lesson that only some are capable of understanding and appreciating the powers of the human intellect, that the human mind is really just a bundle of powers, and that not all of us have the capacity for the development of the whole range of intellectual virtues. But if we act in this fashion, we abandon all claim to wholeness and integrity of the human intellect, that is, to intellectual self-reliance.

We need not believe that everyone can become a practitioner of each and every one of the arts of intelligence. But institutional commitment to the education of the whole intellect must take seriously every student's potential to understand the many different ways human beings encounter and live in our world. Few of us, or of our students, will be research chemists, or discoverers of new mathematical theorems; but each one can come to know what the researcher and the mathematician do. Few of us will play the violin professionally. This is no excuse to fail to appreciate the virtuosity of the performing artist.

It is precisely because most of us will not be involved in scientific research, mathematical theory, or the performing arts that we must aspire to some grasp of what they are. We cannot become intellectually self-reliant in ignorance of the diverse places and points of view by which humanity has sought and found meaning in life. This capacity for perspective, for personal intellectual coherence, J. Glenn Gray called generosity:

> Generosity in its philosophical sense is the capacity to participate imaginatively in others' experiences, to explore freely many worlds, and to give ourselves to them for their own sake without calculation of returns. . . . The genius of a generous education is its intent to aid each person to become what he alone can become.[32]

The generous mind may safely rely upon itself; it is reliable because it thinks *for* itself, but is not all alone. The generous mind—the self-reliant mind—can help us avoid the worst consequences of the multiplicity of disciplines that separates us as faculty. The practitioners of one discipline are often scornful of or indifferent to the work done in others. James Q. Wilson and Richard Herrenstein describe this phenomenon with respect to criminology:

> Although interdisciplinary by its very nature, criminology became a sociological specialty by the 1940s, and this created a barrier to the flow of knowledge from physical anthropology, not to mention biology and psychology.[33]

Criminology is not alone in this. Just as we are sometimes tempted to say that some of us cannot learn some art or another, or that the curriculum must somehow lay claim to including everything worthwhile, so we may fall into thinking that one discipline necessarily excludes others, and that each of us is confined within the limits of his or her particular field of study. But, as in other cases, we must recognize that the human intellect can, and must, transcend these supposed limits, and that we as faculty *must* do so as well.

If scholars, teachers, administrators can come to think of themselves in these ways—and some of them already do—and devote themselves to their institutions and students, much of what is lamentable in education can be overcome. Change for the worse can be slowed, and curricular disarray from winds of fashion can be stopped. Under such conditions, inertia is not inevitably a disadvantage; it can preserve what is sound.

If, in face of the many curricular possibilities, we despair at making reasonable choices, we are left only with random, arbitrary selections subject to the prevailing tastes or agendas of individual teachers. In such a state of affairs, no appeal to coherence or quality will be of any avail. We may mask our failure to face the central questions by appealing to a process of accommodation and compromise that results in the appearance of a coherent, high quality set of courses and requirements, but we will have failed nonetheless.

We can, instead, face the task of reflecting on and articulating a set of common purposes. Doing so will require that our institution not only permit such an endeavor but require it. The very being of an educational institution cries out for a faculty actively engaged in the study of what is conceived to be worthwhile. In this sense, the key to curricular reform, and so to genuine educational reform, is the ongoing growth of a faculty as a community of learners actively engaged in inquiries not merely *about* the curriculum as such, but *in* those issues and questions that become central to any particular curriculum the faculty offers.

In a way, the ensuing vitality and durability are analogous to the truths Socrates brought to light about the achievement of knowledge and the insecurity of right opinion. Right opinion, because it has no anchor in reasoned understanding, is vulnerable to deterioration. Like the statues of Daedalus that ran away when unchained, right opinion has nothing to hold it in place. In institutions of higher learning, nothing prevents loss of coherence and quality except a faculty and administration resolved to preserve and advance them. When a curriculum is nothing but a patchwork to which nobody is really committed, or when it has no more anchor than some consensus accepted by the present faculty for things that are distinct from education—academic turf, prestige, and the like—it is as fleeting as those statues.

A faculty becomes a *faculty* by making itself a learned body through mutual commitment to the life of the intellect. Thus, we must return to fundamental faculty development if we are to respond to those who find the current state of many precollege and undergraduate programs so dismal. And administrators and trustees must establish within our educational institutions solid programs of faculty development as part of the regular life of the institution. They must raise the money to buy the time. It is not a one-time task; it is the very life of an educational institution. By a common commitment to the rigors of intellectual discipline, we make ourselves fit to exercise educational authority, to design the instruments of education for students, and to bear the public trust.

These goals may appear to be more realizable in colleges and small private schools than in universities and larger public or private schools. How are a university of twenty thousand or more students enrolled in different colleges, or a school of several thousand students in college preparatory, agricultural, or business programs to achieve anything resembling a community united by common purposes?

This is one of the questions a core curriculum is intended to answer. It unites the institution by providing a common course of study for all until students go their separate ways into specialized areas. Distributive requirements are established in the areas believed essential to the educational mission of the institution or essential to becoming an educated person. Traditionally, this concern was also addressed by admission requirements in mathematics, history, foreign languages, natural sciences, English composition, and so forth.

Perhaps there are no better curricular means of achieving common purposes, however halting and transitory in practice. In any event, common purposes must be based on the conviction that the institution is composed of teachers and administrators who take discipline of mind seriously and who will not fill students' minds with bargain basement furniture. Better for students to take a fine course in business than a shabby course in Western civilization, meet a fine teacher of machine shop than a weak teacher of writing. Institutions whose teachers and administrators deserve each other's confidence are better suited to bear the public trust than those that merely establish curricular commonalities. Let us have colleagues who can be trusted to design courses worthy of students and to teach them with loyalty to high standards. Above all, whatever colleagues teach—engineering, business, education, arts, sciences—let us not ever isolate them from the highest ideals of the profession of education by dismissing the importance of what they can do for students.

Every institution can aspire to capture something of the spirit David Riesman admires in good liberal arts colleges:

> The superiority that I believe the liberal arts college has in preparing students to be scholarly and original and to become independent-minded later on does not come about because they have studied any particular subject matter in traditional areas of learning. It does not come about even, as in the University of Chicago's undergraduate college, because they have experienced an unusually integrated program. Rather, the issue is one that goes beyond particular courses and even particular departments to the general spirit of the place.[34]

LEARNING FROM EACH OTHER

If national debate is not likely to be very useful, faculty and administrators in diverse institutions can nonetheless learn from each other. Every school, college, and university can find examples of curriculum strength. These might well suggest ways to improve their own curriculum while allowing for local differences. Principles that lead to curriculum strength in one setting may be applied wisely to another.

For example, St. John's College in Annapolis and Santa Fe has a single prescribed curriculum for all undergraduates. Every student studies mathematics for four years; takes one year each of biology, inorganic chemistry, and physics; participates in chorus and studies music in the first two years; takes two years of Greek and two of French; and participates in four years of seminars based on great books in literature, philosophy, history, religion, and other disciplines.

Few institutions could or would want to replace their own curricula with this one. Most have many features of institutional structure and program content that have taken years to build and should be preserved. Past successes make radical overhaul imprudent and unnecessary. St. John's was able to establish its program in 1937 only because its financial circumstances were disastrous. It was very small, and it faced possible loss of accreditation. But St. John's curriculum embodies principles that may be applied elsewhere.

First, the liberal arts are taken to include the natural sciences and mathematics, in the tradition of the Trivium and Quadrivium. Inquiry in these areas is taken to be intimately connected to inquiry in the rest of the liberal arts, and by it a sense of the wholeness of human intelligence is conveyed.

Second, while the exclusion of all but great books from the curriculum limits acquaintance with current works, it eliminates trivial texts. It also provides a fertile acquaintance with the foundations of human inquiry and discovery.

Third, students begin to study demanding texts on their first day at St. John's; they come quickly to expect all students to prepare for class so that all can contribute. They are sometimes disappointed, but this is far superior to no expectation that fellow students will take their work seriously. Because the work of freshmen is as important as any other, and because coherence is sought through the four years, freshmen gain ready access to the most experienced faculty members.

No one at St. John's would claim that the curriculum should be maintained exactly as it is. Weaknesses have been identified in student writing, and the college is trying to address long-standing inadequacies in the fine arts. Furthermore, some faculty members think it lax that St. John's has no written examinations. But St. John's offers other institutions an instructive vision of the human intellect, a productive commitment to study of worthwhile books, and a strong reminder that freshmen and sophomores deserve to be taught by experienced faculty members.

Such principles can be applied in different ways. Two interesting variants are the Program of Liberal Studies at Notre Dame and the "Great Theorems" course in mathematics taught by William Dunham at Hanover College in Indiana.

Notre Dame's purposes are not the same as St. John's. Notre Dame's three-year program, established in 1950, and "anchored in the Western and Catholic traditions," tries to teach students "how to go about seeking a solution to a question and communicating the solution to others. . . . The intent of this wide reading is not cultural relativism, but a clear recognition of the universal values and the common problems of perennial interest to human beings. . . . A third dimension of the program seeks the integration of faith and reason." Notre Dame evidently places greater emphasis on writing than does St. John's; beginners are said to write with confidence "in their ability to reach the truth. The intention of the Program is not to dash this confidence but rather to encourage it." By the time they are seniors, "students write with ease and increasing elegance."[35] Many types of institutions may learn from Notre Dame's experience how to advance rigor in student thought and effectiveness in student writing.

At Hanover College, Dunham, of the Department of Mathematics, is fearful that "too often we fall into the easy trap of stressing only the applications of mathematics to commerce and computers. . . . I am afraid that the mathematics professor of today tends to ignore the centuries-old conception of mathematics as an artistic exercise in pure reason that can provide fascinating glimpses into the logical relationships of number and space."[36]

With a regard for colleagues that vividly illustrates professional kinship and common purposes, Dunham explains that, when "we ignore an important mathematical tradition dating back to classical times . . . we run the risk of undercutting our liberal arts colleagues in literature or history or music, whose disciplines cannot promise their students lucrative job offers after graduation."[37]

Dunham has designed and taught his course with these ideas in mind. His purpose is explicit: "Like the art historian, my objective is not the acquisition of skills but the appreciation of greatness."[38] Accordingly, he wanted to delve into mathematics, not just talk about it, and so he required students to be proficient in calculus to gain admission. He chose theorems with ingenious proofs and broad implications from giants in the history of mathematics that could be understood by his students. "In short," he writes, "I was looking for masterpieces—the 'Mona Lisas' or 'Hamlets' of mathematics."[39] Around the proofs of the theorems, he "wove the historical and biographical components of the course."[40]

Dunham's way of thinking about his colleagues and about students can be useful to teachers in all disciplines in diverse institutions. Every teacher and institution profits from such clarity of purpose. Who would not want for his or her own students what Dunham saw in those who succeeded in understanding the theorems: "a sense of awe in recognizing the genius of others" and "a degree of personal satisfaction that one can, indeed, comprehend the works of a master"?[41]

The fifty-year old Plan II Honors Program at the University of Texas in Austin and recent work on curriculum at Brooklyn College may also serve as examples for other institutions.

The Plan II Program began at Texas in 1935. It admits only about 150 students per year; classes range from a high of sixty students to a low of fewer than eighteen. Faculty are chosen from throughout the university and often include the most distinguished teachers and scholars. Courses require a full year, larger classes are supplemented by smaller discussion groups, and the Plan II Major is genuinely interdisciplinary. By this design, Texas is able to provide the advantages of a liberal arts college while maintaining access to the resources of a great university; the program may be the most successful anywhere at achieving the benefits of both types of institution. Notably, it does so at a fraction of the price normally charged by liberal arts colleges and smaller, private universities.

The program is conspicuously free of grade inflation, and students are expected to maintain a B average. Special attention is given to advising students, and this contributes to even greater student access to fine faculty. Admissions standards are high.

The curriculum is rigorous, with substantial work in the sciences, including six hours in biology. The greatest weakness is that there is no longer a mathematics requirement. Proficiency through the fourth semester of foreign language study is required. Philosophy, literature, and history are emphasized; notably, in humanities and fine arts, two courses must be taken in *one* area. For example, students may study art history, music history, or drama history, but they cannot satisfy requirements by taking only one course in any of these areas. The program includes unusually high expectations in writing. Only one semester of study in social science is required. By careful selection of elective courses, a student can achieve the equivalent of a second major. The university does not award dual degrees, but, in fact, a student can complete two majors. Courses may also be arranged to allow for double concentrations such as Plan II/Engineering and Plan II/Pre-Med. The combination of curricular rigor and flexibility is a mark of imagination in institutional planning that can be useful elsewhere.

The Texas program has been built and sustained on the conviction that we can say what an educated person is, and that students can and do aspire to become educated. It achieves, as John Silber describes his experience as a teacher in the program, "intense traffic between one professor and another through the mediation of the students."[42] It is thus genuinely interdisciplinary, and yet it does not spurn the specialism of its greatest teachers *or* the aspiration to specialized learning among students. This spirit of respect for the arts of intelligence is beautifully captured at the university in a reading list published by the College of Liberal Arts and called "The Texas List of Unrequired Readings." Perhaps other colleges and universities should provide their students with such an engaging invitation to intellectual maturity.

Brooklyn College of the City University of New York has made remarkable strides with its "common experience core requirement." In fact, Ethyle R. Wolfe, provost and vice president for academic affairs at Brooklyn College, writes: "Let no one assume that achieving consensus about the content and form of a uniform core was an easy task for Brooklyn College.

Indeed, the birth of a common and integrated core at our institution in 1980 seems in retrospect to have been a miracle. I think it would be hard to find a less likely candidate for success in planning or achieving curricular coherence and commonality at that point in time than our institution."[43]

At the beginning of the 1970s, Brooklyn College adopted an open admissions policy. It grew rapidly from fifteen thousand to thirty-six thousand students. The college was divided into six different schools to accommodate growth; their curricula became a smorgasbord, with the college divided by partisan interests. Five years later, the financial crisis of the city of New York caused some dramatic changes: reduction of enrollment to eighteen thousand, retrenchment of faculty, abolition of open admissions, and establishment of tuition. Given such profound changes, Wolfe asks, "Is it any wonder that the faculty of the college was left exhausted, demoralized, and with its mission confused?"[44]

Not surprisingly under these conditions, the faculty almost unanimously adopted a resolution to institute a college-wide core curriculum and a single set of general education requirements. As Frederick Rudolph and other historians have pointed out, educational institutions are sometimes most capable of aspiring to common purposes and improvement when their circumstances are most dismaying. Other kinds of institutions, including nations on the brink of war and communities faced with cataclysm, show this tendency as well.

Naturally, the nearly universal belief in the need for a core curriculum among faculty and administrators did not answer the questions about what it should contain. But the faculty supported a decision to abolish the separate schools, rejected the proposals of a blue ribbon committee for a specific core curriculum, and elected a second committee. The contemplation and deliberations of this committee, in cooperation with many faculty members, proved decisive. These conversations sought "a common solid foundation" for majors and electives and a program "which would in its inner structure provide for progression in content and level of sophistication."[45] Ten courses were built from scratch, required of all students, and designated Core Studies 1–10 as an indication that "they are by birthright considered college offerings, not departmental property, whose integrity must be safeguarded as a college-wide responsibility."[46] Potential teaching faculty designed the courses to be proposed to the Faculty Council.

The proposed core was adopted—but not with the idea that it would take care of itself. Brooklyn College understood that identifying common purposes and rebuilding a curriculum was not a job to be done once and for all. Instead, it established a standing Faculty Committee on the Core Curriculum, arranged for annual appointment of a group of coordinators to form a network across the disciplines, and mandated provisions for ongoing discussion and refinement of the program. The college treated its own common purposes and means to their fulfillment as objects of *permanent* institutional concern.

These actions contain instructive lessons for other institutions; all must take their individual circumstances and aspirations into account of course, but if they do, they may be able to profit from the experience of Brooklyn College without suffering its ordeals. Certainly, they may benefit from Ethyle Wolfe's insight:

> I do recognize that the attainment of full coherence is an unrealizable goal, and I consider its unrealizability to be the secret weapon that keeps our core alive. The fact that integration of the core courses remains an endless task guarantees that the core will be subjected to continuous discussion, change, and refinement.[47]

Perhaps most suggestive of all is her observation that "the most important lesson we learned is that you can't have curriculum development without faculty development. They must go hand in hand."[48]

Because Brooklyn College had the courage to ask what an educated person is, and what its educational obligations to a highly diverse student population should be, the courses of its core program are broad without being trivial. The core provides thirty-four hours of undergraduate study—just over one-fourth of a student's work toward graduation—and it takes seriously the disciplining and furnishing of the mind in studies of both the old and the new. Every student studies the classical origins of modern culture; fine arts and music; American social organization and European and American history since 1700; mathematical reasoning and computer programming; literature from Dante and Chaucer to a nineteenth- or twentieth-century American novelist, including one work from a non-Western tradition; basic concepts and laboratory in chemistry, physics, biology, and geology; African, Asian, and Latin American cultures; and perennial philosophical questions about knowledge, existence, and values. There is a foreign language requirement from which students with three years of high school study in a language are exempt. Because the college insists that the ability to write well is a mark of an educated man or woman, writing exercises are part of every core course.

Any specialist could look at the readings of the core courses and think that other authors should have been included, even at the price of excluding some who are present. For example, I would try to include Epictetus and Seneca among the classical authors; feature Montesquieu in the course on power, authority, and social organization in America; and emphasize the *Federalist Papers* in American history since 1700. But the authors who have been chosen are in nearly every case worthy of inclusion, and that matters most. Overall, the work is exemplary, an instructive model of an institution making the most of its opportunities in adversity. Above all, it shows what can be done for students when an institution faces up to the problem of achieving common purposes by striving to make itself an intellectual community.

Learning from each other need not be confined to higher education. In *First Lessons: A Report on Elementary Education in America,* William Bennett points to accomplishments of Frye Elementary in Chandler, Arizona; St. Matthew's School in Dorchester, Massachusetts; the Futures Academy in Buffalo, New York; Garden Gate Elementary in Cupertino, California; Johnson Elementary in Bridgeport, West Virginia; and Caloosa Elementary in Cape Coral, Florida. And, as we have seen above, such secondary schools as Langley High School in McLean, Virginia, are striking examples of curricular soundness.

In each of these elementary schools, Bennett explains, "goals are clearly stated and forcefully pursued by principal and staff. Their teachers find opportunities for professional development and the act of instruction transcends method. Parents are involved. The school enjoys community support. Good schools know what to teach and to teach well—and by keeping sharply focused on their instructional mission, they can truly teach well."[49]

At Johnson Elementary, "high expectations are set . . . . Acquisition of basic skills has the highest priority. . . . Homework is an integral part of the curriculum. It is never given out as punishment or 'busy work,' and it is usually begun in class under teacher supervision."[50] At Garden Gate, "the science materials are old—but the sixth graders have planted a forest in a nearby vacant lot. The library needs to be upgraded, but the students really *read* what is in it, because the school provides quiet reading time after lunch."[51] At Caloosa Elementary, "Principal Mary Santini sees that her teachers have numerous opportunities to consult, to review programs in other schools, and to grow in their own knowledge. Teachers work 'across disciplines' in order to learn what information their students lack . . . . Recently, one class wrote books during English class and then bound them in art class. There is a special emphasis on drawing material from various subjects in order to build critical thinking and independent reasoning."[52]

At all levels of education, faculty and administrators can learn from each other. Not tendentious debate but constructive sharing of efforts to serve students faithfully can advance specific purposes in each institution. Colleges and universities can learn from elementary and secondary schools, and vice versa. If we try to work together in such a spirit of cooperation, we may succeed in building even more fertile and diverse institutions, each of which is, in its individuality, worthy of the trust of its students and their families, its benefactors, and the citizens of the nation.

Finally, if we do this, we will surely find opportunity to overcome the dispirited lament that so typifies educational discourse, to find satisfaction in what is being accomplished, and to take joy in what is possible for us and our children in the fruitful exercise of our liberty. We will still have failures and disappointments, and heartache over opportunities lost or mistakes made. But we are not likely to be vulnerable to the despair of having no idea where to turn, no sense of shared purposes.

8

Informed Choices and Institutional Merit

If a man has any greatness in him, it comes to light, not in one flamboyant hour, but in the ledger of his daily work.[1]

—Beryl Markham

INDIVIDUALS, INSTITUTIONS, and nations have hours that are fine and hours that are not so fine. But for each of them, greatness consists in the quality of day-to-day conduct. None can become great by episodic infusions of enthusiasm, passion, opportunity, or money, because greatness is not an episode but a matter of habit. In education, the application of this truism concerns whether each institution and its staff can achieve habits of learning, teaching, administering, governing, and behavior that serve students faithfully in accordance with purposes worth sharing.

In the preceding chapters, arguments have been advanced that the greatness we should seek in education is the greatness of individual schools, colleges, and universities and their personnel. Frederick Rudolph observed, for example, that "George W. Pierson, coming up for air after being long submerged in the history of Yale, gasped, 'One is appalled at the incoherence of American higher education.'"[2] I have argued that the individual institutions that bear the trust of the public for formal education must have coherence. By coherence I do not mean any loss of diversity, because diversity need not signal incoherence or chaos, provided institutions recognize that pluralism rests on shared intellectual and moral ideals.

I have argued that no institution can rise above the quality of its personnel, and that forms, including curricular forms, cannot replace qualified professionals in the classroom, in the conduct of student life, and in administrative office. To be educationally sound, each institution must put priority on the study of the disciplines of human intelligence, make all policies support this, and invest resources in the continuing development of teachers and administrators.

Other of my arguments are that a seamless educational profession is imperative and that cooperation among schools, colleges, and universities is indispensable to this end. The work of an educational institution cannot be done by anyone else—not by the nation, the government, the educational associations—but no institution has to do its work in isolation from others.

All of these arguments are linked to the theme that every school, college, and university is obligated to identify and declare the intellectual and moral purposes it intends to work conscientiously to achieve.

Most of these arguments concern the internal affairs of educational institutions. They do not cover two basic elements of external affairs. Specifically, they do not cover the goals to be pursued by institutions in cooperation with prospective students and their families. Neither do they address the difficulty of achieving institutional merit in a sometimes unfavorable legal and political environment. How, then, can institutions help prospective students and their families to understand them correctly, and how can families make reasonably sure that their choices are informed ones? And, how can institutions counter legal and political pressures that threaten to impair the quality of their educational programs?

UNDERSTANDING EDUCATIONAL INSTITUTIONS

As a college president, I met at the beginning of each year with the parents of entering students and introduced them to key academic and administrative personnel, each of whom made a brief presentation and invited questions. At the opening of these meetings, I said to the parents:

> You and your sons and daughters have placed a great trust in my colleagues and me. I hope that as your loved ones leave St. John's, either at graduation or earlier in order to pursue other opportunities

in life, you will have reason to say, "St. John's bore our trust faithfully and well. We believe that it honorably fulfilled our expectations and its obligations." I promise you that St. John's will put the intellectual maturation of your sons and daughters above all other callings; that we will invest our resources in the finest teachers and academic programs we can secure; that we will seek to advance your sons' and daughters' powers of reading, writing, speaking, listening, translating, demonstrating in mathematics, and experimenting in the sciences by rigorous studies in the fundamental disciplines of human inquiry and discovery; that we will welcome them to the community; get to know them as students and friends; give them our attention and make ourselves available to them; and provide rich opportunities for healthy and pleasurable social, recreational, and athletic participation. We will try by example, by policy, and by our serious educational expectations to help them avoid dangerous excesses and callous behavior.

Institutions can do much in this respect to help prospective students and their families find suitable educational opportunities by explaining clearly what they stand for and how they seek to fulfill their purposes. Because of the great diversity in higher education and variance in quality and price, students and their parents must be able to make informed choices. To a considerable extent, they must be able to rely on the trustworthiness of the institutions from which they seek information. But it is useful for them to know what information to seek, and the institutions should help them to secure it.

It is an old but not very funny joke in education that college and university catalogs belong in the fiction section of libraries. Many catalogs are basically truthful about institutional purposes, academic programs, and student life, but any sampling reveals cases of overstatement and self-aggrandizement. Educational institutions eager to recruit sufficient numbers of qualified students sometimes paint an unjustifiably rosy picture of themselves. But thoroughness by parents and prospective students can get them past the image of to the facts about the institution.

Parents and prospective students do well from the outset to look for one basic sign of institutional weakness. As anyone who visits educational institutions soon discovers, some of them encourage students to adopt the mistaken belief that only *that* school takes students seriously, provides teachers who really care about them, or encourages real intellectual maturation. These are mean falsehoods, because they tend to create snob-

bish students and encourage cynicism about education generally. Institutions that advance themselves by claiming that all
other institutions are indifferent to students and are educationally impoverished exhibit both ignorance of the fine institutions
in America and a lack of conviction about their own strengths. A
parent or a prospective student should therefore disqualify any
institution that celebrates its virtues by denigrating other institutions.

Much that is misleading can be avoided by students and their
parents if they review catalogs carefully, consult standard guides
to colleges, and ask direct questions in person and in correspon-
dence of admissions and other college and university officers.
Schools, colleges and universities ought to help them to learn
the fundamental questions, because they should want enrolling
students to know what they are choosing.

Questions worth asking include the following:

1. Does the admissions office arrange for prospective students to attend classes during visits to the college? The answer
will suggest the extent to which the institution considers academic work its first priority and whether it wants prospective
students to know what to expect. Also, how much daily homework is typical in a course.

2. Does the institution have a core curriculum, that is, a set of
requirements that every student must satisfy in order to graduate? If it does not, why not? If it has, does the core tend toward
broad and shallow topics, or toward the rigorous and demanding? Does it neglect any of the principal arts of intelligence, that
is, does the core include emphasis on reading and writing, on the
use of verbal and mathematical symbols, and on history, literature, natural sciences, philosophy and logic, and foreign languages? If the core curriculum does not include these emphases,
it is likely to be both intellectually mushy and inadequate to
instilling sound habits of learning. If the school has no core
curriculum, it is vulnerable to the winds of fashion and not
educationally solid.

3. How large are typical freshman and sophomore classes?
Are large lower level undergraduate courses taught by distinguished faculty members or are they left to junior faculty and
graduate assistants? Do *not* be misled by college claims about

low student/faculty ratios. The issue is not the ratio, but the size of classes and the accessibility of top quality, experienced faculty members. Large classes by teachers who deserve to be entrusted to lecture are often excellent, especially if they are supplemented by small discussion groups.

4. How are students advised during their consideration of major areas of study at the upper undergraduate level? What questions are they taught to ask about the choice of a major? How large are upper-level classes? What are the senior requirements for completion of the undergraduate degree? How many students annually change their major and why? Does the institution help students to change majors as their interests and judgment mature?

5. How many courses may a student choose or elect in four years? How much access is there to electives, that is, are the courses listed in the catalog actually open to all who want to take them or are some of them window dressing that only a handful of students gets to take?

6. Ask for syllabi of a sampling of required major and elective courses. If these are unavailable, ask whether they can be provided within a reasonable time. If the institution cannot provide syllabi, ask what students are given by their teachers as each course begins. How are students to plan their work, and to do recommended as well as required reading efficiently without detailed course descriptions in advance?

7. Can visitors meet faculty members to discuss the institution and its expectations? If so, ask about the adequacy of library resources for faculty scholarship, laboratory facilities for student and faculty research, cultural programs in the school and community, including visiting faculty and artists, and about the extent to which students are motivated to take advantage of the opportunities. These tell a good bit about the environment a new student is entering. Ask as well about office hours faculty members normally keep and whether they are genuinely available to students at all levels. This question can be asked of students, too.

8. What are the best places for students to study? Are space and carrels available in the library? For freshmen and sophomores? Is the library open on weekends? Are there problems with book theft? If so, how are they met? Do students have

difficulty getting the books required or recommended for courses and placed by faculty on restricted reserve? If so, what is done?

9. Are the dormitories suitable for study? Are there quiet hours for study and are they enforced? Are there adult or upperclass dormitory resident advisors? How are they trained for their duties? How are dormitories organized—are they coeducational by floor, by building, or not at all? If coeducational, how is privacy maintained?

10. How is campus security ensured? How are security personnel instructed to deal with violations of institutional policy and of the law? How many thefts, burglaries, assaults, drug violations, and rapes are reported annually (totally *and per capita*)? How are food and medical services provided? Are professional nutritionists and medical personnel actively involved? Do female students have ready access to a gynecologist? The answers to all of these questions are indications of professionalism and quality; for example, gynecological services normally indicate thoroughness in medical programs for men and women alike. Beware of "peer health counselors."

11. What is the composition of the student body and the faculty? Are they diverse in ways that expose students to a variety of backgrounds and experience? Are any of the institutions sanctioned by the college or university, such as fraternities and sororities, discriminatory on grounds of race or religion?

12. Ask for a detailed description of the extracurricular activities available, including intramural sports. Also ask about parties and social events. When you have the *institution's* answers, ask *students* so that you can compare answers.

13. What is the attrition rate of students in the freshman and sophomore years? Is the percentage high or very low? If high, it may mean that students did not find what they expected, and so close scrutiny of the institution is even more important. If it is very low, it may be a good sign, but it may also mean that standards and work loads are not demanding and that students are complacent. In either case, seek an explanation.

14. How do academic credits transfer to other institutions? What percentage of students go to graduate school? Where do they go? What percentage are admitted to their first choice? How is academic advising for graduate school conducted?

15. What services are provided by the career and placement office? Are freshmen and sophomores encouraged to discuss their plans for the future and to learn how to gain access to jobs? Do they learn the differences between a career and a succession of jobs? How are the academic work of the faculty and the work of the counseling and placement office coordinated so they are not at cross-purposes? What are the patterns of opportunity for graduates? Where do alumni work, in what fields, for what firms, and in what positions? Ask specifically about members of the two most recent graduating classes.

16. What are *all* the financial aid programs—need-based and merit—offered by the institution? What payment and prepayment options are available? Are summer job programs or internships in corporations and government available to students? What percentage of the education and general budget is paid by tuition? Does the institution expect this percentage, and tuition itself, to rise? For parents who have the financial background, a careful look at the most recent audited financial statement of the institution can reveal financial strength or weakness and the likelihood of tuition increases; so can a look at the past five years of tuition increases. If tuition contributes more than 65 per cent of the education and general budget, take a thorough look at the economic circumstances of the institution and the size of the endowment, and ask about plans to reduce the percentage.

17. What percentage of alumni make contributions to the institution annually? This is a significant indication of the extent of their personal satisfaction with the institution.

When these questions have been answered, prospective students and parents can compare the answers with the written account in the institution's charter, catalog, and student handbook. If the accounts square, the institution is probably trustworthy. If there are significant discrepancies, great care is called for. Finally, watch students and faculty as they move about the campus. Are they cheerful and spirited? Downcast and listless? What feel do you as parents get for the people and environment a member of your family may enter?

Assessing institutions along these lines can lead to fruitful investment of time, money, and effort. It is important to understand that, if a school fails expectations, there is no reason to panic. So long as transfer of credit is assured from the outset, a move to a more suitable institution is possible without great hardship. This, too, the institution should explain, along with the steps it would take to help students transfer elsewhere.

It is prudent to ask such questions, because some schools have outlived their reputations and some are better at marketing themselves than they are at offering good educational programs. Further, high price is not always a reliable guide to quality, nor does low price mean low standards. Very few institutions conduct themselves on the principle of *caveat emptor;* most are genuinely interested in the well-being of students. Straight questions can distinguish good intentions from successful conduct.

Institutions can, moreover, learn important things about themselves by reviewing such questions. By generously understanding prospective students and parents, the institutions can discover oversights or areas of weakness that need attention.

MERIT, LAW, AND POLITICS

For a school, college, or university to achieve its highest potential and its greatest level of educational merit, it must behave with generous understanding of its own personnel and of the students and families the institution serves. It must also take into account its legal and political environment.

Carelessness in these areas can jeopardize identification, appointment, and retention of highly qualified personnel and lead to compromises that threaten the educational merit of the institution. Discrimination is both illegal and wrong, but respect for distinction is both right and obligatory. Sometimes the legal and political climate can endanger the latter without successfully preventing the former.

This danger is highlighted by the increase in litigation against educational institutions. Although the charges range from the ridiculous to the very serious, lawsuits in education are often grueling ordeals for both plaintiffs and defendants. Frivolous charges can sometimes be overcome quickly. I was once involved in a mercifully short set of discrimination hearings in which the principal evidence was uneaten cookies; the fact that the cookies were not eaten by colleagues was offered as evidence of prejudice against the employee who had baked them.

But where the issues are not so frivolous, all the litigants generally suffer.

George A. La Noue, a recognized trial expert in academic discrimination cases, and Barbara A. Lee, a member of the National Institute of Education's Commission on the Conditions of Excellence in Higher Education, explain:

> Institutions "win" the overwhelming majority of decisions, but litigation still has many negative consequences. First, the publicity almost always is harmful. . . . Second, litigation that drags on is bad for institutional morale. . . . Third, litigation can be hard on plaintiff's peers. . . . Fourth, costs in time and money are burdensome. . . . Plaintiffs report being in a kind of limbo for three to five years or longer. . . . Litigation often breaks irreparably the collegial bonds upon which academic life depends.[3]

The institutional consequences—even of "victorious" litigation—are thus often so painful that there is a powerful motive to settle suits before trial, and as early as possible. In the case of *Rajender* v. *The University of Minnesota,* for instance, "Realizing the damaging publicity that would ensue, the regents decided a settlement was necessary even though many administrators and faculty were convinced the university had not discriminated against Rajender."[4] The settlement placed the university "under judicial supervision for 10 years, paid plaintiff's attorney's fees of more than $2,000,000, and incurred other settlement costs of at least another $1,000,000."[5] The university sacrificed much more than money: it sacrificed its own authority in personnel decisions.

My own experience confirms that the temptation to settle in order to spare an institution all the ordeals of extended litigation can be very strong. Even though federal courts generally impose high standards of proof on the plaintiff, rulings on discovery sometimes result in expensive and time-consuming reproduction of documents, lengthy review of previously confidential files, discussion of other faculty members, and extensive involvement of institutional personnel. Confidentiality is sometimes hard to preserve, and high feelings can cause conflict and bitterness no matter the outcome. These conditions may obscure the importance of defending the institution from present or future legal extortion.

This battery of facts should be sufficient to set before institutions two basic questions. The first is a question of morality: Are we fair and just and do we make all of our decisions on relevant grounds? The second is a question of prudence: Are we in a position to defend ourselves if accused of discrimination?

Because the process of discovery is often extensive in discrimination cases, prudence must instruct not only the procedures of the institution but also the quality and detail of its documentation. La Noue and Lee urge that "in evaluating claims of individual discrimination, the key is consistency: Did the institution consistently follow its own criteria and rules in making the disputed decision? Were the various levels of review consistent? Was the decision consistent with those made about other faculty members?"[6]

Of course, it is not enough to be consistent. Institutions must be able to prove consistency. This depends on the establishment of rigorous procedures for documentation of the process and the substance of each case of academic peer review. The nature of these procedures and the documentation they yield should be examined by each institution's legal counsel in light of existing law and judicial precedents, and institutions should have their lawyers conduct an annual review.

But if these steps cover the basics of prudence for an institution, they are insufficient for institutional morality. Even if every candidate for reappointment or tenure has the benefit of procedural consistency, it does not follow that any review is conducted with integrity and candor. An institution can be consistently bad in peer review.

The decency of an institution depends in part on the willingness of peer reviewers to examine thoroughly the relevant facts about teaching, research and publication, and intellectual and moral quality. It depends as well on their willingness to express their judgments candidly and to go on record in writing about their conclusions and the reasons for them. Without such courage in peer review, the fundamental considerations in a decision may be forever obscure no matter how procedurally consistent the institution has been; and where there is obscurity there is the possibility of subtle prejudice and moral failure.

The importance of such courage is increased by rulings of the United States District Court for the Eastern District of Pennsylvania and the United States Court of Appeals for the Third

Circuit. In 1981, a French professor at Franklin and Marshall College was denied tenure; he filed a charge of discrimination against the college with the Equal Employment Opportunity Commission (EEOC), alleging discrimination based on his French national origin. Despite Franklin and Marshall's strong record of tenuring faculty of foreign background, the EEOC issued a subpoena requiring the college to provide it with "all notes, letters, memoranda or other documents considered during each case"[7] of tenure granted or denied at the college from November 1977 until 1981 and also other previously confidential records. Franklin and Marshall College appealed for relief on the grounds that preservation of confidentiality is essential to peer review and to academic freedom. The District Court and the United States Court of Appeals for the Third Circuit have upheld the EEOC subpoena. The Supreme Court has denied review.

Circuit Judge Carol Los Mansmann wrote: "We are not unmindful of nor insensitive to the importance of confidentiality in the peer review process. . . . We recognize that permitting disclosure to the EEOC of confidential peer review may perhaps burden the tenure review process in our nation's universities and colleges. In the face of the clear mandate from Congress which identified and recognized the threat of unchecked discrimination in education, however, we have no choice but to trust that the honesty and integrity of the tenured reviewers in evaluation decisions will overcome feelings of discomfort and embarrassment and will outlast the demise of absolute confidentiality."[8]

This ruling lessens even limited confidentiality in academic peer review throughout America. Is such a measure likely to safeguard individuals from discrimination, and is the probable price worth paying?

The fundamental purpose of peer review is to secure the services of trustworthy teachers and scholars. The interests of students are most at stake in the process because they will be either the beneficiaries or the victims of the decisions.

Congress and the courts are, at the same time, concerned over, and bound by law to diminish, "the threat of unchecked discrimination in education." Judge Mansmann urges that the mission of an institution can be conscientiously fulfilled without traditional confidentiality if the reviewers in peer evaluation

have sufficient honesty and integrity. Unfortunately, if an institution is already susceptible to "unchecked discrimination," the
integrity and honesty of its personnel are questionable. On the
one hand, this suggests that there is even more reason to prevent
them from using confidentiality to hide their prejudices. On the
other, it suggests that they may be cunning enough to generate
documents to protect their biases. Anyone can build files and
records so as to provide a convincing appearance of justice. For
these reasons, the courts' remedy for discrimination is power-
less to erase the worst threats of discrimination and the worst
kind of bad faith. Intelligent ruthlessness is not so easily
checked, and, in any case, it can seldom be combatted from
outside an institution.

But such cases are rare; in nearly twenty-five years of professional life, I have met only a few teachers and administrators
who were ruthlessly prejudiced. In most cases, a seeming discrimination is not actually ill will or overt bigotry but a subtle
blindness. In this respect, the academic community is not exempt from human imperfection and weakness.

But if most people in academe try to be fair, will less confidentiality dispose them to do even better? It seems to me that, while
it will invite them to be more careful about documentation, they
will be less rigorous in controversial cases. Where there is
disagreement, the benefit of doubt will probably fall to the
individual under consideration.

We may be tempted to celebrate this prospect by analogy to
the legal principle that people are innocent until proven guilty.
But the analogy is inapplicable and destructive. Questions of
merit in education are not questions of guilt or innocence. The
issue is whether the person under review has conclusively
shown ability—and the promise of continuing ability—to advance the mission of the institution. Where there is reasonable
doubt, the benefit of it should not fall to the individual but rather
to the people the institution is obligated to serve. Specifically,
the benefit of doubt should fall to students, and this implies that,
where there is reasonable doubt, a decision on tenure should be
negative.

Because I believe that the rulings of the courts in this instance
will obscure the overriding status of students, I conclude that
they will impair the ends of education. But this does not mean

that educational institutions themselves *must* of necessity lose sight of the priority of their obligations to students in academic peer review.

Nothing *can* replace integrity and honesty in peer review—or in the rest of intellectual life. But they cannot flourish without courage, and with confidentiality reduced, the need for courage will be greater than ever. Much depends on how academics respond to this change. If reduction of confidentiality leads them to self-indulgent despair, their institutions will become worse. But if they rise to the fact that the task of conscientious peer review has become more demanding by asking more of *themselves,* they will have a chance to compensate for any legal contingency.

That is, the question is whether academics are willing to place institutional mission and duty to students above the safety and comfort of confidentiality in their judgments. If they act on the conviction that they must do so, this judicial decision cannot destroy the power of their institution to fulfill its purposes. This much is within their control even though such judicial rulings are not.

In this respect, academic institutions and their personnel are like all others in the human condition. For all of us can still accomplish our purposes even when circumstances change for the worse. We can do so through active virtues that can, in large measure, compensate for unfavorable conditions. It is preferable, of course, for peer review to be conducted in confidence because privacy reduces the need to rely on individual courage. But when confidentiality is lost, courage can still get the job done. So long as courage obtains, the ultimate safeguard of academic quality remains intact. But it is nonetheless perilous for students whenever courts destroy *institutional* protection of their interests and disregard the danger of trusting everything to individuals.

Because institutions must rely on the character of the people who work in them, no amount of demonstrable consistency in decision making is sufficient for the moral well-being of the institution. Decisions about appointments and tenure are, in the end, matters of judgment, and not merely of rules or criteria. The buck must stop somewhere. The members of an institution must be willing to judge, to do their level best to judge fairly, and to go on record. Their acceptance of responsibility for judgment and their willingness to go on record obliges the institution to stand behind them. For this reason, the counsel of La Noue and Lee is wrong:

> Finally, not every decision, even if correctly made, is worth defending at any cost, so settlement should be considered if reasonable terms can be achieved.[9]

If an institution has established responsible procedures and criteria, and if its personnel have conscientiously judged on publicly-known criteria of merit in accordance with the procedures, then what terms of settlement could possibly be reasonable? The institution cannot rightly abandon the judgment of its own personnel; it cannot decently agree to any terms that cloud their conscientiousness; it cannot rightly override them. Presumably, then, "reasonable terms" are limited to buying off a plaintiff with token amounts of money or less-than-candid letters of recommendation and the like. This may only encourage others to sue the institution whenever they feel aggrieved or disappointed. In any case, settlement will not replace serious attention within institutions to their own prudence and morality. It may even lead them to grant appointment or tenure in order to avoid possible lawsuits.

Judgments about institutional quality and resolve in such matters are akin to other judgments in politics. Uncompromising respect for merit does not imply unwillingness to compromise in other matters. The question is, rather, what sorts of compromises are worthy of the institution, worthy of it in the sense that they are faithful to its ideals and to the staff who are doing their best to advance those ideals. If an institution is procedurally weak, or weak on documentation, it may have to settle or suffer worse. But if it attends to prudence and morality, it has a better chance to stand its ground and to make compromises that do not sacrifice its principles or mission.

In my experience, not all cases of litigation involving educational institutions are fundamentally spiteful. I have been involved in discrimination hearings in which I was convinced that the plaintiffs and the defendants alike were truly concerned that the institution be as educationally strong and as morally decent as possible. There were disagreements about past conduct and current practices, and judgments concerning the professional excellence of individuals. Sometimes feelings ran high. But by trying to understand generously—trying to see why things seem as they do to an adversary whose intelligence and character you respect—members of institutions can sometimes discover how to improve policies without sacrificing anything in the way of educational mission.

My experience of the worst ordeals of litigation is limited to hearings or lawsuits already in progress; occasionally I felt terribly sad that some things had been allowed to reach the litigation stage before anyone had listened to anyone else or genuinely tried to understand. Such circumstances make generous understanding very hard. Sometimes, as my own experience has also demonstrated, an adversary in litigation deserves neither respect nor compromise, and the better you listen, the more clearly you know it. This helps to dampen the temptation to compromise for the sake of economy or convenience.

A sense of humor is a great asset. I will never forget a beloved colleague turning to me during a lengthy lawsuit and saying, "I always knew you were as bad as plaintiff says, but I just can't understand these terrible misjudgments of me." That wonderful moment of friendship and laughter helped to achieve our purposes.

9

Public Policy and Public Self-Reliance

What enables men to know more than their ancestors is that they start with a knowledge of what their ancestors have already learned.[1]

—*Walter Lippmann*

T HOUGH WE rely on schools, colleges, and universities to make themselves worthy of students, we cannot expect them to do so alone. They cannot provide proper educational opportunity to students without public support, including financial support. Many of the most important policy questions for the nation, the states, communities, private foundations, and individual benefactors therefore concern funding for education.

How can government and private benefactors contribute most effectively to education? And what must Americans do for themselves if formal education is to be fruitful?

EXTERNAL SUPPORT OF EDUCATION

Currently, federal funding for education supports the Department of Education, the National Endowment for the Humanities, the National Endowment for the Arts, the National Science Foundation, and programs of the Veterans Administration, among others. The largest financial investment is in and through the Department of Education.

This department finances over one hundred different programs in elementary, secondary, and postsecondary education. It conducts research and distributes information about the con-

179

dition of educational institutions and the performance of students at all levels. It provides information about effective teaching and learning, and celebrates the accomplishments of fine institutions. Its publications, as, for example, its monographs on "What Works" in education, are very useful. But the greatest portions of the funds are spent on financial aid to students in postsecondary and higher education and on programs for disadvantaged children in schools. Postsecondary financial aid, especially, has given rise to controversial questions.

Financial Aid

With very few exceptions, financial aid is awarded not to educational institutions but to students. Eligible students are entitled by law to federal loans or grants. Because the money is used by students for tuition and fees, it reaches the institutions indirectly. But since students have a choice, no educational institution enjoys a legal entitlement to the money. Many nevertheless rely on the grants and loans to balance their budgets, and to do so they must secure adequate enrollment. Currently, about one-third of all postsecondary student costs are met by federal grants or loans. Most arguments for the expansion of federal aid programs are couched in terms of opportunity, the need for an educated public, and the importance of limiting indebtedness after graduation. Occasionally, but not often, I have been involved in private conversations where concern for institutional revenues was expressed as well, especially where levels of enrollment were in jeopardy. But even in these rare instances, the mixture of motives is not necessarily base or self-serving, because most educators are genuinely concerned about increased educational opportunity for students from families that cannot afford higher education. In practice, many institutions commit a major portion of their own resources to student aid, but few are wealthy enough to provide all that is needed. Thus, both the institutions and their students have come to rely on federal aid.

The nation's interest in an educated public makes it appropriate to provide federal support for students. The questions are: How expansive should it be and what forms should it take? Should it consist mainly of grants, guaranteed low-interest loans, College Work-Study programs, or a combination of these

and related programs? Few people question the correctness of
federal support, but strong disagreements persist about levels
and types of funding.

The principal arguments for outright grants are that they
provide genuine equality of opportunity in both access and
choice, and that they limit the burden of debt students must bear
after graduation. The main arguments against are that the grants
require taxpayers who have never enjoyed the benefits of educational opportunity to help provide them for other people, and
that they are costly to the nation—especially in light of rising
national debt. The principal arguments for loans are that they
offer equality of opportunity *and* call for the recipient of the
benefit to pay a major portion of its costs; repayment eases the
financial load on the nation. The main argument against loans is
that the prospect of debt or market interest rates discourages
many students from continuing to go to school.

The College Work-Study Program enables colleges and universities to offer part-time jobs to students. The government and
the institution share costs. The main arguments for the program
are that it helps students to earn their opportunities, enriches
their educational experience by giving them work responsibilities, reduces student debt, and makes institutions and the nation
partners.

The main arguments against are, first, that few institutions
actually provide jobs that join work and study, as with library
and laboratory assistants. Many actually use the program to
employ students in service jobs that are unrelated to studies and
are services the institutions are obliged to provide. In addition,
critics argue that providing the money directly to institutions
reduces student choice; that the program is more costly than
loans and yields less cost-sharing; that the funds sometimes
support students who do not need them; and that there already
are ample employment opportunities for college students.

A main thread runs through these pro and con arguments: The
education of the American people is achieved by institutions in
the independent sector and the state sector. Those in the latter
category charge lower tuition because they enjoy vastly larger
state appropriations. If the main sources of federal financial aid
are loans, more students will attend the less expensive schools;
such a pattern will require costly expansion of the state institu-

tions and involve massive waste of the facilities and educational resources of independent ones. Without federal financial aid, the argument runs, many of our finest colleges and universities would be genuinely accessible only to the wealthy. Such a situation would reduce independent education to an elitism of wealth.

These issues cannot be separated from other basic questions concerning the national economy—inflation, corporate productivity, and employment. When the economy is highly inflationary, tuition and fees rise generally, but often the real income of teachers and administrators cannot keep pace, expensive but necessary plant maintenance is deferred, and institutional levels of financial aid lag behind. Similarly, if corporations and individuals suffer in a weak economy, charitable contributions to educational institutions decline. Such patterns in the national economy have long-term consequences for students, because educational institutions tend to continue to raise prices to recoup costs after inflation rates have declined. In some cases, institutions raise tuition because they find it easier than raising endowment funds and because tuition increases will not adversely affect enrollment. But many institutions work faithfully to secure endowment, control costs, and keep price increases as low as they can while still maintaining their facilities and trying to pay decent salaries. It is very difficult to tell the extent to which tuition and fee increases in any particular institution are justified without a careful look at its financial resources, its patterns of expenditure, and its habits of budgetary control.

Those who make federal policy would do well to address questions about direct forms of aid to students and to education with due regard to the overall economic context. As the late Arthur F. Burns explained, "one of the clearest lessons of our history and that of other countries is that bigotry, class hatred, and discrimination have the best chance to thrive when a nation's economy becomes depressed and the ranks of its unemployed multiply. A healthy and strong economy is therefore essential to our way of life so that justice and fair treatment to all citizens alike may be preserved and indeed enlarged in our country."[2] To this may be added the fact that, since social justice depends on distributing wealth for the sake of opportunity, there must be wealth to distribute. The economic well-being of the country is fundamental to the well-being of educational opportunity because, as Michael Novak observes, "The main problem of social justice is not distribution; it is *production* . . . The ethic of productivity precedes the ethic of distribution."[3]

Within this broad context, then, we must provide forms of financial aid that promote real opportunity not only in access but in choice; that are fair to the taxpayers; that promote educational service by institutions in both the independent and the state sectors; that develop the intellectual capital of America; and that use the nation's financial resources prudently. These ends require a combination of grant and loan programs and an emphasis on programs that make institutions and the states partners in sharing costs. For this reason, revolving state and institutional loan funds whose costs are shared by the nation, the institutions, and the states, and need-based grants from the states and from colleges and universities to limit borrowing by students are especially important. Policies for loan repayment should be sensitive to individual income so that debt can be repaid without undue hardship. At the same time, we must minimize default on repayment of loans because default impairs opportunity for subsequent generations of students.

If we are to develop most fruitfully the intellectual capital of the American people, we must also look beyond need-based financial aid to financial support of high academic performance. We cannot afford to neglect academic merit, irrespective of need, especially in times when popular attitudes favor "entitlement" over achievement.

Many of my colleagues in education oppose merit scholarships on the premises that, if good students want to go to college, and they have the money, they *will* go, and, that if good students do not have the money, they will be eligible for need-based financial aid.

These arguments seem to me unpersuasive. Even our best students can be discouraged from pursuing education to their fullest advantage if they are concerned about personal or family debt, if they attend undemanding institutions, or if they assume that academic merit does not count for much. The proper issue is not so much whether academic accomplishment should be celebrated and rewarded, but by whom. Prevailing attitudes, however, may dramatically limit rewards for students' merit from the country, the states, and the educational institutions themselves; we should not allow this to happen—at any level.

The Department of Education has proposed rescinding all Work-Study funds after 1987 on the grounds that these grants do not join work with study; that they increase college revenues but do not necessarily provide aid to needy students; that providing income to institutions rather than individuals tends to reduce students' chances to attend the institutions of their choice;[4] and that more total money can be provided students by state and federal participation in loan programs.

The fact that a program does not always accomplish its purposes or that it is subject to misuse is not, however, a sufficient reason to eliminate it. If it were, we would have to eliminate all social programs, for none of them is perfect. In my judgment, the principal issue in this case is whether college jobs must be directly related to academic study for the program to be justified.

A job that enables a student to help pay his own way to college provides educational opportunity and may teach important lessons about personal diligence and responsibility, no matter whether the job is filing in an admissions office or assisting in a laboratory. Is this not justification enough for such job programs? I am sympathetic to the idea that students should work to pay a portion of their own educational costs. I am also mindful of the temptation that working students may come to think of themselves not primarily as students, and that time spent working may inordinately divert attention from study in the scholarly and scientific disciplines. I think work-study programs should emphasize that students are, above all, *students,* by requiring that eligible jobs be directly related to academic progress. Such an emphasis is one more means by which government can contribute to the development of intellectual capital.

Financial aid is not of course the whole of the federal budget for higher education. A much smaller portion provides grants directly to educational institutions. These competitive grants are awarded by such agencies as the National Endowment for the Arts, the National Endowment for the Humanities, and the

Fund for the Improvement of Postsecondary Education. Projects in curriculum development, faculty development, and expanded student opportunity have high priority, and the earlier themes I have addressed have special implications for policy in these areas.

Curriculum Development

As the development of sound curricula depends on institutional purposes, priority should be given to institutions with clear commitments to intellectual discipline. No funds should be awarded without evidence that the institution is trying to make conditions of student and faculty life *and* the curriculum supportive of educational mission.

The curriculum is a program of study and should reflect the intellectual priorities and convictions of the institution's faculty and administration. They must teach it, and thus they should build it. Therefore, funding should not be provided to develop academic curriculum packages by educational organizations outside educational institutions. Such packages diminish the importance of faculty knowledge; they function by analogy to "teacher-proof" curricula. If the members of a faculty are sufficiently knowledgeable to bear the trust of classroom duty, they are competent to design sound courses. If they need academic packages, they are not sufficiently knowledgeable. It *may* be worthwhile to fund highly rigorous packages by corporations, especially in technological areas where their competence is an addition to the resources in academe.

As work on curriculum strength is not episodic but continuous, grants should be awarded only to institutions that commit some portion of their own resources to ongoing work. Quick-fixes of curricula are illusory, so money should not be wasted on them.

Faculty Development

Faculty development means both the intellectual progress of individual faculty members and the forging of faculty members into a collegium. Because institutional gridlock is a dreadful obstacle to improvement, grants to institutions should support the latter over the former. For the same reason, proposals that also emphasize the involvement of administrators should be given priority. Individual faculty study can be supported through other research grants.

These priorities indicate that faculty development grants should provide opportunities for faculty and administrators within institutions and across institutional lines, as between schools and colleges, to study objects of shared interest. These interests derive their significance from the educational purposes of the institutions; thus, each request for funds should be assessed in terms of its visible relation to educational mission. The development of the intellectual power of a faculty is distinct from the development of curriculum; accordingly, faculty development grants should not be awarded for curriculum development.

Strong faculties and administrations do not develop in fits and starts any more than do strong curricula. Thus, in faculty development, too, the issue is the extent to which institutional resources are sought and secured for support of continuing programs that release faculty for shared study. Grant priority should be given to institutions that establish, or are working to establish, permanent programs, and not to support sporadic faculty development.

Because the significance of faculty development derives from institutional purposes, grants should not be awarded for the pursuit of current fashions. If, for example, an institution believes that it is essential to its mission for faculty and students to grasp concepts in ethics, and it designs a program of continuing faculty development for that purpose, then funding is worth consideration. But if an institution seeks funds to attract students to courses hastily conceived because of the public visibility of problems—such as government scandals, business corruption, or health care issues—there is no reason for confidence that faculty knowledge will be advanced or a collegium nurtured. Accordingly, there is no warrant for funding.

Expanded Student Opportunity

Every curriculum excludes much that is worthy of study. Time rather than lack of merit makes limits necessary. For this reason, many institutions seek external funding of special courses and programs for students. In addition, as admissions standards are relaxed, many institutions admit students who need remedial courses. Here, too, one fundamental question is whether the institution shows resolve to be effective in remediation in a way that reflects its educational purposes. Remediation is not simply a classroom enterprise; it depends on student recruitment, orientation, and advising, and on rigorous evaluation of progress and failure. Funding should be awarded only when there is evidence of comprehensive planning for remediation. Likewise, special courses should be funded only when they can be regarded as means of access to the intellectual mainstreams of the institution.

Private Foundations

These considerations also apply to the funding guidelines of private foundations. Like government, private foundations should consider greater investment in merit scholarships. Some, such as the Beneficial-Hodson Trust, have already moved in this direction. The Beneficial-Hodson Scholars programs at Johns Hopkins University, Washington College, and Hood College deserve consideration by other benefactors. They are programs that are used to draw students of demonstrated academic accomplishment and to provide financial support for four years, thereby enriching the experience of all their students.

Some institutions oppose privately funded merit scholarships on the grounds that they deprive needy students of funds. This argument presumes that allocation of merit funds and need-based funds is zero-sum. It is a false presumption. Many benefactors who do not contribute to financial aid of any other kind may be persuaded to support merit scholarships. Furthermore, there is no injustice in trying by merit grants to provide all students with intellectually fertile companions, while there *is* injustice in failure to show the highest regard for performance.

There is a problem with colleges and universities that simply buy students, because there is no necessary connection between wealth and quality; thus, an exceptional student may be enticed to a school that is wealthy but does not offer educational programs of sufficient intellectual power to make the most of the student's potential. The student may discover this and transfer, but the problem does not always resolve itself that way.

It is a hard problem to tackle. Wealthy institutions are not always self-critical, but they are eager to draw highly able students. They are not likely to relinquish any of the advantages that attach to their wealth. This means that foundations and individual benefactors must be judicious and thorough in deciding which institutions and which forms of institutional improvement should have priority. For example, a foundation that considers funding merit scholarships when it knows that an institution's curriculum is in disarray or its retention of highly qualified faculty is falling off, could do more good by trying to help the institution face its fundamental problems first.

When the educational quality of institutions is above question, foundations may want to consider the utility of Bard College's tuition equalization plan. In that plan, students of superior accomplishment are charged the tuition they would pay at the public universities of their home state—one form of merit scholarship for which partial foundation funding is often required. The plan also promotes economic diversity among students in independent higher education.

Private foundations that support curriculum and faculty development should also determine what elements of continuity are needed for the investment of their resources to be productive. For them, too, the funding of episodic projects is not likely to result in long-term institutional improvements.

RECENT POLICY RECOMMENDATIONS

The National Commission on Excellence in Education

In April 1983, the National Commission on Excellence in Education, appointed by Secretary of Education T. H. Bell, submitted its report, *A Nation At Risk: The Imperative for Educational Reform*. The report declared:

> [T]he educational foundations of our society are presently being eroded by a rising tide of mediocrity that threatens our very future as a nation and a people. . . . Our society and its educational institutions seem to have lost sight of the basic purposes of schooling, and of the high expectations and disciplined effort needed to attain them.[5]

Declining student achievement, high rates of functional illiteracy, increased need for remedial courses, and unreadiness of many high school graduates for work or college contributed to this conclusion: "Secondary school curricula have been homogenized, diluted, and diffused to the point that they no longer have a central purpose."[6] "Too many teachers are being drawn from the bottom quarter of graduating high school and college students."[7]

The commission described one "common expectation: we must demand the best effort and performance from all students, whether they are gifted or less able, affluent or disadvantaged, whether destined for college, the farm, or industry."[8] To this end, the commission proposed expanded high school requirements for all students in English, mathematics, science, and social studies; foreign language study beginning in the elementary grades; elevation of admission standards in colleges and universities; improved textbooks; increased homework; an extended school year; development and enforcement of fair codes of student conduct; sanctions for absenteeism; higher salaries for teachers including eleven-month contracts to ensure time for curricular and intellectual development, with similar investment in superintendents and principals; and adequate financing by the states, with leadership at the national level. It called each parent, as a child's "first and most influential teacher," to be "a *living* example of what you expect your children to honor and emulate."[9]

If elementary and secondary schools are able to rise to such standards, students will be ready for the best that higher education has to offer.

The National Commission on the Role and Future of State Colleges and Universities

In November 1986, the National Commission on the Role and Future of State Colleges and Universities issued a report called *To Secure the Blessings of Liberty*. Described by the association as a "political" document, the report notes that "only 8.8 percent of black Americans, 7.8 percent of Hispanic Americans, and less than 1.5 percent of Native Americans have a bachelor's degree. Nearly 50 million American families have never had a college graduate in their households."[10] The report argues that educational opportunity will be curtailed unless state colleges and universities maintain low tuition and receive more federal money. Appealing to the reliance of democracy on an educated public, to standards of equity, and to the economic and international power that derives from high levels of education, the report cautions against elitist policies, i.e., educational opportunity only for the rich and the very bright.

The report projects a dearth of new and qualified schoolteachers and encourages close cooperation among state colleges and universities and schools to achieve good academic standards and to address current pedagogical problems. Furthermore, "Because the crisis in teacher education is national in scope, the Commission recommends that Congress reinstitute the student loan forgiveness program for college graduates entering the teaching profession."[11]

The commission proposes that state colleges and universities adopt "a set of minimum academic skills and levels of proficiency that all students should attain, preferably by the end of the sophomore year. . . . Each college and university should further specify . . . the means by which it will facilitate their acquisition by every student. . . . "[12]

The central theme of the report is that "America has far too many people whose abilities are never awakened," and that this is a "staggering waste and dissipation of our most precious resource" resulting in "unemployment, unenlightened citizen participation or nonparticipation in elections and other processes of democracy, reduced productivity, and personal stagnation leading to frustration, crime, and abuse of freedom."[13]

These claims and inferences are often overstated. For example, it is true that many Americans never aspire to make much of their intellectual gifts, and that this places them and the country at a disadvantage. It does not follow, however, as the report implies, that greater investment of money for higher education by the federal government would necessarily change this for the better. Improving schools and restraining troublemakers take precedence. Closer cooperation between higher education and the schools in order to build an academic profession with shared ideals is needed if we wish even to speak of schoolteachers entering "the teaching profession"; alliances between local schools and colleges require more local or state funds to provide released time for schoolteachers.

Minimum academic standards within each college and university are absolutely obligatory; without such standards, what are the state institutions offering to students in return for tuition and to taxpayers in return for subsidization? Now, in fact, many state schools are among the best colleges and universities in America; their standards are far above any minimum, and they should be emulated by others.

The 91 per cent of black Americans, 92 per cent of Hispanic Americans, or 98.5 per cent of native Americans who do not have bachelor's degrees are by no means all unemployed, indifferent citizens, criminals, or a drain on the country. Many of them are deprived by circumstances of some of the fundamental blessings of liberty, and no one of any sense would deny it. But we should look to the quality of their schooling, their neighborhoods, their protection by the law, their family circumstances, and the health care available to them before concluding that increased spending for higher education is *the* key to increasing their educational achievement.

Nothing is guaranteed by increased federal funding for drawing more people into college except that more people will be drawn into college. Race makes no difference; sex makes no difference; ethnic heritage makes no difference. Mere entry means *nothing* unless the education provided is intellectually fertile and students are prepared to take advantage of it. If colleges and universities have serious admission requirements, more money will not gain entry for unprepared students. And, if the colleges are open to everyone, they have, mainly, three ways of proceeding: They can, as many have, establish remedial programs; they can lower academic standards; or they can fail students who were never prepared to do the work but were nevertheless admitted. The first path forces the work of the schools onto colleges and takes the meaning out of "higher" education; the work of schools should be done primarily in schools and we should persist in trying to improve them. The second path cannot benefit either students or the nation; the third path drives unprepared students into a slaughterhouse and is scarcely more than "opportunity" to be doomed to failure from the outset.

This problem of federal funding and admissions can be addressed only by forthright thinking and action in favor of standards in each institution, standards that give substance to the word *opportunity*. A qualitative problem of this kind cannot be solved by financial aid for higher education because it is not a financial aid problem. When the problems of *quality* have been addressed by schools, colleges, and universities, and they have some shared sense of what constitutes preparedness for higher education, then many students of all backgrounds who are adequately prepared but cannot afford to go to college should be helped. Financial aid for them will deserve high priority.

Even so, we must remember that those who cannot afford college are not in the same category as those who must incur some reasonable debt in order to do so. Some prospective students will be hampered by counselors who do not know enough to explain financial options to them. Where better counseling is needed, along with greater outreach, the educational institutions are obliged to provide them. Financial aid ought not to spare them this obligation. Historically, many among us have incurred debt for the sake of education, and there is no reason to conclude that opportunity must be universally debt-free.

As for attracting future teachers, loan forgiveness is a trifling consideration in the choice of one's life work, and people should not be encouraged to make the choice to bear the public trust for a few thousand dollars. If what we seek is a more substantial applicant pool and greater permanence among schoolteachers, we must address the problems of working conditions, including student discipline, opportunities for intellectual maturation, and overall compensation. The reallocation of financial resources is crucial, but loan forgiveness will not begin to achieve it.

Because these issues cannot be dealt with entirely at the federal level, every effort should be made by the federal government to encourage and sustain local and state funding and other conscientious action. The states' move to compulsory schooling in the 1930s is instructive: The federal government had no authority to make schooling compulsory, but it strongly encouraged the states to do so. The federal government can play this part again. Along these lines, the Department of Education, for example, included $80 million in the 1988 budget for teacher training and improvement, with 80 per cent of the funds to be used for state and local programs.[14]

The Carnegie Foundation for the Advancement of Teaching

In the 1987 Carnegie Foundation report *College: The Under-graduate Experience in America,* Ernest L. Boyer, president of the foundation, writes:

> A quality college is guided by a clear and vital mission. The institution cannot be all things to all people. . . . A coherent curriculum is only the beginning. Good faculty are essential to a good college.[15]

Rarely, however, does a good faculty emerge from a good curriculum; the faculty, not the curriculum, are the beginning. But Boyer does stress the need of staff and trustees with intellectual and moral virtue:

> In addition to the traditional functions of setting policy, selecting presidents, and approving budgets and key personnel appointments, trustees should participate in shaping institutional priorities, involving themselves especially in reviewing the quality of the undergraduate experience. . . .[16]
> In the end, governance is to be measured not by the formality of the structure but by the integrity of the participants, by the willingness of individuals to work together in support of shared purposes.[17]

To achieve these purposes, Boyer proposes two important steps. First, for orientation of students, he urges "a short-term credit course for new students, perhaps entitled 'The College: Its Values and Traditions.' Such a seminar . . . should pay special attention to the academic traditions of the college and help students understand how scholars carry on their work."[18] The college president should "be a leader in introducing students to the college."[19] Second, as a culminating exercise for the under-graduate, Boyer proposes "that students be asked to write a senior thesis that would relate the major to historical, social or ethical concerns," and "participate in a senior seminar, with no more than twenty other students, where students would present their reports orally and criticize the papers of fellow students."[20]

In practice, few orientation programs initiate students in the common purposes of civilized intelligence and the ideals of higher learning in free countries. Indeed, few students learn of the resources available to them in a school, college, or university, let alone how to make effective use of them. Well-designed courses for orientation—introducing students to the reasons for which the institutions they attend have been created and sustained—would be profoundly valuable, especially if they included fine readings in addition to sound lectures and discussion. The involvement of the president of the institution is highly desirable, because the president cannot adequately represent the institution to donors, trustees, and parents without knowing what students are being taught about common purposes. And he can hardly encourage loyalty to common purposes without investing personal effort in their behalf.

For the senior thesis to be worthwhile, it must be more than merely an overgrown term paper. To stimulate reading, writing, and thinking throughout the undergraduate years and to invite the application of specialized knowledge to broad issues, the thesis must be an exercise for which students are carefully prepared throughout the undergraduate program. Only then can it help them to overcome the shallowness of mere breadth and the narrowness of mere specialization.

Specifically, if the thesis is to make the most of both core studies and studies in the major, it must presuppose that high levels of skill and content retention are achieved by students over four years. Comprehensive examinations at the end of the sophomore and/or junior years are very likely necessary to ascertain whether the levels of retention are adequate for undertaking the senior thesis. And, to make the thesis as rigorous as possible, emphasis must be placed not only on reading and writing, but also on mathematics and the natural sciences. Lack of attention to these severely impairs intellectual rigor.

If the senior thesis of each student were advised by faculty members from different departments, the process could contribute to faculty development as well. And, if trustees review the "undergraduate experience," as Boyer suggests, they should read the essays of seniors and attend orals. To the extent possible, they should read the texts of the orientation course as well, and, when they are on campus, they should attend these and other classes. If the board of trustees as a whole is unable to do all this, a visiting committee composed of qualified members who are able to be on campus with some regularity should be chosen.

Boyer is especially concerned about the transition of students from high school to college. He recommends that the Educational Testing Service (ETS) and the College Board, among others, "establish regional advisement centers throughout the country" to teach high school counselors more about the range of colleges and universities in each region. He urges the same agencies to provide grants to enable schools to strengthen counseling services and to enable counselors to visit colleges and universities. The American Council on Education is called upon to establish a code of conduct for student recruitment, and accreditation associations are asked to review recruitment procedures as a part of their evaluation.[21]

As well-intentioned as these recommendations may be, it would have been better to encourage public libraries in each community to make known their available reference books on colleges and universities. The colleges and universities that prepare high school counselors, not ETS and the College Board, are obliged to see to their knowledge of higher education and to their competence to advise students. Centers are not necessary if the educational institutions do their work properly. Perhaps regular mailings with relevant information about colleges and universities should be prepared by ETS and others, on the assumption that the counselors are sufficiently conscientious to read them. Moreover, schools should be expected to enable counselors to visit colleges and universities in their region. This should be a duty of every school, and its fulfillment should not depend on external grants that come and go.

National codes of conduct and accreditation reviews are less useful than responsible governance by the institutions themselves; if the institutions lack the character to tell the truth about themselves, national codes will not improve them, and accreditation reviews are seldom sustained long enough to detect anything but the most obvious deficiencies. Here, as elsewhere, we must finally depend on schools, colleges, and universities themselves to treat the trust of the public with respect and even reverence. They must provide the facts necessary for students and their families to make informed choices.

Corporations may be of direct service to their neighborhood schools by establishing grants for counseling and advising students. Many companies presently award college scholarships to students in local schools. It would also be useful for companies to inquire how many local students who want to go to college do not do so for lack of funds. Where this is an issue, corporate grants for counselors to secure information on available funds, to travel to institutions in the state, and to invite college and governmental financial aid officers to visit and explain how to secure grants and loans, may provide greater benefit to more students than a single corporate scholarship. But the counseling grants should be provided every year until the schools fund the activities adequately, and the corporations should insist that their grants are intended only to provide time for the transition.

CONCLUSION: PUBLIC SELF-RELIANCE

Even if schools, colleges, and universities throughout America attend to the achievement of common purposes with liberty, and even if the wisest possible institutional and public policies are implemented, the well-being of our children and their children will not be secure. Formal education, no matter how sound, is not the entirety of education. Educational opportunity, no matter how hugely financed by public and private funds, is not the totality of opportunity.

Members of the public should be able to trust the schools, colleges, and universities they and their children attend. They must also earn their own trust as mothers and fathers, as citizens.

As C. S. Lewis explains in *The Abolition of Man,* "When a Roman father told his son that it was a sweet and seemly thing to die for his country, he believed what he said. He was communicating to the son an emotion which he himself shared and which he believed to be in accord with the value which his judgment discerned in noble death. He was giving the boy the best he had, giving of his spirit to humanize him as he had given of his body to beget him."[22] The propagation of the spirit of daughters and sons by mothers and fathers is crucial to human maturation. Formal education cannot provide it.

Parents must give their children the best they have at home, their most deeply held and considered convictions, along with their love, and they must try to make their best good enough. If children learn at home that classrooms are not part of the real world, schooling will seldom be able to do them much good intellectually. If they learn from their parents that the sole purpose of education is to make money, they will treat everything in their schooling not obviously connected to this end as superfluous. If at home they learn indifference to informed judgment as citizens, their courses in civics, history, and political theory will be taught at a disastrous disadvantage. If they learn to look out only for the proverbial Number One, emphasis in formal education on justice and liberty will accomplish little. If they learn at home that subjects they don't like are a waste of time, no core curriculum will have a fair chance to cultivate fully their natural talents. Education can be undermined at home as surely as it can be encouraged. Every parent who lovingly understands a child, every parent who seeks to grasp the world as a child does, knows how powerfully true this is.

If parents want the education of their children to be fertile, they will have to plow the ground at home. This takes devotion, and it takes attention to basic questions: What kind of mind do I want my children to have? How can they achieve good judgment? It does not matter whether a child studies the liberal arts, the fine arts, or the manual arts; whether the curriculum emphasizes philosophy, physics, drama, or automobile mechanics, the questions to ask are: Do you want your children to be able to make wise decisions about how to behave toward others? Then teach them by example how to behave decently. Do you want your children to detect bias in propaganda and the misleading aspects of advertising? Then read the paper and watch commercials with them. When a commercial sells a bill of goods, explain how; when an aspirin company says that more doctors recommend the *ingredients* in its brand, ask your children why the commercial is careful not to say that the doctors recommend *its* brand. Ask them why advertisements describe automobiles as "previously owned" rather than "used"; watch how they react to advertisements for "genuine artificial" mink coats. Again: Do you want your children to have abundant imagination? Then act out fables with them—fables like that of the crow in the desert who cannot get his beak into a pitcher to reach the water; with great patience, he places one pebble after another in the pitcher until the water rises to his beak. Do you want your children to be safe drivers who are less vulnerable to the foolishness of other drivers? Then teach them to use their eyes, ears, and minds, to observe and predict as much as possible, and show them how you observe and predict, and how you exercise caution in the face of uncertainty. Their schools will then be better able to teach them to observe and predict in a laboratory. Teach them, too, how to avoid unnecessary risk, just as Madison avoided unnecessary risk by building checks and balances into government. Again: Do you want your children to understand that sexual promiscuity is morally, emotionally, and physically dangerous? Then help them to see that human sexuality is a matter of profound importance that affects the deepest dimensions of personality and character and also the way we think of ourselves and other people. *Show* them how loving parents treat each other.

In everything that happens every day to everyone, the crucial issue is the power of mind we bring to living. The point is exactly the same in writing a scholarly work, repairing a transmission, seeking a job, or going on a date: Are you able to exercise good judgment? Can you trust your own mind to grasp what is going on and to make decisions knowledgeably? No matter what, specifically, we want for our children—scholarly attainment, professional standing, a good income, decency, happiness—*this* fact of the human condition applies to us all, and it never changes.

Thus, if we want our children to profit fully from formal education, we must, as parents, nurture attitudes and respect for ideals and the qualities of mind that illuminate the possibilities of schooling. And, if we want them to enjoy the blessings of a free country that enable genuine education rather than manipulation and propaganda, we must alert them to the effort and vigilance that are the indispensable guardians of liberty.

To do this, we can encourage our children as they grow in the ways Mentor Graham encouraged Abraham Lincoln:

> After Lincoln had been to school for a short time, he told the schoolmaster, "I believe I can go it alone. I can read and write and cipher a bit." Graham responded, kindly, "Yes, so you can, and better than most; but that is only the introduction to knowledge, only the keys."[23]

And when Lincoln, at the age of twenty, in the process of "ketchin' up" on schooling, would grumble that "larnin' ain't such great shakes; no farmer has a needin' to larn sechlike," Graham was ready with a response about the life of citizens and their country: "Lazy minds make a dying nation, young man."[24]

These lessons—that it is foolish to quit learning when you are just a beginner and that it is dangerous to ignore your opportunities as a citizen—should be taught our children at home. These are lessons of love, and they are blessings adults should deliver to their own young.

All of this takes time, and of course it often seems that the pressure of other activities limits the time parents can devote to their children. We speak, therefore, of the importance of "quality" time, but quality is not the only thing that matters. *Being* together matters, because the intimacy of parental love matters. Of course, the lessons learned in companionship are important, but few are more telling than the simple lesson that we love our children enough not to be rushed away to other things.

Perhaps we should recall "A Cradle Song" by W. B. Yeats, for it describes how precious is the time we spend with our children:

> *The angels are stooping*
> *Above your bed;*
> *They weary of trooping*
> *With the whimpering dead.*
>
> *God's laughing in Heaven*
> *To see you so good;*
> *The Sailing Seven*
> *Are gay with his mood.*
>
> *I sigh that kiss you,*
> *For I must own*
> *That I shall miss you*
> *When you have grown.*[25]

In the embrace of love, propagation flourishes. For the propagation of the spirit, mothers and fathers must be able to rely, above all, on themselves. If, as Hutcheson insisted, the country is to "preserve our objects of endearment to us," and if formal education is to advance their well-being, it is as surely true that we must give the best of ourselves to our children. No one can bear this trust for us. No one can bear this trust except us.

Notes

CHAPTER ONE

1. Alexis de Tocqueville, *Democracy in America,* trans. George Lawrence, ed. J. P. Mayer (Garden City, New York: Anchor Books, 1969), pp. 197, 440.

2. Alexander Hamilton, James Madison, and John Jay, *The Federalist Papers,* Introduction by Clinton Rossiter, (New York: Mentor Books, 1961). In *Federalist 1,* Hamilton refers to the experiment: "It has frequently been remarked that it seems to have been reserved to the people of this country, by their conduct and example, to decide the important question, whether societies of men are really capable or not of establishing good government from reflection and choice, or whether they are forever destined to depend for their political constitutions on accident and force" [p. 33]. In *Federalist 14,* Madison refers to our "experiment of an extended republic" [p. 104].

3. *Northwest Ordinance,* Article Three.

4. Alfred North Whitehead, *The Function of Reason* (Princeton University Press, 1929), p. 2.

5. *The Digest of Education Statistics* (Washington, D.C.: United States Department of Education, 1987), pp. 15–18.

6. *Sweezy* v. *New Hampshire,* 354 U.S. 234, 262–263 (1957), Frankfurter, J., concurring.

7. Francis Hutcheson, *A Short Introduction to Moral Philosophy, In Three Books; Containing the Elements of Ethicks and the Law of Nature* (Glasgow: Printed and Sold by Robert Foulis, Printer to the University of Glasgow, 1747), p. 347.

8. Francis Hutcheson, *A System of Moral Philosophy in Three Books* (Glasgow: R. and A. Foulis, Printers to the University of Glasgow, 1755; reprint ed., New York: August M. Kelley, 1968), p. 285.

9. Ibid.

10. Ibid., p. 335.

11. Smith Hempstone, "Carnegie visits the colleges," *Washington Times,* November 21, 1986, p. E1.

12. Judith Block McLaughlin and David Riesman, "The Shady Side of Sunshine," *Teachers College Record,* Volume 87, No. 4 (Summer 1986), p. 471.

13. Ibid., p. 487.

14. J. Myron Atkin, "Washington vs. The Public Schools," Ethics and Public Policy Center Reprint Number 26 (December 1980), p. 87.

15. Ibid., p. 91.

16. James B. Conant, *The Education of American Teachers* (New York: McGraw Hill, 1963), p. 38.

17. Smith Hempstone, "Carnegie visits the colleges," p. E1.

18. Ibid.

19. Fred M. Hechinger, "Learning by Rote," *The New York Times,* October 28, 1986, p. C11.

20. Bernard J. Weiss et al., *Freedom's Ground* (Units 4–6), Holt Basic Reading Teacher's Edition (New York: Holt, Rinehart, and Winston, 1983), p. T–481; also *Great Waves Breaking* (Level 17), pp. T–26, T–88.

21. Abraham Lincoln, *The Collected Works of Abraham Lincoln,* ed. Roy P. Basler (New Brunswick, New Jersey: Rutgers University Press, 1953), Volume III, p. 362.

22. Bruce De Silva, "Better Textbooks? Dim Outlook Ahead," *Curriculum Review,* (November/December 1986), p. 9.

23. *Mozert* v. *Hawkins County Public Schools,* 647 F. Supp. 1194 (E.D. Tenn. 1986), appeal docketed, No. 87–5024 (6th Cir. Jan. 13, 1987).

24. Horace Mann, *1837 Annual Report to the Massachusetts State Board of Education,* in ed. Herbert M. Kliebard *Religion and Education in America: A Documentary History* (Scranton, Pennsylvania: International Textbook Company, 1969), p. 68.

25. "Youth Suicide Prevention Act," *U.S. House of Representatives Report 99–667* (July 14, 1986), p. 2.

26. Carol E. Floyd, *Faculty Participation in Decision Making: Necessity or Luxury?,* ASHE-ERIC Higher Education Report No. 8 (Washington, D.C.: Association for the Study of Higher Education, 1985), p. iv.

27. Edward Shils, *The Academic Ethic* (Chicago: University of Chicago Press, 1984), p. 16.

28. Gerald Grant, "Education, Character, and American Schools," Ethics and Public Policy Center Reprint Number 32 (December 1981), pp. 147, 148.

29. Gilbert Highet, *The Art of Teaching* (New York: Random House Vintage Books, 1950), p. 60.

30. Ibid., p. 31.

31. Immanuel Kant, *Education,* trans. Annette Churton (Ann Arbor, Michigan: University of Michigan Press, 1960), 1.4, 5 pp. 3, 4.

32. Thomas Sowell, "Patterns of Black Excellence," Ethics and Public Policy Center Reprint Number 5 (December 1977), p. 5.

33. Ibid., p. 56.

34. "College Chiefs Gather at Harvard for Answers to Rising Flood of Criticism," *The Newark Star Ledger,* November 14, 1986, p. 7.

35. Robert L. Jacobson, "Efforts to Assess Students' Learning May Trivialize the B.A., Boyer Says," *Chronicle of Higher Education,* October 15, 1986, p. 41.

36. "Coach Says He Padded Players' Grades," *Washington Post,* October 9, 1986, p. B2.

37. "Langley Coach Is Fired In Eavesdropping Incident," *Washington Post,* October 9, 1986, pp. E1, E3.

38. Edward B. Fiske, "Free Speech Debate," *The New York Times,* October 4, 1986, p. B25.

39. George Will, "Not Your Basic Beach Book," *Newsweek,* July 7, 1986, p. 68.

CHAPTER TWO

1. Alexander Hamilton, James Madison, John Jay, *The Federalist Papers,* Introduction by Clinton Rossiter (New York: Mentor Books, 1961), p. 59.

2. Alfred North Whitehead, *The Aims of Education* (New York: Free Press, 1957), p. 13.

3. Laird Bell, Detler W. Brooks, Paul H. Bucks, John E. Millett, et. al., *Nature and Needs of Higher Education* (New York: Columbia University Press, 1952), pp. 31, 32.

4. Rene Descartes, "Discourse on the Method of Rightly Conducting the Reason and Seeking for Truth in the Sciences," *ab. init.,* in *The Philosophical Works of Descartes,* trans. Elizabeth S. Haldane and G. R. T. Ross (Cambridge: Cambridge University Press, 1911), Vol. 1.

5. Saint Augustine, *The City of God,* ed. Vernon J. Bourke, trans. Gerald G. Walsh, S. J., Demetrius E. Zema, S. J., Grace Monahan, O.S.U., Daniel J. Honan (Garden City, New York: Doubleday, 1958), especially: "In fact, the city of man, for the most part, is a city of contention with opinions divided by foreign wars and by the demands for victories which either end in death or are merely momentary respites from further war" (p. 327);"The simple truth is that the bond of common nature makes all human beings one. Nevertheless, each individual in the community is driven by his passions to pursue his private purposes. Unfortunately, the objects of these purposes are such that no one person (let alone, the world community) can ever be wholly satisfied. . . . The result is that the city of man remains in a chronic condition of civil war" (p. 392); "What, then, men want in war is that it should end in peace. Even while waging a war every man wants peace. . . . And even when men are plotting to disturb the peace, it is merely to fashion a peace nearer to the heart's desire; it is not because they dislike peace as such. It is not that they love peace less, but that they love their kind of peace more" (p. 452).

6. Antoine de Saint Exupery, *Wartime Writings 1939–1944,* trans. Norah Purcell (New York: Harcourt Brace Jovanovich, 1986), p. 32.

7. Thomas Hobbes, *Leviathan,* ed. C. B. Macpherson (Baltimore: Penguin Books, 1968), Part 1, chap. 13, p. 186.

8. Ibid., Part 2, chap. 17, p. 223.

9. Thomas Hobbes, *"De Cive",* in *Man and Citizen,* ed. Bernard Gert (Garden City, New York: Doubleday, 1972), chap. 5, section 8, p. 170.

10. Tocqueville observes that a slave, because he understands that he is not responsible for himself, "peacefully enjoys all the privileges of his humiliation." *(Democracy in America,* p. 318.) This, too, gives the tyrant purchase on the lives of the oppressed.

11. Isaiah Berlin, *Four Essays on Liberty* (New York: Oxford University Press, 1969), p. 167.

12. Michael Crozier, *The Trouble With America,* trans. Peter Heinegg (Berkeley, California: University of California Press, 1984), p. 83.

13. B.C. Brymer, *Abraham Lincoln in Peoria, Illinois* (Peoria, Illinois: Edward J. Jacob Printer, 1926), p. 103.

14. James Q. Wilson and Richard Herrenstein, *Crime and Human Nature* (New York: Simon and Schuster, 1985), p. 27.

15. Ibid., p. 66.

16. Alexander Hamilton, James Madison, John Jay, *The Federalist Papers,* Introduction by Clinton Rossiter (New York: Mentor Books, 1961), p. 79.

17. Ibid., p. 322.

18. Ibid., p. 346.

19. Aleksandr Solzhenitsyn, *A World Split Apart* (New York: Harper and Row, 1978), p. 21.

20. Ibid., pp. 21, 23.

21. Reinhold Niebuhr, *The Children of Light and the Children of Darkness* (New York: Charles Scribner's Sons, 1972), p. viii.

22. J. Myron Atkin, "Washington vs. The Public Schools," Ethics and Public Policy Center Reprint Number 26 (December 1980), p. 97.

23. Edward Shils, *The Academic Ethic* (Chicago: University of Chicago Press, 1984), p. 6.

24. Marcus Aurelius, *Meditations,* trans. George Long (South Bend, Indiana: Regnery-Gateway, Inc., 1956), Book II, 7, p. 14.

25. John A. Beach, "The Management and Governance of Academic Institutions," *Journal of College and University Law,* Vol. 12, No. 3 (Winter 1985), p. 338.

26. Ibid., p. 332.

27. Ibid., pp. 339, 340.

28. "Sexual Harassment Policies Under Review by Colleges," *Chronicle of Higher Education,* December 17, 1986, p. 16.

29. William J. Bennett, *To Reclaim a Legacy: A Report on the Humanities in Higher Education* (Washington, D.C.: The National Endowment for the Humanities, 1984), p. 25.

30. Ibid.

31. Lloyd H. Elliott, "Changing Internal Structures: The Relevance of Democracy," in *The Future Academic Community,* ed. John Calfrey (Washington, D.C.: American Council on Education, 1969), p. 50.

CHAPTER THREE

1. Josiah Royce, *The Religious Aspect of Philosophy: A Critique of the Bases of Conduct and of Faith* (Boston: Houghton Mifflin Company, 1885), pp. 157–162. The passage is William James's abridgement of these pages of Chapter 6:5, "Altruism and Insight," as it appears in "On a Certain Blindness in Human Beings," in *The Writings of William James,* ed. John J. McDermott (Chicago, Illinois: The University of Chicago Press, 1976), pp. 633, 634.

2. John Dewey, "Teaching Ethics in the High School," *The Early Works of John Dewey, 1882–1898* (Carbondale and Edwardsville, Illinois: Southern Illinois University Press, Feffer and Simons, Inc., 1971) Vol. IV, p. 57.

3. Stephen Crane, "War is Kind," in *The Portable Stephen Crane,* ed. Joseph Katz (New York: Penguin Books, 1977), p. 548.

4. II Maccabees, 6:24–25, *Anchor Bible,* Introduction and Commentary by Jonathan A. Goldstein (Garden City, New York: Doubleday and Company, 1983), p. 281.

5. Ibid., 6:31, p. 282.

6. Jon Moline, "Teachers and Professionalism," in *Against Mediocrity: The Humanities in America's High Schools,* eds. Chester E. Finn, Diane Ravitch, and Robert T. Fancher (New York: Holmes and Meier Publishers, Inc., 1984), p. 207.

7. John R. Silber, "Soul Politics and Political Morality," *Ethics,* Vol. 79, No. 1 (October 1968), p. 22.

8. Ibid.

9. William James, "On a Certain Blindness in Human Beings," in McDermott, *The Writings of William James*, p. 629.

10. Ibid., p. 630.

11. Ibid.,

12. Thomas Hobbes, *Leviathan*, ed. C. B. McPherson (Baltimore: Penguin Books, 1968), Part I, chap. 13, p. 184.

13. Martin Luther King, Jr., "Letter from Birmingham Jail," in *A Testament of Hope: The Essential Writings of Martin Luther King, Jr.*, ed. James Melvin Washington (San Francisco: Harper and Row, Publishers, 1986), p. 292.

14. William James, "On a Certain Blindness in Human Beings," in McDermott, pp. 630, 631.

15. Antoine de Saint Exupery, *Wartime Writings 1939–1944*, trans. Norah Purcell (New York: Harcourt Brace Jovanovich Publishers, 1986), pp. 13–15.

16. Winston Churchill, *The Gathering Storm* (Boston: Houghton Mifflin Co., The Riverside Press, Cambridge, 1948), pp. 325, 326.

17. Martin Gilbert, *Winston Churchill: The Wilderness Years* (Boston: Houghton Mifflin Co., 1982), p. 227.

18. B.C. Brymer, *Abraham Lincoln in Peoria, Illinois* (Peoria, Illinois: Edward J. Jacob Printer, 1926), p. 100.

19. Kunigunde Duncan and D.F. Nichols, *Mentor Graham* (Chicago: University of Chicago Press, 1944), p. 164.

20. Jacques Barzun, *Teacher in America* (Lanham, Maryland: University Press of America, 1986), p. 31.

21. Gilbert Highet, *The Art of Teaching* (New York: Random House Vintage Books, 1950), p. 248.

22. Joyce D. Stern and Mary Frare Williams, eds., *The Condition of Education, 1986 Edition* (Washington, D.C.: National Center for Education Statistics, 1986), p. 154.

23. Victoria Churchill, "Proposed Schools for the Disruptive Debated Again in P.G.," *The Washington Post*, December 21, 1986, pp. B1, B5.

24. Thomas Sowell, "Patterns of Black Excellence," Ethics and Public Policy Center Reprint Number 5 (December 1977), pp. 33, 54.

25. Nancy B. Dearman and Valena White Plisko, eds., *The Condition of Education, 1982 Edition* (Washington, D.C.: National Center for Education Statistics, 1982), p. 88.

26. Ibid.

27. Mary Hatwood Futrell, "The Cabbage-Patch Teacher," *Washington Post*, December 14, 1986, p. H5.

28. Gerald Grant, "Education, Character, and American Schools," Ethics and Public Policy Center Reprint Number 32 (December 1981), pp. 143, 144.

CHAPTER FOUR

1. A.E. Housman, *Introductory Lecture Delivered in University College London, October 3, 1892* (New York: MacMillan Company, 1937), pp. 32,33.

2. Plato, *Gorgias*, trans. W. C. Helmbold (New York: The Bobbs-Merrill Company, Inc., 1952), 485a–486a. pp. 53–55.

3. Seneca, *Letters from a Stoic*, trans. Robin Campbell (New York: Penguin Classics, 1969), Letter 27, p. 75.

4. Soren Kierkegaard, *Fear and Trembling and The Sickness Unto Death* (Garden City, New York: Doubleday and Company, Inc., 1954), p. 165.

5. Benito Mussolini, *My Autobiography* (New York: Charles Scribner's Sons, 1928), p. 22.

6. John Dewey, "Democracy and Education," in William K. Frankena, *Philosophy of Education* (Toronto, Ontario: Collier-MacMillan Canada, Ltd., 1965), p. 22.

7. Cicero, "On Friendship," in Cicero, *On Old Age and On Friendship,* trans. Harry G. Edinger (Indianapolis: Bobbs-Merrill, 1967), section 20, p. 51. Cicero's points have a long tradition. For the notion that "perfect" or "complete" friendship can exist only between good men, cf. Aristotle, *Nicomachean Ethics,* 8.3 1156b7, 8.4 1157a18. For the tyrant's lack of friends, we have Plato's account in *Gorgias,* 576a; *Republic,* 9, 576a; and his specific example of Dionysius in *Letter 8,* 331e, 332a, etc.

8. Ibid., section 52, p. 63.

9. John Dewey, "Self Realization as the Moral Ideal," *John Dewey, The Early Works 1882–1898* (Carbondale, Illinois: Southern Illinois University Press, 1971), Vol. IV, p. 50.

10. Seth Bernardete, trans., *Plato's Sophist: Part II of The Being of the Beautiful* (Chicago: University of Chicago, 1986), 246ab, p. 39.

11. Louis Raths, Merrill Harmon, and Sidney B. Simon, *Values and Teaching* (Columbus, Ohio: Charles E. Merrill Publishing Company, 1966), p. 54.

12. Michael Silver, *Values Education* (Washington, D.C.: National Education Association, 1976), p. 27.

13. Hans Oberdieck, "Who Is To Judge?" *Ethics,* Volume 87, No. 1 (October 1976), p. 77.

14. Ibid., p. 86.

15. William Arrowsmith, "The Future of Teaching," *The Public Interest,* Number 6 (Winter 1967), p. 54.

16. Jacques Maritain, "Education at the Crossroads," in William K. Frankena, *Philosophy of Education* (Toronto, Ontario: Collier-MacMillan Canada, Ltd., 1965), p. 41.

Chapter Five

1. Gilbert Highet, *The Art of Teaching* (New York: Random House Vintage Books, 1950), pp. 5, 14.

2. Richard Cohen, "Back When Schools Taught Values," *Washington Post,* October 7, 1986, p. A17.

3. Eloise Salholz, "Morals Mine Field," *Newsweek,* October 13, 1986, p. 92.

4. *Mozert* v. *Hawkins County Public Schools,* 647 F. Supp. 1194 (E.D. Tenn. 1986), appeal docketed, No. 87–5024 (6th Cir., Jan. 13, 1987), Plaintiff's Trial Brief, July 3, 1986, pp. 23, 25, 2.

5. Horace Mann, *1837 Annual Report to the Massachusetts State Board of Education,* in ed. Herbert M. Kliebard, *Religion and Education in America: A Documentary History* (Scranton, Pennsylvania: International Textbook Company, 1969), p. 68.

6. Ibid., p. 69.

7. *Science* (1096) PACE Series (Lewisville, Texas: Accelerated Christian Education, Inc., 1986), p. 31.

8. Stephen H. Balch and Herbert I. London, "The Tenured Left," *Commentary,* Volume 82, Number 4, (October 1986), p. 43.

9. Ibid., pp. 46, 43.

10. Ibid., p. 45.

11. Edward Shils, *The Academic Ethic* (Chicago: University of Chicago Press, 1984), p. 22.

12. John Stuart Mill, *On Liberty,* ed. Elizabeth Rapaport (Indianapolis: Hachett Publishing Company, Inc., 1978), p. 5.

13. C.S. Lewis, *The Abolition of Man* (New York: MacMillan Publishing Company, Inc., 1947), p. 35.

14. Learned Hand, *The Spirit of Liberty: Papers and Addresses of Learned Hand,* ed. Irving Dillard (New York: Alfred A. Knopf, 1959), p. 105.

15. Justus Hartnack, *Wittgenstein and Modern Philosophy* (Garden City, New York: Anchor Books, 1965), p. 5.

16. Alexander Meiklejohn, *What Does America Mean?* (New York: The Norton Library, 1955), pp. 82, 83.

CHAPTER SIX

1. Brand Blanshard, *Reason and Goodness* (London, England: George Allen and Unwin, Ltd., 1961), pp. 425, 434–435.

2. John Palmer, "Teacher Education: A Perspective from a Major Public University," in *Colleges of Education: Perspectives on Their Future,* Charles W. Case and William A. Matthes, eds. (Berkeley, California: McCutcheon Publishing Corp., 1985), p. 52.

3. Edward Shils, *The Academic Ethic* (Chicago: University of Chicago Press, 1984), pp. 41, 44–48.

4. Andrew Oldenquist, *The Non-Suicidal Society* (Bloomington, Indiana: University of Indiana Press, 1986), p. 35.

5. Ibid., pp. 36, 37.

6. Joyce D. Stern and Mary Frare Williams, eds., *The Condition of Education, 1986 Edition* (Washington, D.C.: National Center for Education Statistics, 1986), p. 141.

7. Jon Moline, "Teachers and Professionalism," in *Against Mediocrity: The Humanities in America's High Schools,* eds. Chester E. Finn, Jr., Diane Ravitch, and Robert T. Fancher (New York: Holmes and Meier, 1984), p. 201.

8. Chester E. Finn, Jr., and Diane Ravitch, "Conclusions and Recommendations: High Expectations and Disciplined Effort," in *Against Mediocrity,* eds. Chester E. Finn, Jr., Diane Ravitch, and Robert T. Fancher (New York: Holmes and Meier, 1984), p. 255.

9. Liz McMillen, "'Alliances' of Teachers and Faculty Members Create Links Between Schools and Colleges," *Chronicle of Higher Education,* January 7, 1987, p. 12.

10. Ibid., p. 13.

11. Steven L. Dubovsky, "Coping With Entitlement in Medical Education," *The New England Journal of Medicine,* December 25, 1986, p. 1672.

12. Ibid.

13. Ibid., pp. 1672, 1673.

14. Ibid., p. 1673.

15. Chester E. Finn, Jr., and Diane Ravitch, "Conclusions and Recommendation: High Expectations and Disciplined Effort," pp. 255, 256.

16. Jacques Barzun, *Teacher in America* (Lanham, Maryland: University Press of America, 1986), pp. 7, 9.

17. Palmer, "Teacher Education: A Perspective from a Major Public University," p. 64

18. Peter Brimelow, "Are We Spending Too Much On Education?", *Forbes,* Volume 138, Number 14 (December 29, 1986), pp. 73, 74.

19. "Goldilocks Takes Fall in Children's Mock Trial," *Santa Fe New Mexican,* May 3, 1983, pp. A1, A9.

20. Philip S. Foner, ed., *Voices of Black America* (New York: Simon and Schuster, 1972), pp. 100, 101.

21. D.H. Lawrence, "Fenimore Cooper's Leatherstocking Novels," in *Selected Literary Criticism,* ed. Anthony Beal (New York: Viking Press, 1956), p. 329.

22. For information, contact Eve Bither, superintendent of schools, Portland, Maine.

23. Budget of St. John's College, adopted by the Board of Visitors and Governors, April 1986.

24. Alfred North Whitehead, *The Aims of Education,* (New York: Free Press, 1957), p. 6.

25. Carolyn Gecan, "Report to the National Humanities Faculty from Langley High School" (McLean, Virginia: Unpublished, March 1976).

26. Nettie Silver, ed., *A Guide for Teachers* (New York: New York State Education Department, 1979), pp. 19, 26.

27. Thomas Sowell, "Patterns of Black Excellence," Ethics and Public Policy Center Reprint Number 5 (December 1977), pp. 50, 51.

CHAPTER SEVEN

1. Edward Levi, *Point of View* (Chicago: University of Chicago, 1967), pp. 84, 85.

2. Elaine El-Khawas, *Campus Trends, 1985,* Higher Education Panel Reprints, Number 71 (Washington, D.C.: American Council on Education February 1986), p. vi.

3. The National Institute of Education, *Involvement in Learning* (Washington, D.C.: United States Government Printing Office, 1984), p. 10.

4. *Integrity in the College Curriculum,* (Washington, D.C.: Association of American Colleges, 1985), p. 1.

5. William J. Bennett, *To Reclaim a Legacy: A Report on the Humanities in Higher Education* (Washington, D.C.: The National Endowment for the Humanities, 1984), pp. 1, 2.

6. George W. Bonham, "Toward One Human Experience," in *The Great Core Curriculum Debate* (New Rochelle, New York: Change Magazine Press, 1979), p. 4.

7. Henry Rosovsky and Phyllis Keller, "Issues and Problems: A Debate," Ibid., p. 51.

8. James Q. Wilson, "A View From the Inside," Ibid., pp. 47, 48.

9. William J. Bennett, *To Reclaim a Legacy,* p. 25.

10. Ibid.

11. John Stuart Mill, *Dissertations and Discussions,* ed. William V. Spencer, (Boston, 1868), Volume IV, p. 341.

12. Barry O'Connell, "Where Does Harvard Lead Us?", in *The Great Core*

Curriculum Debate (New Rochelle, New York: Change Magazine Press, 1979), p. 42.

13. "Prologue and Major Recommendations of the Carnegie Foundation's Report on Colleges," in *Chronicle of Higher Education,* November 5, 1986, p. 38.

14. *Reports on the Course of Instruction in Yale College* (New Haven, Connecticut: Printed by Hezekiah Howe, 1828), pp. 6, 7.

15. Ibid., p. 7.

16. Matthew D. Wald, "College Heads Endorse a World Peace Curriculum," *New York Times,* December 17, 1986, p. A14.

17. Ibid.

18. Antoine de St. Exupery, *Flight to Arras,* trans. Lewis Galantiere (New York: Harcourt, Brace and World, Inc., 1942), p. 80.

19. Walter Lippmann, *The Public Philosophy* (New York: Mentor Books, 1955), p. 27.

20. Alfred North Whitehead, *The Aims of Education* (New York: Free Press, 1957), p. 10.

21. *Missions of the College Curriculum* (San Francisco: Jossey-Bass Publishers, 1979), p. 7.

22. Mortimer J. Adler, "God and the Professors," in ed. Lyman Bronson *Science, Philosophy, and Religion* (New York: Harper and Row Publishers, 1941), pp. 128, 137.

23. Arthur E. Murphy, "Sectarian Absolutes and Faith in Democracy," in *Reason and the Common Good,* eds. William H. Hay, Marcus G. Singer, and Arthur E. Murphy (New York: Prentice Hall, 1963), pp. 290, 291.

24. Ibid., p. 292.

25. Robert Maynard Hutchins, *The Higher Learning in America* (New Haven, Connecticut: Yale University Press, 1936), p. 66.

26. Arthur W. Chickering, David Halliburton, William H. Berquist, and Jake Lindquist, *Developing the College Curriculum* (Washington, D.C.: Council for the Advancement of Small Colleges, 1977), p. v.

27. Henry Wilkinson Bragdon, *Woodrow Wilson: The Academic Years* (Cambridge, Massachusetts: Harvard University Press, 1967), p. 293.

28. Frederick Rudolph, *Curriculum: A History of the American Undergraduate Course of Study Since 1636* (San Francisco: Jossey-Bass Publishers, 1978), p. 19.

29. George Eliot, *Middlemarch* (Middlesex, England: Penguin English Library, 1965), p. 45.

30. Christopher Jencks and David Riesman, *The Academic Revolution* (Garden City, New York: Doubleday, 1968), p. 534.

31. Gilbert Highet, *The Art of Teaching* (New York: Vintage Books, 1950), p. 203.

32. J. Glenn Gray, *Re-Thinking American Education: A Philosophy of Teaching and Learning* (Middleton, Connecticut: Wesleyan University Press, 1984), pp. 80, 91.

33. James Q. Wilson and Richard J. Herrenstein, *Crime and Human Nature* (New York: Simon and Schuster, 1985), p. 80.

34. David Riesman, "The Vulnerability of the Private Liberal Arts College," *Liberal Education,* Vol. 73, No. 1 (January/February 1987), p. 39.

35. "Program of Liberal Studies," University of Notre Dame, 1985.

36. William Dunham, "A 'Great Theorems' Course in Mathematics," *American Mathematical Monthly,* Vol 93, No. 10 (December 1986), p. 808.

37. Ibid., pp. 808, 809.
38. Ibid., p. 810.
39. Ibid., p. 809.
40. Ibid.
41. Ibid., p. 811.
42. John R. Silber, in a panel with Robert Kane and Paul Woodruff, "Current Value Dilemmas: The Revolt Against Individualism," Plan II Alumni Reunion, Austin, Tex.; March 8, 1986.
43. Ethyle R. Wolfe, "Visitors Program Presentation," Brooklyn College, City University of New York, November 1986, p. 5.
44. Ibid., p. 7.
45. Ibid., p. 10.
46. Ibid., p. 11.
47. Ibid., p. 20.
48. Ibid., p. 24.
49. William J. Bennett, *First Lessons: A Report on Elementary Education in America* (Washington, D.C.: U.S. Department of Education, September 1986), p. 19.
50. Ibid., p. 64.
51. Ibid.
52. Ibid., p. 65.

CHAPTER EIGHT

1. Beryl Markham, *West With The Night* (San Francisco: North Point Press, 1983), p. 153.
2. Frederick Rudolph, *Curriculum: A History of the American Undergraduate Course of Study Since 1636* (San Francisco, California: Jossey-Bass Publishers, 1978), p. 2.
3. George R. LaNoue and Barbara A. Lee, "Lawsuits in Academe: *Nobody Wins,*" AGB Reprints (Washington, D.C.: Association of Governing Boards, January/February 1987), pp. 40, 41.
4. Ibid., p. 40.
5. Ibid., p. 41.
6. Ibid., p. 42.
7. *Equal Employment Opportunity Commission* vs. *Franklin and Marshall College,* United States Court of Appeals For The Third Circuit No. 84-1739 (D.C. Misc. No. 84-0675), August 5, 1985, Mansmann, p. 5.
8. Ibid., p. 12.
9. George R. LaNoue and Barbara A. Lee, "Lawsuits in Academe: *Nobody Wins,*" p. 42.

CHAPTER NINE

1. Walter Lippmann, "Education versus Western Civilization," in *American Poetry and Prose,* ed. Norman Foerster, (Cambridge, Massachusetts: The Riverside Press, 1947), Vol. II, p. 1585.
2. Arthur F. Burns, *Reflections of an Economic Policy Maker: Speeches and Congressional Statements: 1969-1978* (Washington, D.C.: American Enterprise Institute for Public Policy Research, 1978), p. 71.

3. Michael Novak, "Productivity and Social Justice," in *Will Capitalism Survive?* ed. Ernest W. Lefever (Washington, D.C.: Ethics and Public Policy Center, 1979), p. 35.

4. *The Fiscal Year 1988 Budget of the United States Department of Education: Summary and Background Information* (Washington, D.C.: Department of Education, 1987), p. 40.

5. *A Nation At Risk,* The National Commission on Excellence in Education (Washington, D.C.: U.S. Department of Education, 1983), pp. 5, 6.

6. Ibid., p. 18.

7. Ibid., p. 22.

8. Ibid., p. 24.

9. Ibid., p. 35.

10. "To Secure the Blessings of Liberty," American Association of State Colleges and Universities (1986), reprinted in *Chronicle of Higher Education,* November 12, 1986, p. 32.

11. Ibid.

12. Ibid., p. 36.

13. Ibid., p. 29.

14. *Fiscal Year 1988 Budget of the U.S. Department of Education, Summary and Background Information* (Washington, D.C.: Department of Education, 1987), pp. 11, 12.

15. Ernest L. Boyer, *College: The Undergraduate Experience in America* (New York: Harper and Row, 1987), pp. 288, 290.

16. Ibid., p. 248.

17. Ibid., p. 295.

18. Ibid., p. 48.

19. Ibid., p. 49.

20. Ibid., p. 259.

21. Ibid., p. 23.

22. C. S. Lewis, *The Abolition of Man* (New York: MacMillan, 1947), pp. 31, 32.

23. Kunigunde Duncan and D. F. Nichols, *Mentor Graham* (Chicago: University of Chicago Press, 1944), p. 129.

24. Ibid., p. 99.

25. William Butler Yeats, "A Cradle Song," in *The Collected Poems of W. B. Yeats* (New York: MacMillan Publishing Co., 1956), p. 39.

Index of Names

213